STAGING BLACK FUGITIVITY

BLACK PERFORMANCE AND CULTURAL CRITICISM
Valerie Lee and E. Patrick Johnson, Series Editors

STAGING BLACK FUGITIVITY

STACIE SELMON McCORMICK

THE OHIO STATE UNIVERSITY PRESS
COLUMBUS

Copyright © 2019 by The Ohio State University.
All rights reserved.

Library of Congress Cataloging-in-Publication Data
Names: McCormick, Stacie Selmon, author.
Title: Staging Black fugitivity / Stacie Selmon McCormick.
Other titles: Black performance and cultural criticism.
Description: Columbus : The Ohio State University Press, [2019] | Series: Black performance and cultural criticism | Includes bibliographical references and index.
Identifiers: LCCN 2019013238 | ISBN 9780814214053 (cloth ; alk. paper) | ISBN 0814214053 (cloth ; alk. paper)
Subjects: LCSH: American drama—African American authors—History and criticism. | Slavery in literature. | African Americans—Race identity. | Racism in literature.
Classification: LCC PS338.N4 M33 2019 | DDC 812/.5409896073—dc23
LC record available at https://lccn.loc.gov/2019013238

Cover design by Thao Thai
Text design by Juliet Williams
Type set in Adobe Minion Pro

*To the ancestors and to my babies,
Zoe, Jackson, Leroy, and Sylvester*

CONTENTS

Acknowledgments   ix

INTRODUCTION   A Body without a Nation   1

CHAPTER 1   Mapping Fugitivity in Black Drama   21

CHAPTER 2   Fugitive Acts   54

CHAPTER 3   Performing Escape   77

CHAPTER 4   Fugitive Intimacies   114

EPILOGUE   Contemplating and Complicating Black Freedom   136

Works Cited   147

Index   157

ACKNOWLEDGMENTS

A LOT OF LIFE happens between the time you begin a book and the moment it becomes a tangible artifact. From the time I began forming the seeds of this project, I had just become a mother. I was living in New Jersey and navigating the uncertainties of the academic job market. I am now living in Fort Worth, Texas, with two school-aged children and still working to achieve that elusive balance of work and life. Near the end of writing this book in 2018, I lost my beloved grandmother, Lillie Pearl Selmon. She was a Mississippi woman, born in the Depression era. However, she never let her present circumstances determine how she spoke about the future. She lifted me up in ways I am still fully appreciating, and I would like to think that this book is somehow a testament to her care and nurturing support—how she modeled it for her children, for my mother, her daughter, my guide. I feel the same sentiment for my grandmother L. G. Riley, a homemaker and domestic worker, whose smile lights up any room. I come from a lineage of black women who are future-minded and resilient. I could never have fathomed their marvelous vision for my life, and that is why I'm so glad they spoke it out loud for me to hear and absorb.

For this reason, I begin these acknowledgements with my family. They are my foundation and without them, none of the achievements of my life could be possible. I am so thankful to my mother, Jana Selmon for her steadfast support and love. I also thank my father Ezell Riley and my stepmother Gladys Riley for their support as well. To my husband, Demetrius, who has been a phenomenal partner and friend: I truly appreciate you and the wonderful father that you are to our children Zoe and Jackson. I thank my mother-in-law, Earlean McCormick, for offering encouragement along this journey. More than encouragement, she, along with my mother, provided countless hours of childcare while I worked on this book. I am indebted to them as well as other childcare providers who gave me the invaluable peace of mind that my children were being loved in my necessary absence. My sister, Angela Sinclair, has been a constant confidant and sounding board. I also thank my brothers, Sidney Riley and Isaiah Riley, for offering laughter and joy. I am also thankful to Claude Riley for your kindness and support. To my aunts Minnie Greer, Rosie Patterson, Adeline Peggy Selmon, Katherine Herron, as well as my aunts Alzena Whitcomb and Alene Riley, who have both passed on, and my uncles Michael Selmon and Ledell Riley—thank you for your enduring love. I count a host of cousins, in-laws, and dear friends among the foundation of my life. I can't quantify what it has meant to have each of you in my corner.

Even before this project was conceived, I had an enriching community of advisors and mentors who guided me in my development as a scholar. I express immense gratitude to Juliana Nfah Abbenyi, Noel Polk (who has passed on), Lisa Langstraat, and Martina Sciolino. These individuals helped me set a vision for a future in the academy. Their encouragement made all the difference.

The early rumblings of *Staging Black Fugitivity* were formed at The Graduate Center, City University of New York. Barbara Webb, Robert Reid-Pharr, and James de Jongh proved to be ideal mentors and readers. I am thankful for their patience and wisdom as I developed this work. Their enduring support means a great deal. Additionally, other faculty at The Graduate Center, such as Mario DiGangi, Talia Schaffer, and Victoria Pitts-Taylor, offered invaluable opportunities for me to grow. My time spent at *Women's Studies Quarterly* working with Talia and Victoria proved to be so consequential in sharpening my perspective and helping me learn more about the process of seeing drafts of manuscripts into publication. Collectively, these dear scholars, whether through reading drafts, writing countless recommendation letters, encouraging one-on-one meetings, or simply making space for me to do my work, model what it means to be a teacher-scholar. I am ever grateful for being able to work with them.

When thinking of all that it has taken to turn my various ideas into the book that it is today, I meditate on the African proverb that "it takes a village to raise a child." I can't be the first person to draw an analogy between this and the "raising" of a book. This project could not have been what it is without the scholarly community that I am fortunate to be a part of. I extend deep gratitude to those in my field who read drafts and offered insight, encouragement, or an engagement in some form with my work. Angela Ards served as my mentor for the Career Enhancement Fellowship, sponsored through the Woodrow Wilson and Mellon Foundations. Angela has read through just about every page of this book. I know that it is so much better as a result. Lisa Woolfork, too, mentored me in the early stages of my project and offered wise counsel on the directions it should take. Much appreciation goes to Douglas Jones, Michelle Commander, Matt Richardson, Shelly Eversley, Cynthia Young, Cedrick May, Soyica Colbert, and those who have offered constructive feedback, be it large or small, on this work.

I am also appreciative of accountability partners and friends who either read and responded to drafts or cheered me on as I went through each stage of the process. Karen Gaffney, Tonya Foster, Lavelle Porter, Fiona Lee, and RaShell Smith-Spears, you engaged my thoughts when they were in their infancy and have remained across time as they emerge into the world. I am particularly thankful to Karen and Tonya who, through many conversations, helped me to refine my ideas. What a journey we have been on together! To my growing village of brilliant scholars whose work inspires me in ways they do not know: Shelagh Patterson, Tatum Petrich, Laila Amine, Aneeka Henderson, Airín Martínez, Rhaisa Williams, Octavio Gonzalez, Darius Bost, Julius Fleming, Jarvis McInnis, Brandon Manning, Robin Brooks, Tayana Hardin, Therí Pickens, Donavan Ramon, Marquita Smith, and Molly Scudder, thank you for everything big and small you have done to make me feel grounded in this process. I also extend special appreciation to Kerry Ann Rockquemore and the National Center for Faculty Development and Diversity. My participation in the Faculty Success Program was such a valuable experience. And to Tawania Harris, Metra Blanks, Christinia Townsend-Clark, Ronda Jones, Joanna Hudspeth, Anntoinette McGee, Carla Blue, and Rashanna Anderson, I can't say how much it means to have individuals like you in my beloved community.

I have benefited from significant institutional support in seeing this project into fruition. I owe a special thanks to the Woodrow Wilson and Mellon Foundations for awarding me a Career Enhancement Fellowship for the 2017–18 academic year. This fellowship provided me with a dynamic community of junior and senior scholars who inspired me to think bigger and reach higher. This project has also received support from Emory University's Stuart A. Rose MARBL Library, TCU's Research and Creative Activity Fund, and their Junior Faculty Summer Research Program, as well as the Lapidus Center for the Historical Analysis of Transatlantic Slavery at the Schomburg Center and their inaugural conference. The funding provided via these institutions made many things possible—including travel, research, childcare, and community—as I developed this work.

I express sincere gratitude for my colleagues at TCU who have embraced me and my work wholeheartedly. I want to thank all of the faculty and staff in the English Department, Women and Gender Studies, and Comparative Race and Ethnic Studies. I am particularly thankful to my American Literature cohort, who has inspired me to greater heights. I feel especially grateful for those colleagues who read drafts and offered wisdom: Theresa Gaul, David Colón, Sarah Robbins, Ariane Balizet, Bonnie Blackwell, Layne Craig, Rima Abunasser, and Chantel Carlson. I want to extend special thanks to my department chairs, Karen Steele and Joddy Murray, who have extended financial and moral support for the development of this project at each stage. I also thank Victor Boschini, Andrew Schoolmaster, Darron Turner, and Nowell Donovan for providing much needed administrative support. I can't thank Merry Roberts and Regina Lewis enough for all that they have done in helping me manage the various tasks that have come with producing this manuscript. I also thank Charlotte "Sarge" Hogg for the spring bootcamps and accountability check-ins. These colleagues have helped me get through some writing humps with cheer and community. I benefitted from a similar warmth from my sister-scholars Fran Huckaby and Melanie Harris. Our writing sessions were restorative and so generative. Thanks in particular to Fran for offering what we have affectionately termed "The Alice Walker Room" in her home as a sacred space to create. I also thank TCU research assistants Linda Davis, Chase Sanchez, Sue-Jin Green, Ann Tran, and Angelica Hernandez for their detailed and enthusiastic work. My graduate classes American Stagings and Contemporary African American Literature: Literary Afterlives of Slavery offered valuable insights that I have taken into account in this book. Thank you for your engaged participation in class and for critically engaging my ideas. I also want to acknowledge Wil Gafney for insightfully engaging my work. To all the women who make up a dynamic group of sister-scholars at TCU, I feel so fortunate for our dinners and community. Moreover, I thank Dean June Koelker of the Mary Couts Burnett Library for providing research space, and I extend gratitude to Ammie Harrison, our amazing humanities librarian, for not only being resourceful but also invested.

I feel very fortunate to be producing this work with The Ohio State University Press. I will never forget the email I received from Lindsay Martin expressing interest in my work. Lindsay saw potential in my work and patiently walked me through each stage of the process from proposal to contract. I am deeply thankful to the series editors for Black Performance and Cultural Criticism, E. Patrick Johnson and Valerie Lee, for their incisive responses to my project. I also appreciate their belief in my capacity to do this work. Thanks especially to the blind reviewers of this manuscript. Their comments transformed this project into more than I could have imagined. This book certainly wouldn't be what it is without their feedback. Kristen Elias Rowley, Ana Jimenez-Moreno, and the staff at OSUP have been amazing, kind, and efficient. Thank you for all of your labor, seen and unseen.

Finally, one need only look at my bibliography to know that I benefit from an excellent body of scholarship. So, I end these acknowledgments by thanking all of the individuals I cite. You offer models and insights that have made me a better thinker and scholar. And to everyone whose path I have crossed (and that I neglected to name here—not deliberately but perhaps due to the fallibility of memory) who might have attended a conference where I presented work on this project and offered meaningful feedback, offered kind words, or simply engaged my work in some manner, I appreciate any and all of the moments that make up the journey of bringing this book to life.

INTRODUCTION

A Body without a Nation

WE LIVE in a present animated by slavery. The long shadow of this history informs modern-day US institutions (political, educational, carceral, and more) despite the social progress that occurs across time. This history remains alive in cultural discourse, fiction, poetry, visual art, film, and certainly in drama. More than any of these aforementioned categories, however, contemporary black drama remains undertheorized for its engagement with slavery.[1] Thus, I came to this project seeking to examine how playwrights and performers represent black subjects grappling with slavery's legacies. More than simply a corpus of work through which to analyze theatrical representation of black pain and trauma borne out of slavery, contemporary black drama provides new critical frameworks for contemplating the "peculiar" institution and blackness itself. This body of work raises important questions: How

---

1. Studies that have considered this body of dramatic production are limited in frame and scope. Valerie Bada's *Mnemopoetics: Memory and Slavery in African American Drama* traces the fluctuating patterns that shape the theatrical memory of slavery in African American drama produced between 1939 and 1996; however, a great deal has developed in African American dramatic production since 1996, and there is a need for an updated study. More recent articles such as Jacqueline Jones's "'We the People': Freedom, Civics, and the Neo-Slave Narrative Tradition in August Wilson's *Gem of the Ocean*," Faedra Chatard Carpenter's "Robert O'Hara's *Insurrection*: Que(e)rying History," and Harvey Young's "Touching History: Suzan-Lori Parks, Robbie McCauley and the Black Body" offer exceptionally insightful analyses but only take on the subject in singular contexts.

does the return to slavery in contemporary black drama illuminate the current public discourse around blackness, freedom, and belonging? What becomes possible artistically and politically when we push against received histories of slavery (those narratives circulated across time that render enslavement and black experience in one-dimensional terms)? How can performances of these dramas enhance our capacity to represent the intricacies of the institution of slavery?

Staging Black Fugitivity examines how black dramas produced in the late twentieth and early twenty-first centuries make critical interventions in our cultural engagement with slavery. Forwarding narratives that disrupt linear, reductive tellings of enslavement and of black experience, writ large, the dramas analyzed in this book approach slavery from myriad perspectives (Afrofuturist, feminist, and queer) in order to produce artistically experimental imaginaries that offer more complex depictions of black experience. These dramas also use slavery as a site of interrogation of the contemporary problem of un/freedom for black subjects. By this I mean black drama's staging of black subjects in constant negotiation of what Saidiya Hartman calls the "afterlife of slavery"– "skewed life chances, limited access to health and education, premature death, incarceration and impoverishment" (*Lose Your Mother* 6). I am also thinking of Rinaldo Walcott's "the long emancipation," which he defines as the ongoing juridical conditions of white civil society that actively preempt black freedom (437).[2] These dramas constitute a critical site for the advancement of experimental practice in black art, and they make valuable interventions in contemporary conversations on how black subjects negotiate the legacies of slavery.

To foreground my exploration of this body of dramatic production, I look to Dread Scott and his 2012 performance art piece *Dread Scott: Decision* because the conceptual concerns of the work dramatize the thematic and theoretical underpinnings of this book. Staged at the Brooklyn Academy of Music (BAM Fisher performing arts theater in Brooklyn, New York) just before the reelection of President Barack Obama, *Dread Scott: Decision* intersects historical text and the contemporary black body in performance in order to probe the relation between slavery and current contradictions of black citizenship and freedom. *Dread Scott: Decision* challenged spectators to consider American democratic ideals in the context of its centuries-long practice of slavery.

---

2. We can also imagine contemporary black drama's engagement with slavery in the context of what Christina Sharpe terms "wake work." Sharpe elucidates that to be "in the wake" means to "declare that we are Black peoples in the wake with no state or nation to protect us, with no citizenship bound to be respected, and to position us in the modalities of Black life lived in, as, under, despite Black death" (*In the Wake* 22).

The performance took its inspiration from the 1857 Supreme Court decision, *Dred Scott v. Sanford*, in which Scott, an enslaved person who lived for many years in the free states of Wisconsin and Illinois, sued for his freedom after the death of his enslaver, John Emerson.[3] The most notable part of the decision, in addition to the failure to grant Scott his freedom, was the declaration that neither blacks, whether enslaved or free, nor their descendants could ever become citizens of the United States and therefore could not sue in federal court. The decision predictably outraged those who desired to see an end to slavery. Correspondingly, it emboldened those who advocated for a continuance of the system and celebrated the decision made by the largely proslavery court. Chief Justice Roger B. Taney's majority opinion infamously asserted that within the United States, the "negro," because of his inferiority, had "no rights which the white man was bound to respect." This precedent-setting language has reverberated across American history and continues to inform struggles for racial equality.

Performed as a sequence of scenes, *Dread Scott: Decision* opens with four nude black men (Clifford Owens, Lawrence Graham-Brown, Wilmer Wilson IV, and "Rock" Belizaire) in the center of the performance space sitting in repose. As two barking German Shepherds enter the space led by handlers, the men eventually stand and form a line that could be read as anything from an auction block to a slave capture to a police lineup or a nonviolent Civil Rights era–style protest (see figure 1). Once the men line up, the audience is directed to form a line and travel through stanchions. The design of the stanchions forces the audience to view the nude men in a kind of discomfiting intimacy, and, were it not for the men standing before them, the scene could have taken place in a department store or a line to see a major motion picture. Some audience members even paused to stare (and, in one case, hug the men) before exiting the line. While this occurs, Scott reads the text of the 1957 Dred Scott decision. As audience members left the space, they were then directed into voting booths positioned behind the men where they received questions in the form of a ballot: "Would you have voted during slavery? Would you vote in a segregated election?"[4] Audience members then received a print out of this "ballot" and were asked to hang it in their homes and talk about it with guests.

In this performance, Scott brings together the textual and the corporeal by reading the words of the 1857 decision as we witness the vulnerable bodies of the black men being displayed in the contexts of Jim Crow, the Civil Rights

---

3. For a background on Scott and the legal contexts of the case, see David Harvey's "Dred Scott, John San(d)ford, and the Case for Collusion" (Harvey 37–66).

4. For greater context on the performance, see the artist's description—http://www.dreadscott.net/works/dread-scott-decision/

FIGURE 1. Film still of *Dread Scott: Decision*, featuring Owens, Graham-Brown, Wilson, and Belizaire

Movement, and the present-day era of mass incarceration. The performance collapses time to show how black Americans have been historically unprotected in the law and that these realities have not been erased by moments of racial progress, even at the dawn of the reelection of America's first nonwhite president. We can read the vulnerable black bodies in this performance as suspended not only between past and present but also between enslaved and free, noncitizen and citizen. They are veritably bodies without a nation.

Much the way Dread Scott problematizes black subjects' relation to the nation, especially when read in the context of slavery, contemporary black dramas draw upon the visual, phenomenological, and symbolic possibilities available in theater to depict the liminal space that black subjects often occupy in the US (suspended between poles of citizen and noncitizen, belonging and non-belonging, past and present). As such, in this book I explore the many forms this critical posture takes and its implications for how we engage slavery in the present. I draw a connective line from Daphne Brooks's theorizing of trans-Atlantic black performers of the nineteenth and early twentieth century as bodies without a nation in her path-making work *Bodies in Dissent: Spectacular Performances of Race and Freedom, 1850–1910* to understand the ways black playwrights and performers dramatize similar tensions in a contemporary context. Brooks asserts that the trans-Atlantic black body is a body that "defies a singular context and national culture. It is a body without a nation and yet in performance . . . it is repeatedly called upon to forge some kind of national consciousness, at the very moments in which its figure exposes and affirms the tenuousness of nationalism and its fictions" (29). Although Brooks references a distinct time and subject, this observation holds powerful resonance when considered in the context of slavery on the contemporary black stage. Indeed, black contemporary subjects utilize the stage as a way to grapple with civic alienation[5] while also forwarding radical performances that imagine alternate modes of freedom and belonging.

In examining how contemporary black drama places itself in ongoing conversations on the tensions of American citizenship and the limits of black freedom, I consider this body of work in relation to the most prominent genre we have for the contemporary depiction of slavery in literary and creative work—the neo-slave narrative. Scholars predominantly look to the genre of the neo-slave narrative as it takes shape in the form of the novel as the primary site for the production of counternarratives of enslaved experience. Yet we lack a thorough assessment for how black drama participates in and departs from this genre in ways that expand the neo-slave narrative's possibilities. In their ability to deploy the black body in performance, contemporary black dramas featuring slavery enhance the neo-slave narrative's capacity to represent the visual, corporal, and affective dimensions of the peculiar institution. Through subverting notions of time, race, gender, and familiar histories of slavery themselves, the dramas under discussion produce *performances of fugitivity*. I define this as subversive, radical, and experimental performances of black artistic and political freedom at the site of slavery. Theirs is an effort on the part of black subjects, past and present, to evade objectification and one-dimensional representations of slavery and blackness. Conversely, this evasion frees up black subjects to present richer, more dynamic renderings of black subjectivity.

STAGING THE NEO-SLAVE NARRATIVE

Without question, the emergence of the neo-slave narrative genre as well as its experimental and often irreverent depictions of slavery constituted a pointed shift in the literary landscape. The roots of this genre were primarily textual via novels such as Margaret Walker's *Jubilee* (1966), a narrativized history of her enslaved ancestors, and William Styron's *The Confessions of Nat Turner*

---

5. See Salamishah Tillet's *Sites of Slavery*.

(1967). Styron's controversial rendering of Nat Turner's voice prompted a flood of responses from literary and nonliterary writers alike. Ashraf Rushdy, whose theories of the neo-slave narrative have proven most consequential for the field, defines the genre as having the following characteristics: 1) they emerge from specific "social, intellectual and racial formations" of the late 1960s and 1970s (3); 2) they aim to salvage the literary form of the slave narrative that white writers like Styron co-opted; 3) they utilize the form of the slave narrative as a return to the mode of writing in which black subjects first articulated their political subjectivity; and 4) they employ intertextuality to explore power relations in the field of cultural production in which black literature emerges from a matrix of literary discontinuities.[6] Drawing upon the strategy of intertextuality allows these writers to situate themselves as belated participants in earlier conversations on civil rights and various social issues concerning black Americans.

Building on Rushdy's foundational formulations, scholars such as Timothy Spaulding, Angelyn Mitchell, and Arlene Keizer have offered new directions for studying narratives that slavery animates.[7] However, there remains a need for new analytics that explore black drama's particular intervention in this genre. Black drama's engagement with slavery tracks thematically and concurrently with the development of the neo-slave narrative in the novel form with dramas such as Amiri Baraka's *Slave Ship* (1967), George Wolfe's *The Colored Museum* (1986), and Robbie McCauley's *Sally's Rape* (1991) to name a few. Given this confluence and the ongoing production of dramas about slavery, this body of work demands greater critical attention and theoretical elucidation.[8]

---

6. While Rushdy's critical framing on the neo-slave narrative is the one with which I am most in conversation, it is important to note that Bernard Bell coined the term "neo-slave narrative" in *The Afro-American Novel and Its Tradition*.

7. Timothy Spaulding defines "postmodern slave narrative[s]" as novels that "create an alternative and fictional historiography based on a subjective, fantastic, and anti-realistic representation of slavery" (2). Among its primary genres are science fiction, the gothic, postmodern metafiction, and the vampire tale. Angelyn Mitchell prefers the term "liberatory narrative," which she defines as "a contemporary novel that engages the historical period of chattel slavery in order to provide new models of liberation by problematizing the concept of freedom" (4). Arlene Keizer reads what she refers to as "contemporary narratives of slavery" in psychoanalytic contexts. These narratives, she argues, cast a wider interpretive net, which allow us to explore how contemporary writers of the African Diaspora use the slave past as a form of release from the postmemory of violent and dehumanizing acts of the past (7).

8. My analysis joins works such as Lisa Woolfork's *Embodying American Slavery in Contemporary Culture*, Salamishah Tillet's *Sites of Slavery*, Maria Bellamy's *Bridges to Memory: Postmemory in Contemporary Ethnic American Women's Fiction*, Christina Sharpe's *Monstrous Intimacies*, Kimberly Juanita Brown's *The Repeating Body*, and Soyica Colbert, Robert Patterson, and Aida Levy-Hussen's collection, *The Psychic Hold of Slavery*, who represent a growing body

As theater, black drama brings to bear embodiment as well as sonic and visual modes of representing slavery not fully available to the written neo-slave narratives. These dramas not only return to the literary form of the slave narrative, but also engage with slavery's extraliterary archives of performance and visuality, which remain deeply resonant in how we know and feel slavery and the enslaved. To be sure, scholars have begun to analyze this body of work with greater frequency. For instance, Jacqueline Jones reads August Wilson's *Gem of the Ocean* (2003) as a neo-slave narrative, yet her analysis centers most firmly on the play's literary devices and sociopolitical valences with little regard to its performance and theatrical strategies. Margo Crawford, too, considers black drama vis-à-vis the neo-slave narrative; she identifies drama as crucial to the emergence of what she names the "post-neo-slave narrative," a genre that instantiates the "move from the literary imagination that fills in the gaps (what historians cannot know) to the refusal to fill in the gaps but to linger in the unknown" ("Inside-Turned-Out" 71). While Crawford's framing is generative for my readings of the shifts occurring within the neo-slave narrative genre, I intend to probe more deeply how black playwrights use text and performance to interrogate irresolvable and unknowable aspects of slavery. I also explore their challenge to received histories of slavery that promote overdetermined representations of the institution and of blackness.

The plays this book hones in on stem from the historical turn in black drama that began in the last quarter of the twentieth century, spearheaded by August Wilson and Suzan-Lori Parks. Many of these dramas rest effectively in the oft-contested category of the post-black, an ethos that is animated by the desire to offer "heterogeneous and heterodox renderings of blackness that are grounded in the contexts and conditions of today" (Elam and Jones xv). This ethos is not very distant from the underlying logics of the neo-slave narrative that Rushdy spells out in his analysis. Consistent with both of these critical categories, contemporary dramas about slavery offer experimental, sometimes radical, representations of slavery that also attend to the sociopolitical conversations of their era, such as state-sanctioned violence against black people largely at the hands of the police. These works articulate what Crawford defines as a "black post-blackness" that is rooted in the "the cultural mood of the Black Arts Movement's simultaneous investment in blackness *and* a type of freedom that broke the boundaries of blackness" (*Black Post-Blackness* 4). These works trouble blackness without worrying about the loss of blackness, centering on the question: "What will blackness be?" Importantly, Rushdy reg-

---

of work analyzing slavery's resonance in contemporary black literary, visual, and expressive culture.

isters the same concern in the neo-slave narrative when black writers grapple with the question: "Who will uninvent the negro?" (21). Given the incredibly powerful overlapping considerations and motivations that originated in the late 1960s and reverberate today, I do not seek to untether contemporary black drama about slavery from the neo-slave narrative altogether. Rather, I aim to interrogate its critical departures from the genre, which call for an analysis that highlights the ever-shifting nature of approaches to representing slavery across form and time. I am interested in exploring the character and content of those shifts on the contemporary stage and their implications for the long-standing genre of the neo-slave narrative.

In considering the broad body of work that constitutes contemporary stagings of slavery, I have identified shared characteristics that allow us to locate drama's interventions in narrativizing slavery. One key element is that this dynamic corpus grounds itself within the neo-slave narrative by engaging with myriad historical texts, debates, and images while staging this work in the theater space. Doing so introduces the phenomenology of performance, visuality, and corporeality into the narrative in provocative ways. Additionally, these dramas utilize black embodiment to critique social constructions of race and to serve as a repository of black memory and historical experience. These dramas also recontextualize slavery—its iconography of cotton, chains, and various aspects of its visual archive—as a means to render the institution (and the black subjects situated at its center) in a new light. Such recontextualizations enable the performance of fugitivity in which stories about black enslaved subjects are rewritten and reperformed in ways that render them as more than what their original narratives suggest; such a rendering, I argue, frees them from the burden of racial representation.[9] Finally, because of the ephemerality of performance, each staged iteration shifts and thereby denies archival containment of the sort that produced the originary representations, which the plays repudiate.

Moreover, dramas featuring slavery call up and produce genealogies of performance. Joseph Roach illuminates,

> Genealogies of performance attend not only to "the body," as Foucault suggests, but also to bodies—to the reciprocal reflections they make on one another's surfaces as they foreground their capacities for interaction. Gene-

---

9. Also, because the telling of slavery is intimately concerned with race, Black theater is uniquely situated to bring forth these aspects of this history. Nicole Fleetwood asserts, "Theater is as much a visual medium as it is one of embodied performance and the live text, or dramatic script. It is in the staging and live moments that the optical regimes of race most clearly unfold" (73).

alogies of performance also attend to "counter-memories" or the disparities between history as it is discursively transmitted and memory as it is publicly enacted by the bodies that bear its consequences. (25–26)

Here, Roach speaks to the reflective processes of performance and the abilities of the body to enact memory. In the dramas I analyze, this critical work takes place on multiple valences: in the signifying on cultural traditions and performances of rituals passed down from the slave era and in the production of counter-memories of iconic enslaved figures. In this sense, the dramas in this study engage in a counterarchival practice that assembles histories of slavery and presents them from the vantage point of the black subject as a way to emphasize that which has been suppressed or denied throughout history.[10]

Performing histories of slavery also counters the ways enslavers constructed black performance as a tool of oppression in order to obscure black testimony. The enslaved were often forced to perform sentiments of happiness and jollity, which largely masked their pain. As a result, the body of the enslaved in performance often spoke the enslaver's truths and served to further augment his power (Hartman, *Scenes* 22). Saidiya Hartman describes these as *scenes of subjection*:

> The pageantry of the coffle, stepping it up lively on the auction block, going before the master, and the blackface mask of minstrelsy and melodrama all evidenced the entanglements of terror and enjoyment. Above all, the simulated jollity and coerced festivity of the slave trade and the instrumental recreations of plantation management document the investment in and obsession with "black enjoyment" and the significance of these orchestrated amusements as part of a larger effort to dissimulate the extreme violence of the institution and disavow the pain of captivity. (23)

Frederick Douglass also reminds us of how the singing of the enslaved was often mistaken for happiness, declaring: "Slaves sing most when they are unhappy. The songs of the slave represent the sorrows of his heart; and he is relieved by them, only as an aching heart is relieved by its tears" (9). Both Hartman's description and Douglass's account show how historically black

---

10. Alexandra Dodd in her analysis of counterarchival practice in the work of South African artist Mary Sibande informs how I invoke the term here. Dodd makes the point that contemporary artists engage in counterarchival work as an act of retrieval of facets of the past in order to reconfigure thoughts and feelings in relation to this history. In so doing, they reveal that which has been largely silenced, heavily exploited, and relegated to the shadows of public discourse (473).

subjectivity has been inadvertently or intentionally distorted to such an extent that the truths of the inner lives of the enslaved often did not emerge in their performances.

In restaging slavery, contemporary black playwrights produce *scenes of objection* that counter the suppression of the voices of the enslaved with figures who speak back to their oppression, telling their histories from an unfiltered perspective.[11] This is much in line with the work of Toni Morrison, who describes her process of preparing to write about the slave past as "a kind of literary archaeology: On the basis of some information and a little bit of guesswork you journey to a site to see what remains were left behind and to reconstruct the world that these remains imply" (Morrison, "The Site of Memory" 92). Her major goal in doing this work is to "rip the veil drawn over 'proceedings too terrible to relate'" (91). Ripping off that veil is itself an act that becomes even more nuanced when we conceive of the veil as the curtain just beyond the proscenium arch.

Suzan-Lori Parks deepens our consideration of Morrison's strategy by situating it within the context of the theater. In her efforts to represent history on stage, Parks, too, envisions herself as an archaeologist seeking to unearth undiscovered aspects of the black past, yet she imagines the theater as a "site of memory" where history can be housed. She explains:

> Since history is a recorded or remembered event, theatre, for me, is the perfect place to "make" history—that is, because so much of African-American history has been unrecorded, disremembered, washed out, one of my tasks as a playwright is to—through literature and the special strange relationship between theatre and real-life—locate the ancestral burial ground, dig for bones, find bones, hear the bones sing, write it down. (4)

Parks's approach to representing history on stage is instructive for understanding the ways the telling of slavery unfolds on the contemporary stage. In unearthing the "bones"—that which has been long buried and repressed—contemporary black dramatists present slavery anew. I understand Parks's notion of making history as an acknowledgment of the theater's ability to produce genealogies of performance that endure each time the drama is staged. With each performance, the history becomes new, operating in an ongoing

---

11. Fred Moten utilizes a similar turn of phrase "scene of objection" in his ground-shifting work *In the Break* where he locates in Aunt Hester's scream as an appositional encounter situated in the space between utterance and response, an improvisation of both speech and writing (22).

process of regeneration, a rewriting of the "time-line—creating history where it is and always was but has not yet been divined" (Parks 5). Parks's notion of creating history reminds audiences that artists have the capacity to represent slavery in a way that speaks back to various historical renderings. Moreover, her articulation of the artistic freedom available to playwrights in representing slavery reflects the critical project of the playwrights covered in this book. They are offering new narratives about this history in ways that do not venture toward historiography but instead reinvention.

The dramas examined in this book offer narratives that ask us to question that which we think we know about slavery and to leave space for the inclusion of narratives we have not yet conceived. This approach is indeed an act of creation, a reinvention, if you will, of slavery and it also constitutes a form of escape from traditional narratives of enslavement that often bind black subjects in time. Hortense Spillers locates a history of facile and oversimplified renderings of blackness in literary works as early as Harriet Beecher Stowe's *Uncle Tom's Cabin*. She argues that Stowe offers up Tom as an authoritative representation of "*the negro*," which works to "rob the subject of its dynamic character, to *capture* it in a fictionalized scheme whose outcome is already inscribed by a higher, different, other, power, *freezes* it in the ahistorical" (180; my emphasis). In what follows, I consider how contemporary black dramas contend with the effects of this capturing, this freezing of black subjects in time, which consequently contains them in a veritable narrative captivity. These dramas aim to not only present slavery in a way that "frees" enslaved subjects from the narrative bondage of overdetermined depictions of their experience, but also to make room for broader possibilities of depicting black experience past and present.

PERFORMING FUGITIVITY

The notion of fugitivity informs my readings of contemporary black dramas and their particular approach to representing slavery. Within this body of work, we see an active attempt to unbind black subjects from the ubiquitous threadbare tropes dating back to Stowe's Uncle Tom and related depictions reproduced across time in the telling of slavery. These dramas intervene in the perpetuation of such representations thereby disrupting the circulation of predictable and uncomplicated representations of slavery and of blackness that desensitize audiences to the surreal and brutal nature of this troubling past. Alongside the artistic, we can also see the concept of fugitivity at work in the political sense where the dramas interrogate the complex question of what it means for black subjects to feel a sense of belonging and home in a nation built on slavery.

My formulation of performances of fugitivity draws on theories of fugitivity in Black (Performance) Studies, namely thinkers such as Daphne Brooks, Saidiya Hartman, Stephen Best; the illuminating conversations of Fred Moten, Stefano Harney, and Jack Halberstam in *The Undercommons: Fugitive Planning and Black Study*; Christina Sharpe; and Keguro Macharia.[12] I am thinking primarily with James Edward Ford who theorizes fugitivity as a "critical category for examining *the artful escape of objectification,* whether said objectification occurs through racialized aesthetic framing, commodification, or liberal juridico-political discipline" (110). His definition highlights ongoing processes of evasion and of inhabiting a slipperiness that eludes containment (i.e., formulations of blackness that deny the very possibility of freedom) among black subjects. Ford's theory also provides a rubric for examining the ways black writers and thinkers have been concerned with escaping objectifying notions of blackness across time. I contend that depictions of slavery on the contemporary stage have forcefully articulated these processes and concerns.

By dramatizing black bodies in various states of surreality (bodies that are suspended in time and space, bodies that cross boundaries of gender and race), contemporary black playwrights stage fugitivity as a means to function outside the confines of the conventions of telling histories of slavery. We can recognize performances of fugitivity in the perpetual project of world-(re)making in which these dramas are engaged. The performances utilize the body as a methodological tool to defamiliarize the familiar via distortions of time, race, and gender. Moreover, performances of fugitivity position the black subject at an intentional critical distance—the space beyond affiliation—to not only critique the ongoing problem of black civic exclusion but also to allow black subjects to exist in a space of possibility. In this way, these performances facilitate the escape of objectification.

Performances of fugitivity also problematize home, depicting homes as troubled spaces that function in some cases as refuge from the exterior world; they also present homes as interior spaces of pain or irrecoverable loss. Echoing Fred Moten's assertion that "homelessness is hard but home is harder" (Harney and Moten 139–40), these performances critique the "master's house," emphasizing it as a founding space of trauma for the unhomed black subject and suggesting that heteronormative notions of home remain hostile to black

---

12. See Best and Hartman's "Fugitive Justice," Daphne Brooks's *Bodies in Dissent,* Christina Sharpe's "Black Life, Annotated," and Keguro Macharia's "fugitivity."

subjects. As such, my invocation of the contemporary black subject as "a body without a nation" speaks not only to the larger issues of belonging and feeling at home within the nation, but also to the ways fugitivity inheres a kind of homelessness with an indefinite end. Thus, performances of fugitivity refashion home in all its protean iterations (whether it be conceptions of Africa as a homeland, the conflicts of feeling at home in America, or the tensions of heteronormative constructions of domesticity).

Staging Black Fugitivity engages fugitivity as a method of reading how slavery is being rendered on the contemporary black stage, considering fugitivity's manifold manifestations and how it enables new articulations of postslavery subjectivity. In doing so, I trace the turn toward slavery in black drama, focusing on the late 1950s and early 1960s as a point of embarkation for experimental approaches to slavery where themes of fugitivity and challenges to canonical histories of slavery emerge. I utilize this genealogy of dramas to make more visible the longer history of this body of work as well as to account for the shifting nature of these representations and how they speak to the exigencies of their present moment. I consider how the Civil Rights and post-Civil Rights era informs the dramas of the 1960s to the early 1990s, an ethos that shifts at the turn of the century in light of the rise of neoliberal discourses of postracialism, the Obama era, and the Black Lives Matter era. As I unpack the various manifestations of fugitivity in the dramas, I do so with the historical backdrop of the contemporary moment in mind. Certainly, the increased attention to police violence against black subjects and the conversations around race and American citizenship engendered by the historical election of President Barack Obama manifest in black expressive culture, with drama being an important site of engagement because of its history as a space around which communities gather and participate in civic and social life.[13] Drawing upon critical reviews of the dramas and playwright interviews, I consider how contemporary issues influence their representations of slavery and how they harness the stage to engage these matters. In addition to considerations of reception and the playwrights' perspectives, I explore the ways the body functions as a central means to articulate the layered implications of fugitivity. Therefore, this book also reads the body in performance as a text with which the dramas under discussion engage. In forwarding this critical approach toward analyzing these works, I do so in the spirit of the dramas themselves, meaning that I envision this critical work as a starting point rather than a destination—like black fugitivity, constantly in motion.

---

13. It is important to note that these conversations have arguably intensified under Donald Trump's presidency; however, the works I discuss in this book are most engaged with the Obama era since the majority of them were produced during that time.

"PAINT THAT DOOR UP BLUE"

In its dramatization of postslavery fugitivity via distortions of time, the troubling of home, and its incorporations of genealogies of performance in the form of ritual and song, Tanya Barfield's 2006 play *Blue Door* indexes key ideas explored in this book and forwards a metaphor that guides my readings of the dramas comprising this work. Although slavery is not the central subject of the drama, it looms large in its narrative framework. The drama follows the internal struggles of Lewis, a black male professor of mathematics at an elite university. We meet Lewis just as his white wife, Kimberly, has left him for reasons that are baffling to him. (She critiques him for not attending the Million Man March and his insufficient housework.) Alone in his home, empty with the absence of his wife, Lewis is visited by the spirits of his ancestor, Simon, a former slave; his grandfather, Jesse, who was lynched after endeavoring to vote; and his militant brother, Rex. Often physically beaten by his father, who arguably enacts his frustrations about racial oppression through violence against his family, Lewis descends from a long line of black men traumatized by racial terror. In spite of all of this, he has been able to ascend the social ladder and attain a PhD in mathematics, another trope Barfield employs to engage the afterlives of slavery. In this Afrofuturist drama, the past and present become enmeshed in what Lewis describes as an "Euclidean universe" with "the past forever vying for the present" (21).

Lewis is a quintessential representation of postslavery fugitivity. Estranged from the world and going through a divorce, Lewis views the world with a conflicting detachment. He is caught between affiliating with an America that lynched his grandfather for attempting to vote while also becoming a part of the academy in his attainment of a doctorate. His brother Rex, who describes himself as Lewis's doppelganger, declares to Lewis "you've been running away" and accuses him of being afraid to be black (17). The irony of this is that Lewis's blackness overwhelms him in the predominantly white spaces of the academy where he experiences microaggressions on a regular basis. Lewis's breaking point comes when he has an encounter with a black male student, whom Lewis accuses of transposing the pronunciation of Heidegger for "House Nigger." In a confrontation with the dean over this issue, the dean recommends that Lewis take time off. He is at once alienated from the academy, his family, and himself. Suspended between space and time, positioned at a critical distance that doesn't allow him to fully find a sense of "home" anywhere, Lewis grapples with racial alienation while also coming to terms with the facts of his family's past (see figure 2).

FIGURE 2. Victor Mack as Lewis in *Blue Door* (2016). Used with permission from David Kinder via Profile Theatre, Portland, OR.

Within the drama, there is also the recurring trope of the blue door, a metaphor for negotiating tensions of home for black subjects. In cases of threatening circumstances brought on by the outside world (whether it be the impending sale of a family member into slavery or the terrorism of the Ku Klux Klan), the members of Lewis's family have historically painted the door blue as a mechanism to keep danger away. The play dramatizes the slave era tradition of painting doors, window shutters, and porch ceilings a "haint" blue color as a means to scare off ghosts (haints)—which could stand in for the threatening white world of the slave and post-Emancipation eras. In Gullah/Geechee tradition, the blue (or indigo) paint represents water that functions as a barrier to haints/ghosts, because according to lore, ghosts are afraid to cross over water.[14] This blue door calls up The Door of No Return of the castles off the Western cape of Africa that enslaved subjects walked through never to return again. If The Door of No Return signaled a severing of home, then the *blue door* symbolizes an attempt to restore this loss—to protect one from structures of power that unhomed millions of black subjects and placed them

---

14. See "The Culture of Gullah" http://www.museumofthecity.org/project/the-culture-of-gullah/.

in an ongoing state of homelessness. The potential of what exists outside the historic danger of the white world and the possibility to imagine safety and freedom animate the blue door. This book is then concerned with the quest in contemporary black drama to manifest what the blue door enables.

The play ends with Lewis and his ancestor Simon painting the door blue as a means to protect him from the problem of blackness in modern life and singing a song, written by Barfield, but employing Yoruba language. Kamari Maxine Clarke documents the maintenance of Yoruba language and spirituality in Gullah Sea Island communities and notes how this practice represents an active rejection of US affiliation and functions as a means to more firmly bind descendants of slavery to Africa.[15] We see this influence in the song Barfield constructs:

Eniyan fo soke	Fly, people
Eye fo soke	Fly, bird
Idiran mi wa sile	Come down, my ancestor
Angeli wa sile	Come down, angel

Here, in addition to her depiction of Lewis and his ancestor Simon performing the ritual of painting the door blue, Barfield calls up genealogies of performance that have resonance in the slave era—meditations on flight in song voiced in the language of the ancestors. The play ends with the sound of the fluttering of a bird's wings—another symbol of flight.[16] The destination of Lewis's metaphorical flight, however, is ambiguous—whether it be to Africa or to another location. Ending with flight (with Lewis being metaphorically suspended in air), Barfield depicts a kind of fugitivity that functions as freeing for Lewis, moving him toward an articulation of his identity outside the confines of objectification. While Barfield ends the play with the enslaved ancestor and Lewis, we should not read this moment as an easy conflation of past and present. Rather, this moment signifies how slavery is still an animating force in black life that must be reckoned with.

MEMORY AND FORGETTING

Within black performance, we find a long and contentious history over just how to reckon with the troubled past of slavery. Debates over how to engage

---

15. See Clarke's "Transnational Yoruba Revivalism and the Diasporic Politics of Heritage."

16. For a deeper consideration of the motif of flight and its continued resonance in African Diasporic cultures and in black speculative fiction, see Michelle Commander's *Afro-Atlantic Flight: Speculative Returns and the Black Fantastic*.

this history in black creative production endure. Resistance to depicting slavery in black performance dates back as early as 1876, where a pageant in Philadelphia, Pennsylvania, marking the Constitution's one hundredth birthday, included a series of floats depicting black Americans' journey from slavery to freedom. Notably, black residents refused to ride on the float depicting slavery (Hill and Hatch 200). Also, in 1898, journalist J. C. Reid objected to the continued performance of the cakewalk after slavery, stating, "What we want to do is put down everything that ever was connected to slavery. We want to forget those days" (Hill and Hatch 201). Unsurprisingly, because these events were so recent in public memory, black Americans sought to distance themselves as much as possible from the institution.

Even today, however, the value of such an enterprise (the ongoing return to slavery in scholarly and creative work) continues to be contested. In a notable instance, Stephen Best's "On Failing to Make the Past Present" issues a challenge to what he perceives as the heavy reliance of critics on the slave past as a "ready prism" for understanding the present. Rather than think of the past in terms of melancholy, characterized by a refusal to detach, Best suggests that we contemplate and represent the past with the ethos of mourning because it offers a more distinct break. Calvin Warren rejects Best's framing of the slave era as a finite historical moment, asserting,

> The violence of slavery constitutes an interminable grief that resists the vectors of the present, past and future. To argue that slavery is a falling away from our present rests on a limited understanding of slavery—one that reduces it to a certain legal, material, and historical incarnation and neglects the epistemological, spiritual, traumatic, and metaphysical dimensions of such violence. (66)

Indeed, black playwrights have been concerned with charting the subject and impact of slavery across time, which speaks to the continual effort to grapple with its interminable effects. Valerié Bada offers a comprehensive history of the dynamic body of work on slavery in black drama produced from the nineteenth century to the late twentieth century, noting plays such as *The Drama of King Shotoway, or the Insurrection of the Caribs* (1822) produced by the African Grove Theatre, William Wells Brown's *The Escape, or A Leap for Freedom* (1858), Pauline Hopkins's *Peculiar Sam, or the Underground Railroad* (1880), extending to pageants of the Harlem Renaissance, the work of Randolph Edmonds and other dramas such as Amiri Baraka's *Slave Ship* (1967), William Branch's *In Splendid Error* (1976), and Daniel W. Owens *The Box* (1989). Bada's work highlights how slavery has always been at the heart of the black theatrical tradition. My work, then, adds another dimension to the conversation initiated by Bada by tracing the continued presence of slavery in black theatrical performance. Specifically, I am concerned with the development of this genre, its increasing intersections with the neo-slave narrative, and how contemporary black dramas construct emancipation as an unfinished process.

CHAPTERS

If a central conceit of trans-Atlantic slavery is that it was world-destroying for black enslaved subjects, then this book's structure calls attention to acts of world-(re)making for black subjects that take place on the contemporary stage. It also takes up how embodiment functions as a critical tool to represent slavery and as an articulation of black fugitivity. In each chapter, I consider how the body is defamiliarized in time and space in order to reconstruct slavery and its meanings for audiences, revealing its subtle indignities, subterranean terrors, and its "as yet unresolved unfolding" (Sharpe, *In the Wake* 14). By examining how contemporary black dramas featuring slavery subvert familiar conceptions of time, place, and space (the who, what, when, and where of history), I locate performances of fugitivity in the dramas I analyze and their capacity to engender new understandings about slavery and black subjectivity. Chapter 1 compiles a genealogy of black dramas presented from the late 1950s to the 1990s that represent an emergence of performances of fugitivity in depictions of slavery on stage. While scholars have rightly identified dramas produced during this period as turning away from realist or naturalist methods of depicting slavery, much of this work has been narrowly theorized in the language of healing or redemptive practice. However, I argue that dramas produced during this time, namely Lorraine Hansberry's *The Drinking Gourd* (1960), Amiri Baraka's *The Slave* (1964) and *Slave Ship* (1967), George C. Wolfe's *The Colored Museum* (1986), Robbie McCauley's *Sally's Rape* (1989), Lorna Littleway's unpublished play *Phillis Wheatley: The Celestial Muse* (1979), and Pomo Afro Homo's *Dark Fruit* (1992), are less concerned with the project of healing the wounds of slavery. Rather, these works constitute early instantiations of black fugitivity in depictions of slavery. I identify patterns of representational strategies that emerge under the rubric of performances of fugitivity that we see occurring in black dramas featuring slavery from the 1960s and into the late twentieth century. I also consider how the development of this dramatic production tracks with the development of the neo-slave narrative, where scholars such as Bernard Bell and Ashraf Rushdy mark the 1960s as an inflection point in black literary production and its engagement with slavery.

In the remainder of the book, I consider dramas that premiered between 1996 and into the twenty-first century for the ways they draw upon the corporeal to defamiliarize and construct new epistemologies of slavery. In chapter 2, I examine how August Wilson treats the notion of Middle Passage in his work that runs counter to the abundance of representations of the Middle Passage, which largely draw upon imagery of abject black bodies tortured on slave ships to present this history. Focusing primarily on *Gem of the Ocean* (2003), I consider how Wilson uses the metaphor of bones to stand in for abused black flesh. He also centers the figure Citizen—a fugitive on the run for stealing a bucket of nails. In upending the familiar tropes of Middle Passage and dramatizing them through the alienated figure of Citizen, Wilson reconfigures notions of loss altogether. In so doing, he also revises America's national myths and constructs new geographies that mark black experience. Wilson frames the prominence of death and grief in the black American body politic as an artifact of American history and ultimately writes black Americans' experiences of grief and loss onto national narratives of mourning.

I turn from the renarrativization of black enslaved experience and the abstraction of black bodies that we see in Wilson's depiction of the Middle Passage to consider the performance of whiteface, as opposed to blackface, in the recounting of slavery. Chapter 3 treats Lydia Diamond's *Harriet Jacobs; A Play* (2008) and Branden Jacobs-Jenkins *An Octoroon* (2014) for how they destabilize the body as a method of critiquing conceptions of race founded in slavery. Working from original texts, *Incidents in the Life of a Slave Girl* and Dion Boucicault's *The Octoroon,* respectively, Diamond and Jacobs-Jenkins stage fugitivity in order to deny an objectifying representation of slavery and call attention to the complexities of black interiority. In their reframing of slavery's graphic economies, depictions of captive black bodies, and interventions in canonical narrative accounts, these dramas engage in a multilayered process of recontextualizing slavery and enslaved subjects (and in the case of Jacobs-Jenkins, modern-day subjects) that perform fugitivity. Theirs is an artistic and political effort on the part of black subjects, past and present, to evade objectification and oversimplified representations of slavery and blackness. The performance of whiteness in both dramas also calls up performance genealogies of blackface minstrelsy that chiefly were designed to caricature black subjects and define them through performance.

Chapter 4 examines the staging of queer subjectivity against the backdrop of slavery. I look to playwright Robert O'Hara in particular to explore how he destabilizes time, place, and space to write the queer into the counterarchive of slavery. I consider two of O'Hara's works in this chapter: *Insurrection; Holding History* (1996) and *Antebellum* (2009) in terms of their depictions of queer fugitivity. These performances of fugitivity rely on the troubling of notions of home—often a site of tension for queer subjects. I argue that this approach brings forth the ways gender was upended in slavery. This method accounts for the buried narratives of queer subjects in slavery—what Matt Richardson calls the "queer limit of black memory." In this chapter, I consider how O'Hara forwards radical practices of intimacy and troubles the intimate space of the home through enslaved queer subjects past and present.

I conclude with a meditation on the ending of Suzan-Lori Parks's *Father Comes Home from the Wars: Parts 1, 2, and 3* and the line spoken by Odyssey Dog, "The Runaways, they still got to run." The runaways in the play flee just before the central character, Hero, now named Ulysses, can read to them the Emancipation Proclamation and announce their freedom. As a result, they never learn that they are free and continue in a perpetual state of fugitivity. I argue that Parks ends the drama in this way to frame emancipation as unfinished. I merge my reading of *Father Comes Home* with Claudia Rankine's 2014 *Citizen: An American Lyric* and its employment of J. M. W. Turner's 1840 painting, *The Slave Ship: Slavers Throwing Overboard the Dead and Dying—Typhoon Coming On* as an expression of the ongoing strife black Americans experience in the contemporary era, which is rooted in slavery. Rankine's work, too, reflects the ethos of this project and serves as a reminder of the extent to which the history of slavery still haunts the present. My work considers the stage as a site where the effects of this haunting are expressed, histories reframed, and new forms of identity advanced.

This book seeks to understand what factors in contemporary black life and developments in black art have contributed to the increased return to slavery, particularly in black drama. Also, how do these representations re-present the slave past? How might these new depictions offer insight into contemporary black subjects existing in slavery's long shadow? The metaphorical blue door that Tanya Barfield presents offers an invitation to ponder these questions. This project ruminates on what exists on the other side of the blue door that runs counter to The Door of No Return. What possibilities might lie beyond its threshold?

CHAPTER 1

Mapping Fugitivity in Black Drama

LORRAINE HANSBERRY'S unproduced 1960 screenplay *The Drinking Gourd* dramatizes slave era life on the Sweet Plantation just before the commencement of the Civil War. Commissioned by NBC producer-director Dore Schary in 1959 as part of a series of shows to mark the Centennial of the Civil War, the screenplay never made it on air, with Hansberry lamenting, "They thought it was 'superb' . . . *and then they put it away in a drawer*" (*Collected Last Plays* 145).[1] Although the production company gave no true explanation for why they did not proceed with producing the show, one need only read *The Drinking Gourd* to gain insight. The play confronts inconvenient truths of slavery (its brutality, its cumulative catastrophe, its corruptive and corrosive qualities) as it depicts the lives of families—both enslaved and not—torn apart by the institution. Perhaps most forceful in this drama is the undercurrent of resistance embodied through the enslaved Hannibal, who secretly learns to read and is then blinded once this fact is exposed. The play ends in a painful confrontation between Hannibal's mother, Rissa, and dying enslaver, Hiram Sweet. As Hiram endeavors to apologize for the brutal actions of his overseer in damaging Hannibal's eyes and causing his vision loss, Rissa retorts with a challenge to his power and exposes his limitations. When Hiram proclaims

---

1. See Robert Nemiroff's introduction to *The Drinking Gourd* in Lorraine Hansberry's *The Collected Last Plays* for an extended analysis of the politics behind the decision.

that she has gone too far, she poignantly asks, "Will your overseer gouge out my eyes too?" and continues, "I don't 'spect blindness would matter to me. I done seen all there was worth seein' in this world—and it didn't 'mount to much" (215).

To end the drama with a meditation on blindness and Rissa's commentary on her bleak reality against the backdrop of a bleak future even as the war for emancipation is commencing at the play's end, Hansberry juxtaposes black subjects unable to envision (literally and figuratively) a future for themselves alongside the ongoing mainstream impulse to "look back" on the Civil War without full attention to the atrocities of slavery. Rissa's words, "I don't 'spect blindness would matter to me," signals a kind of fugitivity that aligns with her sons' active attempts to free themselves from slavery. (Her son Hannibal surreptitiously leaves the fields and learns to read, and her other son Isaiah is rumored to have escaped to Canada.) Rissa distances herself from her location in the world as evinced by her dismissal of the value of sight. She would rather live in darkness than continue to witness the brutal realities of her current state.

I begin with *The Drinking Gourd* because it stands as one of the first dramas on slavery that fully engages the notion of fugitivity and the ambivalence of American citizenship for the descendants of the enslaved. Hansberry's mixed-media autobiography *To Be Young, Gifted and Black* includes excerpts of *The Drinking Gourd,* although the piece never made it to official production at NBC. While we have primarily understood Amiri Baraka as being at the forefront of the movement in black drama to push back against received histories of slavery and center black subjectivity in the telling of this history, it is important to acknowledge Hansberry's contributions to this critical turn, which are not only evident in *The Drinking Gourd* but also in her public writing and contemporaneous conversations.[2] Situating Hansberry as a consequential and key contributor to the critical work of presenting slavery on stage makes clear the contributions of those who produced what Mary Helen Washington terms "Black left literary modernism" (of which Hansberry is included) and the paths these writers made for the radical literary production of the Black Arts era.[3]

In this chapter, I will offer an extended reading of Hansberry's *The Drinking Gourd* in order to place the work within the larger body of black dramatic production on slavery and to give this work its critical due as an innovator in presenting slavery in a new light. Using the conceptual lens, *performances of*

---

2. See *The Collected Last Plays*, which includes more of Hansberry's public writing on slavery.

3. See Mary Helen Washington's *The Other Black List: The African American Literary and Cultural Left of the 1950s.*

fugitivity, that I offer in the book's introduction, I read *The Drinking Gourd* as an early representation of this concept. I will also identify patterns of representational strategies that emerge under the rubric of performances of fugitivity that we see occurring in black dramas featuring slavery from the 1960s and into the late twentieth century. The development of this dramatic production tracks with the development of the neo-slave narrative, where scholars such as Bernard Bell and Ashraf Rushdy mark the 1960s as an inflection point in black literary production and its engagement with slavery. In offering a trajectory of the development of black drama's performances of fugitivity in its representations of slavery, I forward interpretive frameworks for reading the overlapping patterns that emerge in mid-to-late twentieth-century black dramatic production on slavery and its reverberations. These frameworks are not meant to be understood as discrete. Their boundaries are porous and should be considered primarily as facilitating the identification of prominent representational strategies present in a particular drama. This allows for a more effective tracing of early manifestations of fugitivity on the black stage. Moreover, I do not suggest that the dramas I discuss in the pages that follow constitute an origin point for resistant performance practices in black expressive culture. As scholars such as Daphne Brooks, Saidiya Hartman, and Fred Moten demonstrate, this orientation in black performance has a long history dating back to slavery. Put simply, the works I discuss here more effectively allow for a situating of developments in black drama alongside the neo-slave narrative, which in turn moves us closer to the contemporary era that is the primary concern of this book.

To remind, I define *performances of fugitivity* as subversive, radical, and experimental performances of black artistic and political freedom at the site of slavery. In presenting black fugitive subjects of the slave past and beyond, contemporary black drama's performances of fugitivity provide a critical framework for examining these subjects as well as offer a useful way to think about black subjects' ongoing feelings of non-belonging and critical distance from American institutions that have been historically unwelcoming and hostile to them. Performances of fugitivity emerge in black dramas in the following ways: 1) in the centering of black subjectivity more prominently in the telling of slavery in order to forward new narratives about slavery and advance new vocabularies for blackness; 2) in the assertion that emancipation remains an ongoing and unfinished process; and 3) in the troubling of notions of home where black subjects are depicted as disconnected from the nation, holding America at a critical distance to recognize black Americans' unrealized citizenship and civic exclusion as well as their skepticism toward underlying value systems of a nation built on slavery. These dramas also reconceive domestic notions of home by interrogating "the master's house" as a founding and problematic structure of current iterations of black domesticity.

With this in mind, I return to *The Drinking Gourd* to explore the early workings of performances of fugitivity in black drama and its significance for the black dramatic canon. Hansberry wrote *The Drinking Gourd* during a time of major social unrest and rumblings of more to come. Four years before 1959 (the year that she was commissioned to write the drama), Rosa Parks refused to give up her seat on a bus in a move that would spark the Montgomery Bus Boycott. This same year also saw the murder of Emmett Till. Also, the nation was still feeling the reverberations of the 1954 Supreme Court decision *Brown v. Board of Education of Topeka, Kansas* and the *Bolling v. Sharpe* decision that overturned the "separate but equal" doctrine codified into law with *Plessy v. Ferguson*. If, as Hansberry would have it, a dramatist must "thoroughly inundate himself or herself in an awareness of the realities of the historical period and then dismiss it" in order to create human beings "whom you know in your own time" (*Collected Last Plays* 147), then the characters of *The Drinking Gourd* cannot be said to be merely relics of a bygone era, but equally informed by the tumultuous times of the mid-twentieth-century realities with which Hansberry was thoroughly engaged. Hansberry works to represent human emotion in a way that transcends time, and it is clear that *The Drinking Gourd* speaks not only to the revolutionary spirit of the enslaved but also to the social revolution occurring around her in the late 1950s.

Gesturing to the spiritual "Follow the Drinking Gourd" in its title, a song that directs escapees from slavery to follow the long handle of the Big Dipper constellation to the Ohio River, *The Drinking Gourd* centers fugitivity as a mechanism to intervene in misrepresentations of black subjectivity in historical discourse and to reveal slavery's devastating impact on notions of home, particularly for black subjects. Notably, Hansberry came to know slavery through the prism of the fugitive. She recounts her first trip to the American South when her mother took the family to visit Tennessee. Her mother points out the landscape and informs the children that "her father had run away and hidden from his enslaver in those very hills when he was a little boy" (*To Be Young* 53). Hansberry arguably carries this knowledge with her across time when she expresses her objection to a critic reviewing James Weldon Johnson's *Trumpets of the Lord* and his suggestion that the work is influenced by "the 'recent' militancy of Negroes" (*Collected Last Plays* 148). In a 1964 letter to the editor of the *Village Voice,* Hansberry rejoins, "Negro protest and revolt is not new. It is as old as the slave trade. Negroes came here fighting back" (*Collected Last Plays* 149). This letter offers insight into Hansberry's desire to elevate the spirit of revolution for black subjects that has often been misrepresented in historical discourse.

The Drinking Gourd introduces the enslaved subjects in the drama as restless, unhomed, and seeking escape. They sing the spiritual "Steal Away," which calls up a genealogy of performance of black subjects' resisting slavery. The first verse here is particularly poignant:

> Steal away, steal away,
> Steal away to Jesus.
> Steal away, steal away home—
> I ain't got long to stay here.

These lines express longing and a kind of anticipatory action that rejects the realities of "here." The words "Steal away" call up the theft of flesh that often framed the act of running away for the enslaved. To escape was tantamount to stealing from the enslaver. Yet, home persists. To "steal away home," the place that is not "here," means to be in search and unhomed in the "here" and now. I linger on these opening lines because Hansberry layers onto them an interrogation of home and frames the enslaver's house as a site of terror, an undesirable space for the unhomed black subject.

The ironic name of the plantation itself, Sweet Plantation, signals that plantation life is anything but "sweet." Much like the "Sweet Home" that Morrison riffs on in *Beloved*, Hansberry goes to the heart of the matter by challenging any memory or representation of slavery as "sweet." Indeed, the young Hannibal is horrified that his mother has secured a position for him in the Hiram Sweet family home. Hannibal furiously exclaims, "I don't want Marster Everertt's [Hiram's son] bright red jacket and I don't want Marster Sweet's scraps. I don't want nothin' in this whole world but to get off this plantation!" (*Collected Last Plays* 201). Hannibal's refusal to accept what has been framed as a desirable job overturns notions of working in the enslaver's house as honorable. Hannibal rejects participation in the Sweet Plantation's domestic life, which represents for him yet another site of his dehumanization. Moreover, he does not desire to be in the company of the Sweet family, whose interactions are anything but. At dinner, Hansberry depicts the Sweet family in a bitter battle over the future of the plantation and how to defend against the imminent army of Union soldiers preparing to end slavery. Hiram's chief antagonist is his son Everett, who desires to operate the plantation with greater severity and surreptitiously hires an overseer to aid in this effort. The war between the past and the future are thoroughly engaged in the domestic space of the Sweet family home. In this way, Hansberry reveals slavery's cumulative damage and its severing of familial ties for both black and white subjects.

The Drinking Gourd's depiction of Hannibal's efforts to revolt highlights black agency in narrating the story slavery. Yet, it is telling that Hannibal, an individual who so thoroughly sought after freedom, could literally not see the coming freedom that the Civil War purportedly delivered. Clearly, Hansberry does not present an optimistic view of emancipation, ending the drama with Hannibal's blindness and Hiram's death as he collapses outside of Rissa's dwelling. In fact, the play gestures to the ways the tragedies of slavery resonate in Hansberry's 1950s present. This drama marks a turning point in black drama's representations of the slave era where we see a more critical stance taken on how the history of this era has been narrated and how it has often obscured black subjectivity. Thus, this drama offers a strategy of representing slavery that challenges the historical record in order to communicate larger (and often inconvenient) truths about the institution.

I turn now to an assemblage of black dramas about slavery that, like *The Drinking Gourd*, are in conversation with the cultural politics of the 1950s extending to the late twentieth century. These dramas provide valuable context for the contemporary dramas I examine in the remainder of this book. In their groundbreaking portrayals of slavery, these dramas forward countermemories of slavery that critique histories and make new lives possible. Taking into account Margo Natalie Crawford's challenge to those who theorize about the postblack era as somehow a departure from previous approaches to envisioning and representing black aesthetics (Crawford, "'What Was Is'" 23), I call attention to the experimental impulse in black drama from the 1960s to the late twentieth century that has always been present.

While not comprehensive, this chapter locates fugitivity in key works of the Black Arts era and beyond in order to map out frameworks for reading how performances of fugitivity manifest in contemporary black drama. As such, I present categories for understanding the fluid approaches to fugitivity and slavery that each drama takes on. I identify these categories in the following ways:

1. *Revolutionary Fugitivity*
2. *Fugitive Time*
3. *Black Feminist Fugitivity*
4. *Black Queer Fugitivity*

These categories aid in identifying critical strands in this dynamic body of work and serve as a foundation for my exploration of how we see these ideas show up in the works of black playwrights of the late twentieth and twenty-first centuries. I do not mean to suggest that they correlate exactly with the works I examine in subsequent chapters or that they are contained concepts that don't overlap with one another. I am more interested in how iterations of these ideas show up in contemporary black dramas featuring slavery and how they shift or take on new dimensions across time.

REVOLUTIONARY FUGITIVITY

Aligned with the ethos of the Black Arts Era, *revolutionary fugitivity*, as I delineate it, is deconstructive black performance trained on dismantling the white Western social order. Under this rubric, practices of undoing, dismantling, and overthrowing create possibility for black subjects. This ideological posture positions black subjects at a critical distance from America (in the case of black American experience), figuring them as inhabitants of hostile territory. Moreover, this approach to fugitivity also advances notions of separatism and independence as key to black freedom. In keeping with the dismantling of the social order, revolutionary fugitivity refuses closure of traumas brought on by racial terror and state-sanctioned violence against black subjects, particularly that of slavery. Concomitantly, it sees possibility in unceasing mourning, especially in its capacity to elevate devalued black lives and to refuse a resolution for that which the state has not yet atoned.

My definition of revolutionary fugitivity takes its cues from Amiri Baraka and the performance work of Black Arts Movement artists such as Larry Neal and Kalamu ya Salaam, who innovatively presented slavery in the contexts of revolution and fugitivity. I focus here on Baraka because he stands as most prominent for his dramatization of these sentiments. It goes without saying that the heart of Baraka's theater is revolution. In his essay "The Revolutionary Theatre," Baraka presents a forceful mediation on what the goals of revolutionary theater should be. He asserts, "Imagination (Image) is all possibility. . . . Possibility is what moves us" (*Home* 213). The malleable concept of *possibility* sits alongside Baraka's language of "attack," "expose," "accuse," and "destroy" that he deploys throughout the essay. I want to hold on to this as a guidepost for how I read manifestations of fugitivity in Baraka's revolutionary theater. My analysis here is also buttressed by Baraka's 1962 essay "'Black' is a Country," which offers a more nuanced approach to what constitutes black nationalism and expresses a deep ambivalence toward American belonging.

Baraka's "'Black' is a Country" reveals tensions of home for black subjects in America. Written just two years before the 1964 Civil Rights Act, Baraka espouses an ambivalence toward both assimilation and the creation of a black nation. Rather, he advocates for a focus on black *independence* arguing, "The struggle is not simply for 'equality,' or 'better jobs,' or 'better schools,' and the rest of those half-hearted liberal clichés; it is to completely free the black man from the domination of the white man" (*Home* 84). The focus in this passage is less on attaining the characteristic facets of the American dream for black Americans and more on achieving freedom from the white world. To that end, Baraka expresses blackness as all-encompassing, forwarding the notion that "black" itself is a country. He asserts, "The black man has been separated and made to live in his own country of color. If you are black the only roads into the mainland of American life are through subservience, cowardice, and loss of manhood" (85). Separation from the "mainland of American life" articulates black fugitivity. For Baraka, America may as well be another country for black Americans, who, at the time of his writing, remained excluded from social centers of American life even as small elements of progress were being made. Thus a revolutionary fugitivity like the one Baraka articulates remains unmoved by (and even skeptical of) small moments of cultural progress. This kind of fugitivity sees revolution as the best possible action for achieving independence and critiques American ideals for their contradictory applications in the face of ongoing racial oppression. I must note that Baraka's meditations here contain an overarching masculinist slant and emphasis that frame racial terror and oppression as a black male experience. Later in this chapter, I will return to the problems inherent in this framing in my discussion of black feminist fugitivity.

Amiri Baraka's 1964 play, *The Slave*, dramatizes revolutionary fugitivity with its tensions of American belonging and home for black subjects in the aftermath of the Civil Rights Movement. The drive for independence forcefully animates the drama with Baraka, linking the slave past to the troubling 1964 present. *The Slave* depicts an encounter between Walker Vessels, a middle-aged black man; his ex-wife Grace, a white woman; and her current partner Bradford Easley, a white university professor as Walker veritably holds them hostage during what appears to be a riot initiated by black militants seeking retribution for racial oppression. The play ends with Walker shooting Grace and Bradford. It also leaves open the possibility that the two daughters that Walker and Grace produced from their marriage are actually dead as well. Margo Natalie Crawford labels *The Slave* as a post-neo-slave narrative for its emphasis on the unknown and its refusal of closure from the traumas of slavery. She asserts that in the post-neo-slave narrative "being stuck in melancholy is not pathologized, and mourning is not set apart from rage, action, and resistance" ("The Inside-Turned-Out Architecture" 80). Crawford's identification of rage, action, and resistance as a part of the mourning process is key to Baraka's expression of revolutionary fugitivity. The refusal to perform healing or reconcile the devastating past of slavery undergirds Baraka's representation of slavery. We see a continuation of this approach in his play *Slave Ship* where the Middle Passage is represented as a site of originary and unresolved injury for black Americans.

The Slave opens by destabilizing time with the figure of Walker Vessels alone on stage and dressed as an "old field hand slave, balding, with white hair and an old ragged vest" (43). Baraka utilizes this prologue to frame the drama in the context of slavery. Interestingly, however, Walker doesn't speak in dialect or any affectation of familiar representations of the enslaved in popular culture. Instead, the narration is painstaking and contemplative. Alone on stage, Walker opens, "Whatever the core of our lives. Whatever the deceit. We live where we are, and seek nothing but ourselves" (43). In this moment, Walker espouses a philosophy that prompts the audience to consider their own orientations to the world. It denies a passive spectatorship. Walker also challenges conceptions of time, telling the audience, "I am much older than I look . . . or maybe much younger. Whatever I am or seem . . . [*Significant pause*] to you, then let that rest. But figure, still, that you might not be right" (44). He later informs the audience, "Time's a dead thing really . . . and keeps nobody whole" (45). In the disruption of time both in the enslaved figure speaking to a present-day audience in contemporary vernacular and in the unreliability of Walker's age, Baraka approaches his representation of slavery through radical experimentation. He also uses Walker Vessels as a means for audience members to think on their familiar ideals about representations of blackness on stage. To suggest "you might not be right" is to challenge the spectator to question the reliability of their perceptions of blackness. With Walker, Baraka seeks to challenge historical representations of blackness on stage, saying, "In *The Slave*, Walker Vessels, the black revolutionary, wears an armband, which is the insignia of the attacking army—a big red-lipped minstrel, grinning like crazy" (*Home* 214). Gesturing to the trickster figure of blackface, Baraka constructs Walker as an embodiment of black resistance across time. His name even shares phonetic relation to historical figure Denmark Vesey, who plotted a major slave revolt in 1822—even though the government of Charleston, South Carolina, executed him upon learning of the plan. Walker's body, in its timeless state, inscribes enslavement, revolt, and the ongoing struggle for freedom taking place in the 1960s. We can also read his name as signifying on the words "walking vessel" in that he becomes a vessel of history, a living receptacle that suggests that black experience, particularly its histories of racial terror, cannot be confined to a singular moment, but only as a sum of events that produce the black subject.

As the prologue continues, we move progressively forward into the 1960s present of the drama with Walker in poetic meditation. He discourses, "Discovering the last image of the thing. As the sky when the moon is broken.

Or old, old blues people moaning in their sleep, singing, man, oh, nigger, nigger, you still here, as hard as nails, and takin' no shit from nobody" (45). Here Walker negates the attempts to render the enslaved as socially dead and similar efforts after Emancipation to terrorize and marginalize black subjects in public life. The words "nigger, you still here" speak to Christina Sharpe's articulation of black fugitivity as "black life that persists in spite of" ("Black Life, Annotated"). Baraka's black subject gestures to a fugitivity that is resilient and shifting.

This resilience and malleability, however, must also be read alongside Walker's alienation within the main of the drama. After having married a white woman with whom he has two daughters and after attending university, Walker seemingly has attained the American Dream. Yet, he sees that dream dissolve after his divorce from Grace. He lambasts individuals like Bradford, who offer support for racial equality in rhetoric but not action. Walker says, "You never did anything concrete to avoid what's going on now. Your sick liberal lip service to whatever was the least filth. Your high aesthetic disapproval of the political" (74). Walker in this moment articulates a disappointment with the failures of white ally-ship and the limitations he experiences of truly achieving liberation and inclusion in America.

Baraka dramatizes Walker's alienation at the site of Grace and Walker's broken home. Walker's invasion of the home signals his own feelings of unhomeliness and disconnection. His goal is to strike the very heart of his brokenness—Grace's new marriage to Bradford and Walker's separation from the family. Quoting from Yeats's "News for the Delphic Oracle," Walker recites, "Those innocents relive their death, / Their wounds open again" (50). Walker's wounds are laid bare in the home where he ultimately kills Grace and Bradford Easley. The home has now been transformed into a site of terror that represents the historical terror experienced by black subjects and the terror of the present that has forced individuals like Walker to revolt as a means to attain independence.

The play's ending offers a performance of fugitivity with Grace asking Walker if the girls upstairs (their children) are dead. From that point, we hear various shouts and explosions with Walker shouting, "They're dead, Grace," and a child screaming. Margo Natalie Crawford, too, reads this in the context of fugitivity, arguing that "the screaming is a type of fugitivity" ("The Inside-Turned-Out Architecture 80). "Whatever escapes reshapes the container. The psychic hold of slavery is, sometimes, the psychic hold of fugitivity. As Haki Madhubuti advises, 'DON'T CRY, SCREAM'" (80). The guttural sounds of the screaming child and Walker's shouts perform fugitivity by its refusal of closure and the ambiguous ending of the drama. Walker remains a fugitive now surrounded by the dead bodies of his family, whose deaths represent the carnage of Walker's quest for independence. In this sense, Baraka constructs independence as elusive.

Baraka's 1967 play, *Slave Ship*, continues the interrogation of the costs of independence for black subjects and the role slavery has played in limiting that independence. In almost a continuation of the screams that we hear at the end of *The Slave*, Baraka projects the cries and screams of the enslaved traveling the Middle Passage at the open of *Slave Ship*. Returning to the assertion that the act of screaming performs a kind of fugitivity, the first sound the audience hears in *Slave Ship* are the enslaved women on the ship screaming, "AAAAAIIIIEEEEEEEEEEEE"("Slave Ship" 132). Sounds of chains, the lash, and moaning follow and intersperse the screaming. The emphasis on sound centers black pain and subjectivity as a counter to the dehumanizing process of enslavement. Alongside this, the enslaved call on Yoruba gods, Shango, Obatala, and other orishas, spirits that recall an African homeland. The calling on Yoruba gods functions as another manifestation of fugitivity.[4] These moments depict the refusal of the enslaved to adopt Western hegemonic religious ideals and their efforts to maintain connection to their ideals in the face of severance.

Baraka intensifies this focus on resistance as the drama progresses. *Slave Ship* does not follow a narrative trajectory and is told primarily in scenes. Three images ground *Slave Ship*'s unwieldy narrative. The first image depicts the enslaved being brought aboard the ship and taken into the ship's hold where various sexual acts take place (from a white man raping a black woman to enslaved women surreptitiously joining their husbands to copulate). The second image depicts enslavement and the destruction of black collectivity (a marriage, the selling a husband and wife apart, the traitorous house slave, and the preacher who promotes acquiescence). The final image dramatizes a revolt where the slaves accost a white man who begs for his life.

Baraka calls up one notable fugitive slave, Nat Turner, preparing to lead a revolt. However, he is foiled by an enslaved man seeking favor with his enslaver. This scene occurs just after the first frame of images of the enslaved in the hold of a ship, seemingly as a signal for how slavery disrupted black collectivity in irrevocable ways. This moment also echoes Baraka's ambivalence with the notion of black unity. In "'Black' is a Country," Baraka asserts, "The struggle is for *independence,* not separation—or assimilation for that matter. Do what you want to with *your* life . . . when you can. I want to be independent of black men just as much as I want to be independent from the white" (*Home* 86). These lines contain a tension between a desire for a collective

---

4. See Kamari Clarke's "Transnational Yoruba Revivalism and the Diasporic Politics of Heritage."

progress for black Americans and the pursuit of individual independence. This, too, is a representation of fugitivity in which the black subject maintains a critical distance from spaces that deny the possibility of independence.

The tensions between collective action and individual freedom underscore the central themes of the play. At the play's end, the cast participates in a chant that becomes song. It follows:

> Rise, Rise, Rise
> Cut these ties, black Man Rise
> We gon' be the thing we are . . .
> When we gonna rise up, brother. ("Slave Ship" 143)

The song continues with a number of questions beginning with "when." This chant encapsulates the notion of destruction as enabling the kind of possibility that underwrites revolutionary fugitivity. The future conditional "we gon' be" and "when" point to a reality that has not yet arrived. The cast continues to lead this song in their final act where they kill the black preacher (arguably represented as Martin Luther King, Jr.). They also kill a white man who constitutes the embodiment of white supremacy. As the house lights come up, the cast begins to dance and invites audience members to dance. A party ensues. However, in a notable turn, white audience members are not invited to dance. In his oft-cited review of a 1969 production of the play at Chelsea Theatre, Foster Hirsch expresses being "stunned, confused, hurt, angry" at this slight (102). Ending the party with black communion, celebration, and joy also enacts fugitivity in its effort to depict black subjects outside of and actively rejecting white inclusion. The party also carries a kind of irony that, when juxtaposed with the traumatic opening, feels incongruous. Consistent with revolutionary fugitivity, these sometimes jarring emotional shifts enable black subjects to dictate the terms of their mourning of slavery and collectively envision a potential independence.[5]

FUGITIVE TIME

The party that ends *Slave Ship* points to a critical turn in the depiction of slavery in black drama where we see new affective associations being inscribed onto the institution. Significantly, we also see with Baraka's work emergent

---

5. See also Harry Elam's analysis of *Slave Ship* in the context of revolution in his generative work, *Taking It to the Streets: The Social Protest Theatre of Luis Valdez and Amiri Baraka.*

radical modes of representing time as a means to account for slavery's ontologies and its distortive force. When Walker Vessels of *The Slave* explains in his prologue that "time's a dead thing," he is calling up what I think of as *fugitive time*. I define fugitive time as a temporal accounting for the fluidity of black fugitivity during slavery and beyond as a practice of freedom. It represents time as both suspended and atemporal, or outside of time with the fugitive in perpetual motion. In this sense, time contracts or expands depending on the limits of one's freedom. We can understand it as a redoubling of revolutionary fugitivity in its deconstruction of Western conceptions of time as a way to create an alternate space in which black subjects can grapple with slavery's psychic effects and imagine themselves through new modalities. In its Afrofuturistic turns, fugitive time reorders black life, past and present, in ways that account for the infinite psychic damage of slavery and highlights the need for new epistemologies of time for the black subject in motion.

Theorists have pointed to the need to perform a reappraisal of prevailing constructs of time in order to fully comprehend the psychic impact of slavery on black subjects. Anthony Reed makes plain the political urgency of attending to time in the contemporary era. He argues, "We not only need to consider historical gaps and erasures but also to think about and produce inhabitable futures on terms other than those of the present, generating theories adequate to the complexities and contradictions of Black life" (1). Reed forwards the term "freedom time" to describe an impulse in black expressive culture and experimental writing—and its function in naming the fact that liberation has not yet occurred (7). His generative framing can also be read alongside Calvin Warren, who theorizes what he terms as "black time." Warren proposes an alternative temporality of slavery via black time, which he elaborates as "time without duration; it is a horizon of time that eludes objectification, foreclosing idioms such as 'getting over,' 'getting through,' or 'getting beneath.'" (Colbert et al. 56). In positing a new mode for understanding time in relation to slavery, Warren refuses a static demarcation of past and present, beginning and end. Moreover, Aida Levy-Hussen in her term "traumatic time" aims to account for how slavery's trauma disrupts normative conceptual orderings of time and explains that we must account for this in our assessment of literary explorations of trans-Atlantic slavery. She describes traumatic time as "non-linear, dis-unified, and regenerated by the impossible desire for a redemptive return to the past" (20). Cumulatively, these reflections on temporality and black experience undergird my definition of fugitive time as necessarily atemporal and variable in order to make space for an elusive black freedom.

George C. Wolfe's 1986 play, *The Colored Museum*, dramatizes black subjects in flight, both literally and figuratively, in its provocative renderings of black subjectivity made possible through a deployment of fugitive time. The play typifies the "artful escape of objectification"[6] on the part of black subjects speaking from the confines of institutions such as museums, archives, and other spaces where black identity is often circumscribed in narrow terms. By producing the unexpected and introducing humor in his engagement with slavery, Wolfe offers a new lens through which to view this history, one which challenges audiences to conceive of black identity beyond narrative frameworks. *The Colored Museum* walks through black history from the slave era to the 1986 present day. Wolfe ends the play, like Baraka, with a party, but this party involves major characters in the play such as Miss Pat, Miss Roj, as well as individuals such as Topsy (the iconic figure from *Uncle Tom's Cabin*), Nat Turner, Eartha Kitt, Malcolm X, Bert Williams, and a host of other historic black figures. The merging of the various figures from different historical periods serves as an appropriate culmination of a drama that upends time as a means to present slavery and the larger span of black history anew.

The Colored Museum deploys fugitive time from the outset of the drama. The first vignette, "Git on Board" takes place on an airplane called the Celebrity Slaveship. This ship travels the journey of the Middle Passage under the stewardship of Miss Pat, the airline stewardess who stipulates the rules of flight to the passengers. She instructs them on how to "fasten [their] shackles," informs them that they are not to sing or engage in call-and-response songs, and admonishes them not to play drums under any circumstances. In mid-flight, Miss Pat informs the audience in dramatic fashion that they are entering a time warp where they pass through historical events such as the American Revolution, the Civil War, the Great Depression, World War II, and the Vietnam War, among others. They then see historical figures such as Diahann Carroll, Malcolm X, Martin Luther King, Jr., The Supremes, and more. The flight ends with Miss Pat thanking the passengers for traveling the Celebrity Slaveship and expressing that they must take their baggage because "any baggage you don't claim, we trash."

The opening vignette of *The Colored Museum* destabilizes time as a means to upend familiar notions of slavery. By transforming the slave ship into an aircraft, Wolfe engages this history in a decidedly Afrofuturist and satirical manner.[7] The "flight" motif calls up flight in the sense of the fugitive and flight in the folkloric sense where enslaved Africans often imagined (and attempted

---

6. See James Edward Ford's "Introduction" in *Black Camera* vol. 7, no. 1, 2015.

7. See Christina Knight's "'Fasten Your Shackles': Remembering Slavery and Laughing about it in George C. Wolfe's *The Colored Museum*."

to enact) flight back to Africa.[8] Yet, the mixed metaphor of the Celebrity Slaveship signals a kind of ambivalence about slavery's fixed state in the past. The transformation of the slave ship into a modern airplane also gestures to the kinds of technologies and capitalist innovation that continue to maintain the relations of slavery in the contemporary. The time warp fuses modern-day realities with the painful past. However, in another turn, the drama suggests that the baggage of the past must be discarded. Aboard the Celebrity Slaveship, there is no use for such baggage. Miss Pat reminds us that any baggage left behind will be trashed. So, how then does the play invite the audience to reconcile the historical baggage of slavery?

The actual matter of how to grapple with the history of slavery remains an unanswered question in *The Colored Museum*. We see in the various vignettes a recurring theme of pain. The couple in "The Photo Session" confesses, "And everything is rehearsed, including this other kind of pain we're starting to feel. [Girl:] The kind of pain that comes from feeling no pain at all" (10). The Soldier with a Secret who enacts mercy killings for his fellow soldiers, "I know the secret. The secret to your pain" (13). Miss Roj snaps her demons away. Normal Jean Reynolds endures abuse and confinement in a closet because she is underage and pregnant. The drama, in fact, depicts people with incredible emotional baggage, and this pain gets represented in time as compounding, transforming, and mutating but a constant for black subjects living in slavery's shadow.

In a culmination of the effort to represent slavery's psychic toll while also imagining radical new possibilities for black subjectivity, Wolfe dramatizes Topsy (the abused and dehumanized girl-child in *Uncle Tom's Cabin*) in a transhistorical, transtemporal, and subversive way to represent black resilience in the face of slavery. Topsy opens the final scene, "The Party," by recounting a party she attended while also partying in the present moment. The guests at the party that Topsy recalls traverse large periods of time from the nineteenth-century figure Bert Williams to Angela Davis in the present day. Most telling of Topsy's subversion are the following lines:

> And here, all this time I been thinking we gave up our drums. But, naw, we still got 'em. I know I got mine. They're here, in my speech, my walk, my hair, my God, my style, my smile, and my eyes. And everything I need to get over in this world, is inside here, connecting me to everybody and everything that's ever been. So, hunny, don't waste your time trying to label or define

---

8. See Michelle Commander's *Afro-Atlantic Flight: Speculative Returns and the Black Fantastic* for a sustained conversation of the ongoing resonance of the concept of flight in African Diasporic communities.

me . . . 'cause I'm not what I was ten years ago or ten minutes ago. I'm all of that and then some. And whereas I can't live inside yesterday's pain, I can't live without it. (52)

Wolfe utilizes Topsy as a key interlocutor of fugitive time. Situated in time and space as a vector for an empowered black subjectivity, Topsy intersects with "everybody and everything that's ever been." She cautions the audience not to "*waste your time* trying to label or define me" (my emphasis). In this sense, she figures time as personal, a possession that one can use in whatever manner they desire. Because she sees herself as indefinable, she is able to slip through efforts to contain her in time and space, hence her declaration that "I'm not what I was ten years ago or ten minutes ago." Claiming the right to name herself, Topsy refuses the way *Uncle Tom's Cabin* attempted to fix her as knowable. She understands herself as needing to move forward (not living inside yesterday's pain) while also acknowledging the fact that this pain has shaped her and it continues across time. Topsy's mutability and mobility express fugitive time.

Topsy's ability to elude containment in time and space makes possible her claiming of madness as a form of resistance. During the party, she sings, "THERE IS MADNESS IN ME AND THAT MADNESS SETS ME FREE!" (53) and declares that power lies in her madness as well as her "colored contradictions" (53). We can read Topsy's madness as enacting a kind of fugitivity as she transcends conventional time. La Marr Jurelle Bruce theorizes the act of "going mad" for enslaved women. He writes, "Indeed, if Reason is [a] benefactor of white supremacy, proponent of antiblack slavocracy, and patron of patriarchal dominion, a black enslaved woman might fare better going insane instead. Captive behind the barbed fences of slavocratic sanity, she might find some refuge—however tenuous, fraught, and incomplete—in the fugitivity of madness" (305). Conceiving of madness as a deliberate act, an act of survival even, Bruce's theorizing is valuable for understanding Topsy's performance here. She "goes mad" in the sense of rejecting the racial logics that would render her subhuman, a commodity. Coextensively, she affirms Fred Moten's assertion that commodities can and do resist.[9]

BLACK FEMINIST FUGITIVITY

Underneath Wolfe's subversive depiction of Topsy lies a more probing exploration of her interior life. However, this treatment of black female subjectivity is

---

9. See Fred Moten's *In the Break: The Aesthetics of the Black Radical Tradition*.

often uneven in *The Colored Museum* with the satirical and sometimes dismissive representations of black women and their art. This is particularly true for the scene "The Last Mama-on-the-Couch Play," which casts a derisive light on Lorraine Hansberry's groundbreaking *A Raisin in the Sun*. This, alongside the masculinist framing Baraka offers us in his theorizing about black life post-slavery, demonstrates the need for black women's perspectives in the theatrical interrogations of slavery occurring during this time. I argue that black women dramatists of the era offer what I identify as *black feminist fugitivity* in their representations of slavery. Black feminist fugitivity makes a particular intervention into discourses on fugitivity because it attends to the particularity of black women's experience in slavery, which has been often elided and reappropriated in black nationalist and white feminist collectives. Black feminist fugitivity enacts a radical visibility for black women, particularly through embodiment—in the display of abused, wounded, and vulnerable black female bodies on stage. Through the confrontation with the physical and psychical wounding of black women in slavery and the implications of this history of violence for black women across time, black feminist fugitivity aims to free black women, past and present, from the cultural weight of racial and sexual objectification.

My formulation of black feminist fugitivity is informed by Hortense Spillers in her call for more deeply assessing the abuse of black women's bodies as central to understanding women's experiences in the West. Without it, we lose a powerful text of the devastating reaches of patriarchy and imperialism. Spillers makes clear,

> A female body strung from a tree limb, or bleeding from the breast on any given day of field work because the "overseer," standing the length of a whip, has popped her flesh open, adds a lexical and living dimension to the narratives of women in culture and society. . . . This materialized scene of unprotected female flesh—of female flesh "ungendered"—offers a praxis and a theory, a text for living and dying, and a method for reading both through their diverse mediations. (68)

Black feminist fugitivity projects abused and vulnerable black female subjects, often visually displaying scars and other physical marks of pain to elevate a narrative of slavery that often receives little attention—the black female body in pain. The black women participating in this discursive act do not simply emphasize the pain but demonstrate how claiming that pain can function to free black women from narratives that render them both invisible and hypervisible at the same time. In this sense, they not only make space for fuller representations of black women's experience, but they also make and break the narrative, to expand on Alexis Pauline Gumbs's generative framework in *Spill: Scenes of Black Feminist Fugitivity* (xii).

I turn to two dramas, Lorna Littleway's *Phyllis Wheatley: The Celestial Muse* (1979) and Robbie McCauley's *Sally's Rape* (1989) as illustrative of the radical act of visualizing black women's pain in the service of freedom that underlies my conception of black feminist fugitivity. Both works intervene in reductive narratives of Phillis Wheatley and Sally Hemmings, respectively. They also center black women's experience in slavery to combat their relative erasure from twentieth-century black liberation discourses that were largely male-centered and feminist discourses that concerned themselves with issues particular to white women. They elevate the pain inherent in black women's experiences in slavery, particularly in terms of how they were exploited sexually, as well as for their labor and reproductive capabilities.[10] They also illustrate black women attempting to free themselves from the cultural weight of these histories, even as the attainment of such freedom remains inconclusive.

Phillis Wheatley: The Celestial Muse spans the years 1761 to 1784 and traces Wheatley's life from the day that John and Susannah Wheatley purchased her to her marriage to John Peters and her death. Although never performed on stage, the play, like Hansberry's *The Drinking Gourd* indicates a critical turn amongst black playwrights toward slavery and the effort to challenge conventional notions of the institution. In this sense, the drama reflects similar work that dramatized black female subjectivity produced by her contemporaries, such as Adrienne Kennedy, Alice Childress, and Ntozake Shange. Thus, we should situate Littleway within this larger body of dramatists who were offering transformational depictions of black women in drama at the time. The play draws heavily from archival materials and its textual form takes on a scholarly quality with the inclusion of footnotes as a way to highlight the rigor of the research behind the drama. Even as Littleway takes a realist approach to depicting Wheatley's life, there are moments where she takes an experimental route, particularly in having characters address the audience directly. Having Phillis Wheatley address the audience adds greater depth to the limited knowledge we have of her. In fact, in the years leading up to Littleway's drama, critics of the late 1960s and '70s were reassessing Wheatley in an unfavorable manner, thus influencing her legacy and ultimately devaluing her work. Henry Louis Gates chronicles much of this criticism on Wheatley, which notably

---

10. See Jennifer Morgan's *Laboring Women: Reproduction and Gender in New World Slavery*.

labels her as "an early Boston Aunt Jemima" and the like.[11] It is in response to these kinds of critiques that Lorna Littleway frames her work. The play serves as a narrative companion and extension of Alice Walker's vivid portrayal of Wheatley in "In Search of Our Mothers' Gardens," describing her as a young, sickly girl, who was deserving of more sympathy and appreciation than she was being accorded at the time. As in Walker's illuminating essay, *Phillis Wheatley: The Celestial Muse* complicates conventional understandings of Wheatley's life by providing a greater sense of her interiority.

We can see an underlying ethos of black feminist fugitivity in Littleway's depiction of Phillis Wheatley's move from objectified flesh to her efforts to achieve true self-ownership and liberation via her poetry and her life after the Wheatleys emancipate her, although the outcomes of these efforts remain unclear. The market scene that opens the drama elevates Wheatley's physical pain by featuring her experience as a young, sick child brought through the harrowing journey of the Middle Passage. Wheatley herself does not engage the subject deeply in her poetry. One notable instance occurs in her poem, "To the Right Honorable William Earl of Dartmouth" where she writes:

> I, young in life, by seeming cruel fate
> Was snatch'd from *Afric's* fancy'd happy seat:
> What pangs excruciating must molest,
> What sorrows labour in my parent's breast?
> Steel'd was that soul and by no misery mov'd
> That from a father seiz'd his babe belov'd:
> Such, such my case.
> (lines 24–30)

---

11. Henry Louis Gates's *The Trials of Phillis Wheatley: America's First Black Poet and Her Encounters with the Founding Fathers* chronicles much of this criticism, characterizing it as a reflection of the problematic aspects of authenticity discourse within African American culture. I won't rehearse the criticism in its entirety as many are familiar with it, but I will include a few notable points: Amiri Baraka was one of the first to critique what he referred to as Wheatley's "pleasant imitations of eighteenth-century English poetry," which he felt were uncharacteristic of the bold unpublished voices rising up on Southern plantations; Seymour Gross in 1966 argued that Wheatley clearly exhibited "the Uncle Tom syndrome"; other critics referred to her as "an early Boston Aunt Jemima"; and even more disparagingly, Stephen Henderson in 1969 characterized her work as that of "self-hatred" (Gates 77). Gates recounts scores of others, but perhaps the most telling was Angelene Jamison's argument that because Wheatley had been so thoroughly indoctrinated by white values and attitudes, she could "never be used as an expression of black thought" (Gates 79). Angelene Jamison's comment, which shouldn't be read as a dismissal of Jamison's contributions to the study of African American literature or the sumtotal of her views, reveals a tendency of this era to define black thought as expressing a specific set of concerns and ideologies to which Wheatley does not conform.

Here we gain a glimpse into the sure terror she must have experienced being "snatch'd" from her aggrieved parents and being interpolated as flesh. Littleway explores what this must have been like for the young Wheatley and the extent to which she and the other enslaved individuals suffered in their captivity.

Wheatley makes her first physical appearance in the drama as a young enslaved girl on the market. The market scene offers a narrative illustration of Spiller's assertion that the captive body was totally objectified and exploited as flesh in slavery. Under these conditions, "we lose any hint or suggestion of a dimension of ethics" (Spillers 68). We see this initially in the depiction of the Wheatleys as they plan to purchase a slave, a provocative move on the part of Littleway given that they have been largely understood as benevolent and kind enslavers throughout history. The family peruses ads for the sale of slaves—the language reading: "Just IMPORTED from Africa and to be sold . . . a parcel of likely Negro slaves . . . cheap for cash or short credit" (14). Susannah Wheatley requests that her husband John take her to purchase one of the newly arrived slaves, and to this he responds, "I shan't have any raw Africans upsetting this household" (14). The family discusses the purchase as if they are considering acquiring a family pet. John also admonishes Susannah that he will not purchase any children, proclaiming that he does not want a wild African pygmy (14). This portrayal of the Wheatley family offers another context through which to view them. Instances like these remind the audience that this family actively participated in the trading of slaves, thereby supporting this brutal institution.

At the market, captive bodies are shown in various stages of abjectness. Enslavers describe the site as a place too "unseemly for a lady's presence" (19), yet we must counterbalance this reality with the fact that children are being sold there. We see traders bartering to sell children away from mothers, and the selling of a pregnant enslaved woman. A group of nude black children are held together with rope "in various degrees of sickness" (21) and the trader informs Susannah Wheatley that they are kept at a distance because of their smell. As to Phillis Wheatley, she is described as a "flea" and is lowered by a rope so that Susannah Wheatley can survey her. She is informed that if she does not purchase the sick child, then the child will be thrown overboard and fed to the waiting sea creatures. Susannah agrees to her purchase and has her surveyed by a doctor who declares: "Madame, this child lies near death not from disease but abuse. Only the Lord knows the truth of the horrors of their transport. For their own part, the shock obscures their recollection of it" (26). Littleway's detailing of the inhumane treatment of the enslaved illustrates the absence of ethics. The market scene and the subsequent purchase of Phillis

Wheatley intervenes on received histories of Phillis Wheatley's life and de-exceptionalizes Wheatley by portraying her enslavement as not exempt from pain, as many accounts would have it. In their purchase of the young Phillis, the Wheatleys are complicit with the system by helping to perpetuate it. This critical view of the Wheatleys, the slave market, and the casual way that black bodies were viewed as flesh rather than human beings[12] constitutes a major intervention in how we have understood this period in Wheatley's life.

As the drama progresses, we see Phillis Wheatley with greater depth, particularly as she endeavors to give voice to her experience through her poetry, a move that provides her a modicum of freedom. In one instance, Phillis attends a gathering hosted by the Wheatleys that includes the clergymen Samuel Occom, Mather Byles, and John Moorhead. At one point in the conversation, she makes an abrupt exit from the room and later discloses that she was troubled by the condescension of the other reverends to Samuel Occom, a Native American. It is upon her exit that she writes an initial draft of "On Being Brought from Africa to America." (From this point forward, I will refer to Wheatley as Phillis to reflect Littleway's naming.) Susannah Wheatley asks Phillis to share her poem and she complies; however, in her direct address to the audience Phillis expresses fear that she would be punished for the content of the poem and her abrupt departure from the room earlier. She communicates a double consciousness with regard to her writing where she has to balance her desire to express her views with how they will be received by her owners.[13]

Phillis's captive state and her desires to attain freedom become even more magnified in the depiction of her trans-Atlantic travel to England as the guest of the Countess of Huntingdon, a friend of the Wheatley family. Phillis, accompanied by the Wheatley's son Nathaniel, travels to the Countess in an

---

12. In "Mama's Baby, Papa's Maybe: An American Grammar Book," Hortense Spillers argues that in slavery, the black female body was rendered as flesh. She explains that we locate the flesh in a collection of bodily injuries—seared and ripped apart skin, missing eyes and teeth, branded skulls, and so forth (67). The flesh also stood in contradistinction to the body, which Spillers defines as a "liberated subject-position" (67).

13. This breaking of the fourth wall to show Phillis's internal conflicts recalls Daphne Brooks's concept of "afro-alienation" where nineteenth- and early twentieth-century performers defamiliarized the spectacle of blackness to offer alternate racial and gender epistemologies (Brooks 5). In the case of Littleway, her presentation of Wheatley is ultimately destabilizing, and it also signals that a figure such as Wheatley also represented a defamiliarized image of blackness in her time. The scene depicts Wheatley reading her poetry for her white audience, and this calls attention to the fact that she likely performed her poetry. Her eloquence, housed in her black body, surely constituted a visual presentation of alternative racial and gender ideals, especially because she effectively undermined the Enlightenment notion of inherent black inferiority.

effort to gain support for publication of her book of poetry. During her trip, one of her British hosts inquires if she desires her freedom to which Nathaniel responds that she is "neither enslaved nor bound" (116) and describes her simply as his mother's companion. Nathaniel then tells Phillis in private that his mother is ill and has called Phillis to her bedside, so she must end her trip earlier than anticipated. When Phillis resists this request, he exclaims, "Do not ever forget that you are a slave . . . that you deserve nothing . . . that you are indeed mine to do with as I please" (121). Phillis's liminality between captive and free is most vivid here in that Nathaniel reminds her that she is indeed a slave although earlier he declared the contrary. This moment challenges conventional notions that Wheatley did not endure harsh treatment characteristic of enslaved experience, especially that in the American south. As Nathaniel's words reveal, Wheatley likely did not escape the cruel realities of bondage even as she experienced certain kinds of freedom.

Littleway's drama depicts Wheatley as an intensely self-aware individual who used her writing and social platform to push against racial oppression (albeit subversively and less directly) and to obtain a sense of freedom even before she is formally granted it later in life. Phillis interacts with major figures such as John Hancock and Granville Sharp, a noted English abolitionist. In the drama, Hancock acknowledges Phillis's defying of boundaries with her inclusion of political subject matter in her poetry, stating that this was "not a fitting subject for a woman's discourse" (103). Littleway even places Phillis in the courtroom for the famous *Stewart v. Somerset* trial (1772) on the matter of whether or not Boston customs official Charles Stewart had a right to reclaim James Somerset as his slave. Somerset escaped from Stewart, traveled to England and was being held until Stewart could claim him; however, Granville Sharp ordered that Somerset be brought before the English court in order to settle the matter (Cotter 34–35). The case resulted in Somerset being declared free. When we take into consideration her own efforts to live not as a captive subject but as a liberated one, Phillis's presence in the courtroom reminds us that boundaries between slave and free were in continual contestation. Just as future battles regarding slavery and freedom took place in US courts (the *Dred Scott* case a notable one among them), we can see many cases of enslaved individuals using legal means to obtain freedom and resolve their liminal and precarious existences. Wheatley surely negotiated similar internal conflicts that Littleway dramatizes. This new insight into the complexities of Wheatley's life constitutes a key augmentation of the historical record, thereby accounting more thoroughly for Wheatley's interior life.[14] Moreover, this scene calls

---

14. Critics have aimed to offer an accounting for Wheatley's interior life and add depth to the narratives we have of her. Cedrick May's chapter "Phillis Wheatley and the Charge toward

up fugitivity as she sits in the courtroom witnessing a fugitive slave litigate his desire for freedom. Littleway positions Wheatley in critical conversations about fugitivity and freedom, a move that counters perceptions of Wheatley as the contented slave.

Perhaps most illustrative of a black feminist fugitivity is the end of the narrative where Littleway depicts Wheatley as free but in poverty, ill, and enduring a turbulent marriage to John Peters. For Wheatley, liberation has also come at the expense of her health and well-being. We see John Peters frustrated at his limitations as a free black man in New England. He takes out these frustrations on Phillis by devaluing her work and suggesting that she is complicit with the society that maintains racial inequality. He laments, "Silly woman! I have endeavored to serve the cause of African freedom. I flaunt not my preferred status, but work every day to bring the title free man to every slave who toils daily without compensation. And ye who ne'er labored a day in bondage cannot endure the slightest hardship as sacrifice for our brethern's freedom" (144). Because slavery continues to reign in American society, Phillis and John's freedom have yet to be realized. In showing the devaluation of Phillis by her husband, Littleway explores the manifold oppression that Phillis Wheatley endured. Within mainstream American society, Phillis's freedom was elusive at best. Perhaps symbolic of this foreclosure is the fact that Wheatley dies alongside her child. Littleway ends Phillis's narrative just as she began it—by centering her pain. The tragedy of her death speaks to her unfulfilled liberation in life. What this also points to is black women's continual struggle to obtain recognition and value because forces of racism and sexism often dismiss their subjectivities. That the play ends on such a note signifies the ongoing aspects of that battle. Even at manumission, Wheatley remains in pursuit of liberation. Her struggle foretells the hardships of the subjects Robbie McCauley takes up in *Sally's Rape* where black women post slavery continue to deal with the pain of the past and grapple with the elusiveness of freedom in the present.

Progressive black Theologies" in his book *Evangelism and Resistance in the Black Atlantic, 1760–1835* cites Wheatley's bringing together of various spheres of knowledge within eighteenth century evangelicalism, which actually made her a controversial figure (50). Arlette Frund in her essay "Phillis Wheatley: A Public Intellectual" reassesses Wheatley's role as a public figure and intellectual arguing that her choice of subject, poetic mode and forms, reveal her attempt to exercise social, religious, and political power. Finally Tara Bynum's "Phillis Wheatley on Friendship" looks closely at Wheatley's correspondence with friend and fellow slave Obour Tanner (someone that Littleway includes in her 1979 work, thus illustrating her extensive research). Bynum reads these women's relationship as evidence of how their friendship bonds constituted the maintenance of self-affirming community among slaves.

Robbie McCauley's *Sally's Rape* explores the long-standing conditions of black women's unfreedom stemming from slavery and enduring into the contemporary. Premiering in 1991,[15] the play represents a departure from Littleway's approach in that McCauley does not dramatize the titular character's (Sally Hemings's) full life, but gestures to her and the many other "Sallys" who endured similar sexual oppression that the enslaved Sally Hemings experienced at the hands of Thomas Jefferson, although accounts occasionally imagine otherwise and figure their relationship as consensual. The facts of the matter are that Hemings was an enslaved woman without the power to give consent or have a violation of that consent be adjudicated in the court, especially given Jefferson's social stature. *Sally's Rape* is an improvisational drama constructed as a dialogue between two characters: Robbie McCauley and her white counterpart Jeannie Hutchins. (When referring to the play and the characters, I will use "Robbie" and "Jeannie," which are McCauley's designations for each speaker.) Although the play does not adhere to a narrative structure, it centralizes the experiences of these two women working through historical trauma, particularly the systemic rape of enslaved women and our lack of accounting for it in the present. It is composed of eight sections of dialogic performance: 1) Prologue: Talking About What it is About, 2) Confessing About Family and Religion and Work in Progress, 3) Stating the Context, 4) Trying to Transform, 5) Moment in the Chairs, 6) Sally's Rape, 7) In a Rape Crisis Center, 8) Epilogue: Leaving the Audience Talking. At points passing out food to audience members, McCauley and Hutchins construct an intimate connection between themselves and audience members. They invite the audience to participate and to consider the contemporary impact of slavery on the descendants.

McCauley places herself at the center of this drama in order to draw a line from past to present and illustrate the long-term effects of the unresolved traumas of rape in slavery. Doing so enacts a radical depiction, consistent with black feminist fugitivity, of black women's experience because the realities of rape for black women have often been suppressed in the narrativizing of slavery or exploited to dehumanize them and justify ongoing sexual violations against them. In many respects, McCauley represents Christina Sharpe's "postslavery subject," who rewrites and rescripts genealogy and displaces shame to articulate the "weight of freedom borne by the black female body" (*Monstrous Intimacies* 13). The "monstrous intimacies" between enslaver and enslaved that

---

15. The version of *Sally's Rape* that I am using appears in *Moon Marked and Touched by the Sun: Plays by African-American Women*. There are transcriptions from other performances notably, *The Kitchen*, in New York City in 1991. Because the play is an organic piece, the versions vary to a small extent, but the central dialogue scenario is consistent throughout each version.

produce the postslavery subject recirculate across time, space, race, ethnicities, and nation. McCauley deploys her own body as an "ancestral body"[16] in order to bear witness to the history of her ancestors. Because she has to continually grapple with the implications of this history in the present, she is a liminal subject bound by the past even though she is technically free. As she complicates how we see her, she also brings forth the interiorities of the enslaved women she portrays by depicting the ways they were often caught between captive and liberated subject positions.

McCauley begins with the body as a metaphor for the lack of critical conversation about black women's experience and how those conversations are often framed in the context of sex that largely define them in binary frameworks—saint or whore, church lady or slut, etc. Thus she describes black women as experiencing *tightness* because they get "stuck in the inside of sexual images and in the way [they] internalize what [they are] supposed to do and what [they are] not supposed to do" (216). She locates that tightness between the thighs and asserts that there is "no good sex there" (216). Her project, then, aims to not only challenge prevailing historical narratives about black women's experience but also to address the legacies of pathologizing black female sexuality. In performing black feminist fugitivity, McCauley inscribes a new American grammar, to call up Hortense Spillers, onto the black female body that addresses the historical erasures and pervasive misrecognitions.

Sally's Rape seeks to write black women's historical and ongoing experiences of sexual violence into public discourse where this violence has often been minimized or erased altogether. Robbie addresses insufficient narratives perpetuated about slavery that erase black women's pain. In having a public conversation about this violence, she desires to clear space for black women to freely bare (and bear) their pain as well as their bodies without judgment. Robbie details an exchange at work between her and a Smith College graduate (and history major), regarding the subject of slavery. The woman says, "I never knew white men did anything with colored women on plantations." Robbie responds, "It was rape" and explains to Jeannie that the woman nearly choked on her sandwich and quit the job (225). She also reminds Jeannie "ain't no rape crisis center on the plantation" (233). This framing is powerful because it reminds the audience the extent to which the systemic rape of black women was deliberately ignored and unaddressed. It reveals the incongruity of care that the culture applies to rape victims today versus its lack of care for the pain of black women enduring similar injustices. These correctives bring forth

---

16. Harvey Young refers to McCauley's body as an "ancestral body." He argues, "it represents, and indeed re-presents, the bodies and the embodied experience of her ancestors whose previous actions invoked her current presence" (138).

black women's experiences that have been omitted in the historical record, and they indict the culture as failing to recognize these enduring traumas.

Robbie critiques language, the *American grammar* produced in slavery, as the medium for obscuring the realities of this history. She tells Jeannie, "I can't win in your language" (228). This references how her black skin ties her to this history in ways Jeannie is not, even though she and her ancestors were likely implicated as well. They can, however, conveniently forget. Robbie says to Jeannie, "Let me see if I can use language to say what I feel about your idealism. . . . It angers me that even though your ancestors might have been slaves . . . that history has given you the ability to forget your shame about being oppressed by being ignorant, mean or idealistic . . . which makes it dangerous for me" (228). The danger to which Robbie alludes is the risk she takes in articulating her pain and the history of black women's pain in a conventional discourse that is designed to minimize or dismiss their experience. "Language" here functions metonymically to refer to history. It is also literal in the sense that certain meanings have been inscribed on the black female body that confine black women's identities. So on one level, Robbie embodies enslaved women's experiences as a confrontation with the archive, and she invents new vocabularies in which to read the black female body, past and present. She does this through her interventions in the historical record of black women's experiences in slavery and in dramatizing her own complicated identity that has been shaped by this history.

McCauley first takes on the Sally Hemings story and how it has been sanitized and almost rendered as a love story in cultural memory.[17] She joins other artists (Barbara Chase-Riboud and Annette Gordon-Reed most prominent among them) who challenge the portrayal of Thomas Jefferson in history. These writers emphasize the unequal power relationship between Jefferson and Sally Hemings, which make consent an impossibility. Robbie asserts, "Shit, Thomas' Sally was just as much a slave as our grandma and it was just as much a rape" (252). As she moves between scenes, Robbie imagines Sally Hemings in European tea rooms being treated as a free subject while being held as Jefferson's slave. This recalls Phillis Wheatley, who in Littleway's drama experienced a veritable degree of freedom, but for much of her life she served as the Wheatley's slave. In dramatizing Hemings's captivity even as she experiences relative moments of freedom, McCauley mirrors Littleway in her exploration of how Hemings might have moved between those spaces. She also ties

---

17. See Tillet and Young for extensive historical context on this drama and cultural representations of the Hemings/Jefferson interaction.

Hemings to the larger experience of enslaved women, who faced constant threats of rape.

McCauley deepens her reframing of Sally Hemings as a victim of rape by reenacting the rape of enslaved women, embodying them as a collective archive of pain. She narrates, "In the dream I. I am Sally being (*An involuntary sound of pain*) b'ah. Bein' bein' I . . . I being bound down I didn't I didn't wanna be in the dream, bound down in the dream I am I am Sally being done it to . . ." (231). The stilted prose and the repetition of being "bound" relates a psychic trauma that gets enacted through and read on Robbie's body. In this sense, Robbie produces what Lisa Woolfork describes as "bodily epistemology," a representational strategy that "uses the body of the present day protagonist to register the traumatic slave past" (2). This epistemology becomes complicated when Robbie not only embodies the enslaved women being sexually abused but also embodies her white male ancestor, who doubled as both her great-great-grandmother's rapist and her great-great-grandfather.

Robbie offers a radical depiction of her body as carrying the pain of her black female ancestors while also positioning her body in relation to her white male ancestor. This reinforces the idea that she is an embodiment of socially sanctioned rape of black women. In her act, she makes visible victim and perpetrator all meeting at the site of her body. In embodying the enslaver, she blurs the boundaries of racial identification and brings forward a long-suppressed history. In one instance of this performance, she expresses: "In the dream I. I am being Master. Bindin' Bindin' I . . . I binding down I didn't wanna be in the dream, binding down in the dream I am I am Master doing it to I am down on the ground doing it to binding down didn't wanna be binding down on the ground . . ." (140).[18] This inversion denies a clear understanding of Robbie as separate from either ancestor as she moves back and forth between both individuals. Here McCauley's drama accounts for her conflicted identity reminding us that she is both the product of her great-great grandmother's pain and her great-great-grandfather's brutality.

The auction block scene serves as a culmination of Robbie's dramatization of the troubling legacies of black women's exploitation. After having thoroughly defamiliarized her body, she stands on the auction block to perform the dehumanizing spectacle as well as to claim power over it. Robbie and Jeannie dramatize the auction block by playing the slave and auctioneer, respectively. Jeannie addresses the audience, imploring them: "Bid 'em in" (230). Robbie then removes her clothing and stands nude before the audience. This

---

18. This element of the performance comes from Harvey Young's reading of the drama in *Embodying Black Experience* in which he draws upon a different performance that includes this specific dialogue.

act constitutes the ultimate form of vulnerability in which Robbie is literally bearing her body as a way to force recognition of the varying indignities that the enslaved experienced.

The auction block in particular is a multilayered space. It is at once the site of dehumanization, the site of performance, and the site of commercial exchange. Robbie invokes all of these discourses as she performs the experience. Saidiya Hartman relates that enslaved women's experiences on the auction block evinced the "beastializing display of black bodies on the market, [and] the sexual violation of slave women."[19] This beastializing display sets forth a narrative about black women's sexual availability that Robbie seeks to perform her way out of. Because Robbie exists in the contemporary moment, her body represents a present body that still bears the pain of this dehumanization. Robbie suggests that black women are still not free from being viewed within the contexts of these debasing spectacles and explains, "I wanted to do this—stand naked in public on the auction block. I thought somehow it could help free us from *this (Refers to her naked body)*" (231). Here we see the tightness Robbie wants to perform her way out of. In performing this spectacle of captivity, Robbie hopes the confrontation with this traumatic past will somehow liberate the descendants of these histories in the present. In essence, she strips her body down in order to exercise some degree of control over her objectification and write new definitions onto her body in the process.

The play ends with Robbie and Jeannie opening the conversation up to the audience and inviting them to engage with one another. Robbie explains to the audience,

> It has to do with talking to people, even if you already know 'em, and especially if you don't, how a lot of people in different cultures greet each other, I know some Native American cultures do: "Who are you and who are your people?" And where I come from, African-American folk be like, "Who children you?" (237)

The invitation to discussion signals McCauley's emphasis on how one's history informs one's identity. This moment clears space; however, McCauley ends the drama with a necessary sense of incompleteness. In fact, by ending the

---

19. In order to describe the dehumanizing spectacle of the auction block, Saidiya Hartman presents the story of Sukie, a slave who refuses to mask the pain of the auction block. As her teeth are being examined, she "pult up her dress an' tole de nigger traders to look an' see if dey could find any teef down dere" (40). Hartman explains that "Sukie's gesture to teeth down there, delineates the debasing exhibition of the black body as object of property, as it was common for bidders to feel between women's legs, examine their hips, and fondle their breasts" (41).

play with a continued conversation, McCauley suggests that the work of black female liberation and social recognition is ongoing and constant.

BLACK QUEER FUGITIVITY

Much the way that Littleway and McCauley aim to intervene in narratives that diminish black women's pain and the particularities of their experience in slavery, dramas that assert an ethos of *black queer fugitivity* work toward similar ends. Specifically, I define *black queer fugitivity* as imagining black queer subjects beyond institutions—particularly educational, medical, and domestic—since they are founded upon heteronormative constructs and have been historically hostile to queer subjects in general. For black queer subjects, this holds particular resonance in the context of slavery. As with black feminist fugitivity, black queer fugitivity centers queer subjects who have often been erased from canonical histories of slavery. It intervenes in essentializing narratives of blackness perpetuated in the historical discourse about slavery and challenges white queer allies to recognize the specificity of black queer experience and its consequences, namely the danger black queer subjects face in being harmed on the basis of their race, gender, and sexuality. Black queer fugitivity also presents the problem of home and belonging for black queer individuals as irresolvable, thus demonstrating the ongoing quest to find and potentially build new spaces that embrace black queer subjects.

Matt Richardson's theory of irresolution is instructive for thinking about black queer fugitivity as a means to contest normative frameworks. Richardson, in focusing on the critical work of black lesbian writers, asserts that they are "beneficiaries of and contributors to a reconceptualization of black resistance to include gender variance as well as sexual transgression" (8). Irresolution, then, refuses a normative narrative of queer experience. My formulation of black queer fugitivity is also informed by other thinkers such as José Muñoz, Jack Halberstam, and Karma Chávez. José Muñoz's theory of queer failure is instructive for thinking about queer fugitivity. Muñoz illuminates that within failure we can locate a kernel of potentiality. He writes, "I align queer failure with a certain mode of virtuosity that helps the spectator exit from the stale and static lifeworld dominated by the alienation, exploitation, and drudgery associated with capitalism or landlordism" (Muñoz *Cruising Utopia* 173). This departure from the static lifeworld represents how I read performances of black queer fugitivity. I am thinking along the lines of Jack Halberstam who envisions fugitivity as more than simply escape but a movement toward "spaces and modalities that exist separate from the logical, the logistical, the housed and the positioned" (Harney and Moten 11). Also, I am thinking with Karma Chávez who advocates that queer people of color see themselves as "in but not of" institutions (particularly universities) and to develop new extraorganizational logics beyond those prescribed within institutions (68). Muñoz, Halberstam, and Chávez's ideas cohere around the notion of institutions as being spaces that prohibit a true realization of queer subjectivity. In fact, these spaces repress and require a constant critique as an exercise of freedom for queer individuals. It is in the rejection of affiliation that we see a consciousness emerge that fully embraces queer identity.

The performance group Pomo Afro Homos (Postmodern African American Homosexuals) directly confronts the strictures of institutions for queer subjects in particular, and they intervene in historical discourses that render one-dimensional notions of blackness. The San Francisco-based group was founded in 1990 by Eric Gupton, Brian Freeman, and Djola B. Branner. Marvin K. White would later join the group during Eric Gupton's brief absence. The group formed after connecting via a support group, Black Gay Men United, and eventually disbanded in 1995 to pursue individual projects (Plum 235). Their 1993 work, *Dark Fruit*, stands out as path-making in its articulation of black queer fugitivity.[20] Albeit a latent presence in the work, slavery and the slave era animate key parts of this drama. Like Wolfe's *The Colored Museum*, *Dark Fruit* is presented as a series of scenes ("Aunties in America," "Last Rights," "Black & Gay: A Psycho-sex Story," "Sweet Sadie," "Doin' Alright," "Tasty," and "Chocolate City, U. S. A."). Its seven sketches range in content, but represent what the group envisions as how black queer subjects navigate various communities with a deep ambivalence. This is especially true for the group's confrontation with white queer communities and black communities that often marginalize those who are black and queer, respectively.

Two sketches, "Aunties in America" and "Black & Gay: A Psycho-sex Study" utilize slavery as a lens through which to read the ongoing quest for freedom for contemporary black queer individuals. Both pieces dramatize the desire to escape objectification and the inherent failure of institutions in providing a nurturing space for queer subjects. "Aunties in America" is a playful piece that satirizes celebrated queer dramas such as Tony Kushner's *Angels in America*, John Guare's *Six Degrees of Separation*, and Harvey Fierstein's *La Cage aux Folles*. Portraying the characters: Belize of *Angels*, Paul of *Six Degrees*, and Jacob of *La Cage*, the scene takes these dramas to task for their mammy-fication of queer characters of color. For black queer men, the

---

20. For additional context and an extended reading of this drama, see Jay Plum's "Pleasure, Politics, and the Performance of Community: Pomo Afro Homos's *Dark Fruit*."

mammy trope pervades their representations in similar ways as it does black women where white characters seek heightened awareness and epiphanies through black mothers. Paul laments "You see, Missy Guare has me up there with all these Upper East Side most worrisome white folks, processing all their yap-de-yap get-a-clue-already angst. . . . Like some kind of Hattie MacDaniels meets Mandingo biotech fruit" (324). Here Paul identifies the burden of black male queer characters to be caregivers and sexual objects for white pleasure. At the end of this scene, the actors transform napkins into headrags and dance a short dance to Liza Minnelli's "Mammy." They then smile at the audience, and those smiles transform into a minstrel grimace. The stage directions indicate that they "pull the rags off their heads, drop them in defiance" (325). This opening scene critiques dramatic representations that continue to haunt black characters, namely the mammy and the minstrel, while also working to dismantle them. The drama progressively offers a more complex depiction of black queer experience.

"Black & Gay: A Psycho-sex Study" takes up a similarly harmful objectification of black queer subjects that occurs in institutions such as the medical and educational. The narrative takes place in two contexts: 1) it depicts a scientist enlightening the audience about black gay male sexuality, and 2) it stages an encounter between a black male student (Cliff) and white male student (Paul) at Walt Whitman High, a school that has been working to integrate.[21] This scene opens with "certified psycho-sexologist" Victor Dodson, and according to the program notes from the 1993 performance at NYU, the piece is "adapted 99 percent from an actual 60s pulp/porn pseudoscience novel *Black and Gay: A Psycho-sex Study* by Victor Dodson" (qtd. in Plum 243). Going directly to the heart of medical discourses on black subjects that have long dehumanized and exploited them, the drama offers a critique of these harmful practices.

That Brian Freeman, a black male performer, plays Dodson signals the effort to critique this discourse and present it through the lens of a black queer subject, who continues to be negatively impacted by these notions. It is unclear how much of the book was taken verbatim, but there is an aside within the monologue worth contemplating because Pomo Afro Homos interrogates just how histories about black subjects are told. During Dodson's opening monologue, he claims, "Negro homosexual males have been in evidence since the beginning of history. Accounts of African rituals explicitly describe

---

21. The drama calls up Whitman to stand in for official memory and white canonical authority. Whitman's queer identity complicates this effort, yet his presence reminds us that institutions, no matter how inclusively drawn for black queer subjects, are still bound up in histories of white supremacy and heteronormativity.

homosexual relationships as part of the social makeup of many tribes" (327). On one hand, this narrative advances an important concept in that it situates queerness in a longer history rather than a new phenomenon as some would have it. Yet, the framing here remains problematic because it is used to draw a negative distinction between East and West/white and black. The conflict here represents the struggles for recognition in medical discourses that have a history of dehumanizing black subjects.

The narrative progresses to feature Cliff (who is black) and Paul (who is white), two students at Walt Whitman High. Cliff is a promising young student who comes from what the drama refers to as a "shantytown." His teacher Miss Emory has identified him as an ideal candidate for the Booker T. Washington Scholarship. Notably, the historical figures invoked in this piece perform critical work. Booker T. Washington is a revered figure from the slave era whose ideas of black advancement were often critiqued for their emphasis on manual labor and tolerance for racial segregation. Walt Whitman, a slave era poet, also looms large in that he was a queer man who held inconsistent and contradictory views on slavery.[22] When Cliff and Paul agree to meet one night, they engage in a bit of sexual foreplay until they are discovered by Miss Emory. In response, Miss Emory pledges to keep Paul's secret while letting Cliff know that she intends to tell his mother and withdraw her recommendation for the Booker T. Washington Scholarship. Devastated, Cliff runs away, never to be seen again. The uneven consequences for Paul and Cliff gesture to a larger commentary on the way black queer subjects are marginalized out of spaces on the basis of their black and queer identities. Walt Whitman stands in for a failed white queer allyship where Paul retreats instead of supporting Cliff. This moment also speaks to the failed support of queer subjects within black communities where such individuals have historically faced rejection. Importantly, the drama ends with Cliff on the run. Victor Dodson returns to resolve the drama by explaining, "The town never saw Cliff Wood again. His mother searched but she never found a trace of him. Rumors spread that he made his way north and quickly lost himself in the homosexual jungle they call New York City" (332). Cliff flees knowing that the consequences of staying and facing the impact of Miss Emory's revelation would likely be worse for him. This act signals the inability of institutions to allow Cliff a space to develop as a black gay man. Thus, venturing into the unknown holds more promise. Moreover, Cliff as a runaway calls up narratives of runaway enslaved subjects who traversed to new territories in search of freedom. It returns us to

---

22. Martin Klammer in *Whitman, Slavery, and the Emergence of Leaves of Grass* describes Whitman's ambivalence toward slavery and his problematic views on black subjects.

Rissa's son Isaiah in Hansberry's *The Drinking Gourd,* who is rumored to have escaped to Canada. This representation of black queer fugitivity positions Cliff as a figure in motion attempting to escape the shadow of slavery while asserting himself as a queer subject. In this way, we can read the ending not simply as a "failure" of institutions to recognize Cliff and nurture him. We can also consider how this failure engenders Cliff's ongoing search for spaces that can.

The interpretive frameworks I offer here provide ways of reading a genealogy of emergent performances of fugitivity in mid-to-late twentieth-century black drama. In their shifting and often intersecting approaches to representing slavery, these dramas provide an important foundation for the contemporary dramas about slavery that follow in their path. Tracing this theatrical genealogy also makes visible the parallel development in black drama that was taking place within the textual iterations of the neo-slave narrative genre and elevates a body of work in black drama that actively advanced similar themes in its depictions of slavery. Again, I do not want to suggest that the representational strategies in these dramas, which I read under the rubric of performances of fugitivity, align exactly with the contemporary dramas I examine in the remainder of this book. Rather, my aim is to gather a body of dramas performing similarly path-making work in representing slavery in order to comprehend its significance within the black literary canon.

CHAPTER 2

Fugitive Acts

> The people are having a hard time with freedom.
> —ELIZA JACKSON, *GEM OF THE OCEAN*

IN 1997 August Wilson held a decidedly pessimistic view on realities of life for black Americans. When asked by interviewer Bonnie Lyons if the situation for blacks in America was worse than it was forty years ago, Wilson does not hesitate in answering: "Yes." Lyons follows up on this answer and queries Wilson on what he might do, if he had the power, to make the situation better. Wilson invokes slavery,

> I would make an announcement that slavery is morally reprehensible and will never occur again. The Emancipation Proclamation was a military move, not a moral admission, so this needs to be a policy statement. Then having said that I would tell blacks they are free to participate in American society as Africans, that they don't have to give up their heritage. (209)

In his response, Wilson identifies the contemporary problem of black adversity as rooted in the lack of moral clarity around the ending of slavery. He asserts that the absence of a stated policy condemning the institution of slavery has implications for the past as well as the present. He also suggests that black Americans lack the freedom to participate in society in a way that embraces all facets of their identities. Hence, Wilson identifies the crisis of black life at the ending of one century and the turn of a new one as a problem of language and a lack of freedom. The need to proclaim that slavery has ended and will never occur again suggests an unresolved conclusion. Although Wilson grapples with this conundrum across many of his dramas, he dramatizes this issue most directly in his 2003 play *Gem of the Ocean*. Set in 1904, long after Emancipation but still reeling from its consequences, the drama explores manifold unresolved conflicts from the slave era.

Gem of the Ocean dramatizes a turbulent period for black Americans. In light of the failed efforts of the Reconstruction and rampant terror in the form of lynchings that took place in the aftermath of the post-Emancipation era and continued into the 1950s, black Americans fled to Northern regions in America, intent to free themselves from the brutality of the American South. Yet, as has been well documented, these new vistas or "other suns," as Richard Wright avers, were not welcoming spaces for black subjects hoping to realize a promised life of freedom. We can read *Gem of the Ocean* as capturing the social and political upheaval of this time and its impact on black Americans. Many of the underlying themes of the drama can be expressed in W. E. B. Du Bois's haunting question in *The Souls of Black Folk* (1903), "Why did God make me a stranger in my own house?"

This chapter considers *Gem of the Ocean*'s extended invocation of slavery and its meditation on the limits of emancipation for black subjects still grappling with slavery's devastating effects. I examine how the drama responds to such conditions through presenting what I call "fugitive acts"—actions that the play's characters perform to negotiate feelings of unfreedom and to respond to pervasive attempts to devalue their lives. By maintaining a critical distance from the white mainstream body politic, constructing a counterarchive of the slave past, and enacting practices of radical mourning, characters within *Gem of the Ocean* perform fugitive acts as a means to attain some degree of freedom and self-determination. In depicting these fugitive acts, Wilson narrativizes slavery in ways that center black subjectivity and frame the recognition of black suffering as a political act. In effect, *Gem of the Ocean* stands as a counter-monument to slavery in its attention to the implications for the ways we remember, misremember, or fail to remember this history.

Rather than present a familiar tale of slavery, *Gem of the Ocean* utilizes the drama's central character, the 285-year-old-ancestor Aunt Ester, as a conduit for memory. Although numerous subplots drive the narrative, the drama pivots on a central issue: How do black subjects living just beyond the slave era attain freedom and equality in a world that seeks to deny them both? *Gem of the Ocean* features Citizen Barlow who, after frustration with the inequities he experiences working for a local mill, decides to steal a bucket of nails. When another man, Garrett Brown, is erroneously accused of the crime and drowns in a river after refusing to admit to the accusation, Barlow's guilt brings him to Aunt Ester in order to have his "soul washed." This soul-washing involves a metaphorical trip to the City of Bones, a mythical site commemorating the millions of Africans who lost their lives in the Middle Passage. Aunt Ester regularly takes individuals on this journey as a ritual of remembering, which usually results in a restorative catharsis. In addition to Aunt Ester are a host of other characters that influence Citizen: Solly Two Kings—the community's freedom fighter; Black Mary—Aunt Ester's assistant and apprentice; Eli—Aunt Ester's longtime companion and veritable guardsman for her home; and Caesar Wilkes—Black Mary's brother and the policeman who ultimately kills Solly for setting the mill on fire. *Gem of the Ocean*'s central characters find refuge in the haven of Aunt Ester's home. Citizen, who is a literal fugitive seeking repentance for enacting a deed that cost a man his life, and Solly Two Kings, a former laborer on the Underground Railroad, meet in the space of Aunt Ester's home in a way that connects the fugitivity inherent in fleeing slavery with Citizen's postslavery fugitivity as he continues to seek economic justice and citizenship rights.

Although it is notable for its sustained engagement with slavery, *Gem of the Ocean* does not represent the sum of Wilson's exploration of slavery and its lingering effects on the black psyche. One work that effectively aids in contextualizing *Gem* is Wilson's 1986 drama *Joe Turner's Come and Gone*. I examine this drama in detail here because it contextualizes Wilson's approach to representing slavery and the Middle Passage in *Gem of the Ocean* and demonstrates Wilson's ongoing exploration of slavery's continued resonance in black life. Set in 1911, *Joe Turner* features a collection of characters living in a boardinghouse owned by Seth Holly in Pittsburgh, Pennsylvania. The drama intensifies when Herald Loomis arrives with his daughter Zonia in search of his wife Martha. We learn that Loomis, once a deacon in Tennessee, was captured by Joe Turner and made to labor for seven years. Herald Loomis arrives at Seth Holly's home desperate and shaken by the experience of being veritably reenslaved with no recourse for the act. The drama's critical exploration of the vulnerability of black subjects post slavery and their conditions of unfreedom demonstrates Wilson's sustained focus on unrealized emancipation.

In calling up the lore of Joe Turner, Wilson centers an underexamined aspect of black experience and its consequences. The story of Joe Turner has roots in black American folklore and the very real idea that recently freed black Americans were being reenslaved via chain gangs. Although there are other traceable referents to the figure of Joe Turner in black folklore, one that I encountered specifically intersects with Wilson's interrogation of the failure of emancipation. As told in W. C. Handy's *Father of the Blues: An Autobiography*:

It goes back to Joe Turney (also called Turner), brother of Pete Turney, one-time governor of Tennessee. Joe had the responsibility of taking Negro prisoners from Memphis to the penitentiary at Nashville. Sometimes he took them to the "farms" along the Mississippi. Their crimes when indeed there were any crimes, were usually very minor, the object of the arrests being to provide needed labor for spots along the river. As usual, the method was to set a stool-pigeon where he could start a game of craps. The bones would roll blissfully till the required number of laborers had been drawn into the circle. At that point the law would fall upon the poor devils, arrest as many as were needed for work, try them for gambling in a kangaroo court and then turn the culprits over to Joe Turney. That night, perhaps, there would be weeping and wailing among the dusky belles. If one of them chanced to ask a neighbor what had become of the sweet good man, she was likely to receive the pat reply, "They tell me Joe Turner's come and gone." (146)

Although this is largely lore, it reflects very real anxieties about being lured into reenslavement felt by black Americans in the early twentieth century. Herald Loomis's plight in many ways calls up this history and the long struggle for black Americans to attain full citizenship rights.

Wilson connects Loomis's trauma of forced labor with the trauma of the Middle Passage. Both experiences haunt Loomis's psyche, and it is here that we see the long impact of slavery well beyond its formal conclusion. At the end of act 1 of the play, Loomis relays to Seth Holly and Bynum Walker his recent experience of witnessing bones rising out of the water. In this moment, Seth and Bynum are engaged in dancing the Juba—"a dance performed by African Americans in postslavery times to praise their adopted Christian God through movements, gestures, rhythms that still harkened back to African roots" (Elam *Past as Present* 2). Compounding the allusions to African heritage and tradition here, Wilson incorporates the juba to keep prominent the influences of African culture on black Americans. Loomis interrupts this scene visibly shaken. He then explains that he saw "bones rise up out of the water. Rise up and walk across the water. Bones walking on top of the water" (52). He also relates that these same bones sank back into the water and rose again with flesh on them. He tells Bynum, "They black. Just like you and me. Ain't no difference" (55). Loomis then loses control of his faculties and has difficulty standing up. In this scene, Wilson presents a convergence of conflicting legacies of the Middle Passage: 1) the endurance of African tradition that survived the Middle Passage, and 2) the deaths of those who did not survive. Wilson then does not offer a singular narrative of black experience and slavery; rather, he complicates this narrative to tell a story of resilience as well as one of pain.[1]

With respect to the pain, Loomis's precarious existence aligns with the bones rising up out of the water and becoming flesh. Like the dead-yet-alive enslaved specters, Loomis experiences a veritable living death, where white assailants can abduct him with impunity. That his trauma manifests as him envisioning the bones of those lost in the Middle Passage signifies the unresolved losses brought on by slavery. For Loomis, once Joe Turner releases him, he reemerges from obscurity and endeavors to resume his life, but this proves impossible because he now feels rootless in the world. His unresolved loss, embodied most specifically in his wife Martha, corresponds to the preponderance of unresolved losses that the enslaved experienced as they witnessed horrible scenes of death on board slave ships. With the invoking of the Middle Passage, Wilson weaves together sentiments of individual estrangement from the US and the collective experience of loss that originates in the Middle Passage.

Joe Turner's Come and Gone performs the critical work of illustrating what Sharon Patricia Holland identifies as the failure to fathom black freedom in the minds of many white Americans after slavery. Holland explains, "Not willing to comprehend fully the freed state of formerly enslaved subjects, enslavers and their kin reserved a special place in their *imaginations* for this new being. Although seeing the black subject as a slave was now prohibited by law, there was no impediment to viewing this subject in the same place s/he had always already occupied" (*Raising the Dead* 14). Holland's analysis adds clarity to the unresolved issue of freedom that Wilson explores in *Joe Turner* and continues in *Gem of the Ocean*. Returning to Wilson's statement that opens this chapter, for him the Emancipation Proclamation represented a military move rather than a moral and political mandate. It is clear that like Holland he seeks to depict the consequences of the continued viewing of black subjects as property rather than persons. In such conditions, then, fugitivity functions as an alternative to living under such circumstances. I analyze how Wilson produces performances of fugitivity in *Gem of the Ocean* by first examining what can be understood in the drama as an ideology of marronage that is intrinsic to the Hill District community. I then link that ethos to its material implications by considering how the play functions as a counter-monument to slavery with Wilson's depiction of radical acts of freedom that black subjects engaged

---

1. For an extended reading of Wilson's treatment of slavery in *Joe Turner's Come and Gone*, see Soyica Colbert's chapter, "Rituals of Repair: Amiri Baraka's *Slave Ship* and August Wilson's *Joe Turner's Come and Gone*" in her book *The African American Theatrical Body: Reception, Performance, and the Stage*.

in as a response to their subjugation. I consider counterarchival practices in Wilson's collage techniques, as well as in the reappropriation of artifacts of the slave era and the refashioning of landscapes as black geographies[2] that document and make visible black experience in Western landscapes. All of these efforts reflect critical practices of citizenship that elevate obscured black subjectivities. Finally, I locate performances of fugitivity in the drama in the practices of mourning enacted in the play that reflect a kind of racial melancholia, a conscious refusal of closure that recognizes the losses brought on by enslavement and other forms of racial trauma.[3]

THE HILL DISTRICT AS A MAROON LANDSCAPE

Marronage, a term that conceptualizes the psychological and physical act of formerly enslaved individuals existing outside of the society in order to live autonomously, underlies *Gem of the Ocean*'s narrative framework. The drama, like most of Wilson's work, features the predominately black community of Pittsburgh's Hill District. This community's name unintentionally (but poignantly) calls up James C. Scott's analysis of "*hill people*" who inhabit Southeast Asia and function identically to maroon communities.[4] Indeed, the landscape of the Hill District can be understood as what Sylviane Diouf calls a "maroon landscape," a place of exile where former slaves sought both freedom and self-determination (11). Diouf interestingly focuses on maroon landscapes of the US, which receive less scholarly attention than their Latin American and Caribbean counterparts. Given the social strictures of segregation, even in Northern locales, one could argue that those of the Hill District had very little choice in their social separation, and I do not intend to conflate this segregated community with the complex history of marronage. However, it is notable that the Hill District was also known as "Little Haiti," which gestures to the nation-state of Haiti—a prominent site of maroon communities. The

---

2. Katherine McKittrick defines "black geographies" as comprising "philosophical, material, imaginary, and representational trajectories" located within and outside traditional boundaries of space and place and expose the limitations of such spaces through "black social particularities and knowledges" (7). Sometimes "fragmented, subjective, connective, invisible, visible, unacknowledged and conspicuously positioned," these geographies are places of economic, social and political denial as well as resistance (7).

3. For more on racial melancholia and the neo-slave narrative, see Margo Natalie Crawford's "The Inside-Turned-Out Architecture of the Post-Neo-Slave Narrative" in *The Psychic Hold of Slavery*.

4. See James C. Scott's *The Art of Not Being Governed: An Anarchist History of Upland Southeast Asia*.

Hill District came to be known as such because a large number of Haitians moved to this location after the battle for independence that brought an end to slavery in Haiti.[5] Wilson calls attention to this connection in *Gem of the Ocean* where Aunt Ester mentions "Little Haiti" when she describes a route Rutherford Selig takes as he sales his wares (76). Wilson also brings Haiti into his work more prominently with his character Hedley, who first appears in his 1995 play *Seven Guitars*. Hedley is more concretely described as Haitian in Wilson's 1999 play *King Hedley II*.[6] Thus, in his dramas, Wilson invokes the Haitian influence on the Hill District and draws upon it as a metaphor for an ethos of resistance in the community.

Most centrally, my use of the notion of marronage in relation to *Gem of the Ocean* corresponds with Neil Roberts's theorizing of the term in *Freedom as Marronage*. Roberts utilizes the concept of marronage (which he argues is atemporal and transhistorical) to develop a theory of freedom "that offers a compelling interpretive lens for examining the quandaries of slavery, freedom, and political language still confronting us today" (4). Roberts asserts that freedom as marronage "materializes in the liminal and interstitial social space between our imaginings of absolute unfreedom and the zone of its opposite" (173). If a theatrical articulation of this theory of freedom is possible, then I contend that *Gem of the Ocean* offers it.

Moreover, if the Hill District at large signifies marronage, then Aunt Ester's home on 1839 Wylie Avenue sits at the center as a locus for the workings of marronage in response to oppression and as a means of survival. Aunt Ester's home functions as a site of refuge from various forms of trouble. Individuals arrive at her doorstep in hopes of overcoming their precarious situations, and she offers safe haven. The declaration Eli makes—"This is a peaceful house"—when outsiders attempt to enter indicates the power of this home as a space to flee the social pressures of the white world. Tellingly, Eli's words "This is a peaceful house" open the drama. Black Mary emphasizes to her brother Caesar, "I never been so at peace with myself since I been here" (37). The inhabitants (those who frequent Aunt Ester's home and those who live there) all share some form of desire for escape from a threatening world and for a life free of racial terror. Solly, who has historically sought freedom for enslaved subjects, now pursues it for those desperately seeking to flee the US south and the rampant lynchings taking place. Black Mary and Eli seek to preserve this space as protection from the state-sanctioned violence that even plagues them in

---

5. See Kate Oczypok's "Pittsburgh Neighborhoods: The History of the Hill District" (http://pittsburghbeautiful.com/2017/05/02/pittsburgh-neighborhoods-history-of-the-hill-district/).

6. See Mary Ellen Snodgrass's *August Wilson: A Literary Companion*.

the North. And Citizen comes seeking it because he cannot bear the systemic economic oppression that devalues his labor and personhood.

The house at 1839 Wylie functions not only as a refuge, but also as a site of memory. Aunt Ester performs the ritual of journeying to the City of Bones within the space of her home. It is here that those within the community come to remember enslavement and the harrowing journey of the Middle Passage. The immense cultural value that Aunt Ester's home has for the community explains Eli's efforts to build a wall around the home to protect it. He even employs Citizen to assist him in building the wall, a symbolic act that Anissa J. Wardi reads as facilitating Citizen's "ritual to reconnect with an ancestral homeland" (49). The multiple functions of Aunt Ester's home indicate Wilson's exploration of notions of exile and displacement, which permeate his dramas. As Wardi also observes, Wilson portrays home in a vexed manner reflecting the "pull *toward* and the problem *of* claiming a home" in America (46). In this way, the wall represents a form of power as well as vulnerability. The ability to construct it signals a certain degree of agency for those seeking protection within its walls; however, the need to construct it, particularly because of the representative danger that agents of the state like Caesar Wilkes represent, demonstrates the fear of violence and a disruption of the veritable peace that the home provides. Wilson's complicating of home through Aunt Ester's multifaceted domicile speaks to the ways that troubling home lies at the heart of fugitivity. Here it manifests as both displacement and a refashioning of place. It functions as a temporary space of freedom for Citizen who proclaims, "I ain't got no place" (33) when asked about his homelife by Caesar Wilkes. Aunt Ester and her home exist outside of time. The home provides veritable stability for figures like Citizen who seemingly belong nowhere and everywhere.

Notably, Aunt Ester's home is the site where Solly articulates a theory of unfreedom for black Americans, which very much aligns with Neil Roberts's conceptual investigation of the many meanings of marronage. Noticing the limitations for employment and viability for black Americans post slavery, Solly makes the case that freedom has caused black Americans "nothing but trouble." Eli responds to this saying, "Freedom is what you make it" (29). Solly then retorts:

> That's what I'm saying. You got to fight to make it mean something. All it mean is you got a long row to hoe and ain't got no plow. Ain't got no seed. Ain't got no mule. What good is freedom if you can't do nothing with it? I seen many a man die for freedom but he didn't know what he was getting. If he had known he might have thought twice about it. (29)

Here Solly identifies the problem with static definitions of enslavement and freedom. Freedom, Solly philosophizes, is a malleable concept determined by a number of variable factors. Such factors (racial inequality and segregation, the debt slavery of sharecropping, the criminalization of black subjects and the devaluing of their lives) contribute to black Americans' ongoing sense of unfreedom even though they are technically free from servitude. Rather than participate in this apparent ruse, Solly chooses to live outside of these frameworks submitting to neither ideological pole that would articulate his status as free or enslaved. The critique of social structures that keep black Americans in a state of unfreedom reflects Solly's desire to express a mode of freedom that is unaccounted for. Like the ideology of "freedom as marronage," Solly's definition of freedom conceives of something beyond normative, Western conceptions of this notion.

GEM OF THE OCEAN AS COUNTER-MONUMENT

Solly's critique of freedom and the maroon landscape of the Hill District reveal the tensions between legal definitions of citizenship and freedom versus actual inclusion and recognition. Salamishah Tillet describes this sentiment as "civic estrangement." Tillet interrogates how black artists grapple with the ways black Americans have been "marginalized or underrepresented in the civic myths, monuments, narratives, icons, creeds, and images of the past that constitute, reproduce, and promote an American national identity" (3). In many respects, the effort to infuse black subjects into national narratives, monuments, and so on from which they have been excluded lies at the heart of *Gem of the Ocean*'s critical project. The drama presents fugitive acts in the reappropriation of archival materials from the slave era in order to combat their exclusion from civic myths and narratives. These efforts can be read in relation to James F. Osbourne's counter-monumentality, which works in response to the institutional monument. Osbourne argues, "Counter-monuments thus embody qualities quite opposite from conventional monuments: (a) instead of being permanent, they can be fleeting and transitory; (b) rather than glorifying their subject, they problematize it; and (c) as opposed to being a static representation for the viewer to observe, they actively invite and require viewer participation and engagement" (167). The structure of drama and performances of it correlate well with Osbourne's stated objectives of the counter-monument. Wilson harnesses the ephemerality of performance but also codifies it in text allowing for a fluid troubling of American myths, monuments, and symbols.

The title of the drama itself performs counter-monumentality in its exposure of the incongruence between the myths of American promise and its actual treatment of black American citizens. The title *Gem of the Ocean* signifies on a popular American patriotic song, "Columbia: The Gem of the Ocean" (1843).[7] The words of the tune read:

> O Columbia! the gem of the ocean,
> The home of the brave and the free,
> The shrine of each patriot's devotion,
> A world offers homage to thee;
> Thy mandates make heroes assemble,
> When Liberty's form stands in view;
> Thy banners make tyranny tremble,
> When borne by the red, white, and blue.

The song functioned as an unofficial national anthem until it was replaced by "The Star Spangled Banner." Wilson's appropriation of the title writes the loss of the Middle Passage onto patriotic narratives of freedom, bravery, and liberty. That this song, like so many of the cultural myths established during this time, could be received without irony during a time when whole groups of people were denied freedom and liberty, signals the extent to which the realities of the black experience in America have been written out of its national memory. By recalling this title, Wilson inserts narratives of black experience into this history, thereby making visible what has been erased or never truly acknowledged at all.

Even Citizen Barlow's name strikes at the heart of the unfulfilled promise of citizenship that the Emancipation Proclamation intended to initiate. Citizen explains that his mother named him Citizen after freedom came. Thus his name is largely performative. Citizen's mother calls upon the power of naming after surviving a history of oppression and the declaration of her son as a "citizen" undergirds the narrative. Upon hearing Citizen's explanation of the inspiration for his name, Solly responds "It's hard to be a citizen. You gonna have to fight to get that" (27). Even so, in the naming of her son, Citizen's mother calls upon this speech act as a mechanism to force societal recognition of her son's status as free. Yet, Solly assumes no taken-for-grantedness of American citizenship, declaring that one should not assume that citizenship is bestowed to all American individuals. Solly communicates another layer

---

7. Baraka wrote a piece inspired by his desire to challenge the song "Columbia: The Gem of the Ocean." In a 1973 play of the same name, Baraka used the play to forward a message of black solidary against white oppression.

of Salamishah Tillet's theory of civic estrangement in which black Americans experience a paradox of feeling simultaneously as citizens and "non-citizens." As such, black Americans face "feelings of disillusionment and melancholia of non-belonging and a yearning for civic membership" (3). Citizen Barlow embodies this paradox of American belonging and non-belonging. This paradox, which plays out in the form of refashioning of objects and notions meant to oppress black subjects, occurs across the drama. Their cumulative effect represents a practice of freedom as the characters reappropriate artifacts of the slave era as a form of critique as well as to free themselves of the cultural weight of slavery's enduring material histories.

Though they are largely denied their rights as citizens in the world of the drama, the characters of *Gem of the Ocean* resist marginalization by repurposing symbolic objects to express their resilience in the face of devastating oppression. Wilson takes material objects such as Aunt Ester's quilt, her bill of sale, Solly's chain link, European masks, as well as the materiality of the landscape and shows the characters redefining those objects, thus positioning them as critically engaged citizens more forcefully inserting black presence into American nationalist rhetorics. Elizabeth Pittman explains that the Middle Passage in Wilson's text "draws upon meanings that are accrued through the layering of signs. Furthermore, these signs are interpreted and constructed in a process similar to the way we experience memory—as a part of an entirely subjective process of image and sensory integration" ("Voicing the 'Law of the Sea'" 32). While Wilson's strategic layering of signs can certainly be read as a mimetic portrayal of experiences of memory, these repurposed artifacts are also a central reflection of black American practices of survival, constantly improvising and revising the strictures of their existences. Therefore, Wilson is not simply producing a system of signs that represent the act of memory, but revealing intentional moves by black subjects to articulate their own subjectivity through signs meant to diminish them.

The reappropriation of artifacts of the slave era in *Gem of the Ocean* reflects collage artist Romare Bearden's influence on Wilson. A key figure in the four Bs (Baraka, Jorge Luis Borges, the Blues, and Bearden) that Wilson touts as sources of inspiration, Bearden's art influenced Wilson's aesthetics in a number of ways. Bearden's collage *Millhand's Lunch Bucket,* which depicts a boardinghouse scene at the center of which is a dejected-looking African American man and others around him leaving the house, served as the key inspiration for *Joe Turner's Come and Gone* and *The Piano Lesson*. John Hannah, in his tracing of Bearden's influence in other plays by Wilson, explains that through collagist tension—the continuous and simultaneous interplay between fragmentation and unity—Bearden and Wilson contextualize and represent the African American experience. By replicating and therefore revising the processes of fragmentation arising out of successive forced migrations and ever-changing forms of institutionalization, both articulate the possibilities for unity and balance through a hybrid African American identity, a complex confluence of African retentions and Western appropriations. (122)

We can see strategies of transforming fragmentation into unity via the reconstruction of the material archive of slavery from a black standpoint in *Gem of the Ocean* as well. Wilson draws upon a constellation of images, individuals, and landscapes to produce a complex whole. The collage produced in *Gem of the Ocean* documents black life (and its relationship to American ideals of freedom and patriotism) as a response to how black Americans are often excluded from national narratives.

The theater makes possible Wilson's innovative use of objects in his efforts to reframe instruments of oppression into tools of empowerment. As Bert States argues, the theater theatricalizes images and objects by putting them into an intentional space and thereby neutralizing their objectivity (35). He writes, "Theater ingests the world of objects and signs only to bring images to life. In the image a defamiliarized and desymbolized object is 'uplifted to view' where we see it as being phenomenally heavy with itself" (37). Thus, the objects that Wilson presents take on new meaning via his lens.

Importantly, Wilson ties the reappropriated items in the drama to Citizen Barlow's transformative journey. Before going to the City of Bones and during the actual experience, particular objects facilitate his movement: two pennies, a paper boat, and European masks. With these objects, Wilson historicizes black cultural practice and experience as central to narratives of America. The two pennies that Aunt Ester instructs Citizen to find, and that initiate his journey, gesture to the use of coins in slavery to protect the body from disease, to prevent and release spells. Also, coins have been found next to or on top of bodies in excavations of African American burial grounds, thereby illustrating the connections between coins and burial practices/death ("Creating New Traditions"). Marian Wolbers rightly notes the significance of the penny specifically because it contains the image of Abraham Lincoln, echoing Wilson's underlying commentary on the unfulfilled promise of the Emancipation Proclamation.[8] As he draws upon signifiers of the antebellum era,

---

8. See Wolbers's "Nomos, Mysticism and Power Objects in August Wilson's *Joe Turner's Come and Gone*, *Gem of the Ocean* and *The Piano Lesson*."

Wilson actively re-presents this history from the perspective of the black subject. Alice Rayner sheds greater light on this interplay. Much like Bert States, Rayner sees onstage objects as actively participating in the signifying, narrative, and stylistic fictions of the drama as well as the culture (74). She finds this particularly compelling in the context of re-presenting history in works such as Suzan-Lori Parks's *The America Play* (1995). Rayner asserts, "It is through the intersections of objects and their narratives that history can be written, not in terms of authenticity or of recording what may or may not have happened, but in terms of commentary, often ironic, about such recording of history" (75). In this sense, the objects function as a medium for Wilson to express the notion that we lack a complete history of these objects and this era when black experience and subjectivity are obscured from the dominant narrative.

In addition to his recontextualization of and signifying on the Emancipation Proclamation, Wilson takes up a leg chain, an iconic artifact of enslavement and embeds it into Citizen's journey. When Solly Two Kings notices that Citizen was unable to obtain the iron (another object Aunt Ester instructs him to find) from Jilson Grant, he gives Citizen his broken leg chain, a powerful symbol of his resistance to enslavement. Much like Brother Tarp's leg chain in Ralph Ellison's *Invisible Man* functions as a powerful symbol of the long shadow of slavery, Solly's leg chain functions as a contextualizing mechanism for Citizen both as a representation of America's very recent past of sanctioning slavery and the possibility for overcoming this past. Solly says to Citizen, "That's my good luck piece. That piece of chain used to be around my ankle. Then they tried to chain me down but I beat them on that one. I say, I'm going to keep this to remember by. I been lucky ever since. I beat them on a lot of things" (59). The transformation of the leg chain into a good luck piece becomes a counternarrative of empowerment for Solly. While the chain itself acknowledges Solly's life under slavery, it also speaks to his refusal to allow this system to contain him. For Wilson, both of these narratives are integral to American history. Solly's broken leg chain represents perhaps the most salient evidence of the fugitive acts that occur across the drama. The broken leg chain invokes not only escape but serves as evidence of survival. Solly reappropriates the symbol of his bondage as a good luck piece. That he maintains ownership of this chain also signals his ongoing struggle against bondage.

Extending his refashioning of objects documenting enslavement, Wilson employs Aunt Ester's bill of sale as a critical document facilitating Citizen's journey for spiritual wholeness and belonging. While on the journey to the City of Bones, Citizen must hold in his hand a paper boat, which is made from Aunt Ester's bill of sale. Aunt Ester instructs Citizen to hold onto the boat at all times. When he drops the boat during the frightening reenactment of the Middle Passage experience, he loses his balance and a metaphorical storm overtakes him. Aunt Ester has taken the bill of sale, the symbol of her dehumanization, and has transformed it into a tool that facilitates memory, travel, and transformation. She tells Citizen, "That's a magic boat. There's a lot of power in that boat. Power is something" (56). The power that Aunt Ester derives from the boat serves as yet another reminder that power is rarely if ever absolute. It is through the actions of individuals like Aunt Ester and Solly Two Kings that we see an embodiment of the American ideal of autonomy and self-determination. The European masks utilized during Citizen's journey also complicate notions of power. The masks are significant in that they function as another piece of artwork that Wilson employs on stage, but they also serve to "other" the white presence in a way that challenges whiteness as the standard, a normalized concept. Similar to how Olaudah Equiano details in his narrative being struck with fear at the white faces he encountered before being taken onto the ship, Wilson reframes this vision by portraying white individuals as foreign, masked, and so on. Also, Solly and Eli wearing these masks as they play the role of gatekeepers reappropriate the masks to take power over the image. In this context, Eli and Solly hold the power to give Citizen the freedom he desperately seeks.

Finally, Aunt Ester's quilt functions as a visual history and representation of the community's effort to derive unity from fragmentation. The quilt is at once an art object and a map for Citizen's journey to the City of Bones. Aunt Ester reads the map inscribed on the quilt to Citizen, telling him, "Take a look at this map Mr. Citizen. See that right there . . . that's a city. It's only a half mile by a half mile but that's a city. It's made of bones. Pearly white bones" (54). Aunt Ester's map produces an alternative geography bound up in black Americans' collage art work of quilt-making. In discussing contemporary art work inspired by *Gem of the Ocean,* Heather Nathans reminds us that "the quilts that many African American women produced during and after slavery [were] a means not only of creating a useful everyday object, but of integrating their families' histories into the life around them" ("Visualizing August Wilson's *Gem of the Ocean*" 76). I read Aunt Ester's map as participating in this tradition. Aunt Ester's map holds the history of the Middle Passage and documents a critical geography of the Atlantic that accounts for black experience.

Aunt Ester's map also calls up marronage as it charts an alternative space where black life is honored and remembered. The map takes black Americans in some form of pain (whether it be racially inflected or derived from a different cause) to an alternate space for potential healing. It is an act of power in that it constructs a critical geography that transforms our understanding of cartography as a white, male enterprise and intervenes in traditional cartographic practices. Katherine McKittrick's *Demonic Grounds* is quite informative in helping us register the significance of Aunt Ester's act. McKittrick finds power in the ways that black women disrupt traditional cartographic practices and give a greater sense of the power and possibilities of geographic inquiry. Seeing the slave ship as an "oppositional geography," McKittrick argues, "the ship is a location of black subjectivity and human terror, black resistance, and in some cases, black possession" (xi). The City of Bones that Aunt Ester's map charts serves as an oppositional geography that claims space and possesses the land as well as it reframes the agency of those who lost their lives in the terrifying journey of the Middle Passage.

This oppositional geography also performs the work of the counter-monument. The map, which marks the loss experienced in the Middle Passage, reveals ruptures in the unified narrative of American experience that doesn't fully account for black experience. For blacks in the West, these painful ruptures resonate multiply. Dionne Brand gives language in her account of her lack of access to her family's history because of the erasures caused as a result of the trans-Atlantic slave trade. Comprehending this loss causes her to feel a "rupture in history, a rupture in the quality of being. It was also a physical rupture, a rupture of geography" (Brand 5).

Geographical ruptures also emerge as inconvenient truths in the American landscape. The New York City African Burial Ground stands as an example par excellence. In fact, *Gem of the Ocean* converges with the troubling discovery related to this project. Wilson was engaged in writing *Gem* during the September 11, 2001, attacks on the World Trade Center. As a result of the upheaval caused by this attack, officials located nearly one hundred boxes containing artifacts for the African Burial Ground project in a laboratory basement of 6 World Trade Center (Allen). In 1991, archeologists discovered the remains of free and enslaved Africans (once buried in the segregated Negro Burial Ground) in Lower Manhattan and covered over by development of the area, thus initiating the project to construct a national monument ("African Burial Ground Memorial"). The finding of the boxes in the World Trade Center ignited earlier battles over delays in the construction of the monument and the reburial of the remains. The unburied remains symbolize the unresolved mourning of those who died in slavery and the federal, state, and city governments' deprioritizing of the project. When we consider the fact that Lower Manhattan is the site of Wall Street and a symbol of international exchange, the presence of the remains of enslaved bodies, once exchanged as commodities, reminds us of how this history is imbricated into the foundation of America even as it is rarely acknowledged.

Gem of the Ocean's composition and its temporal confluence with the September 11 terror attacks are coincidental, but the event brings to the fore

Wilson's own critical distance from the nation and his critique of US imperialism as he is composing this play. I contend that the tensions of belonging and non-belonging that are dramatized in *Gem* are informed by Wilson's own resistance to an uncritical patriotism that emerged across various sectors during the aftermath of the terror attacks. Wilson's contemporaneous commentary gives insight. Just before the September 11 attacks, Wilson was engaged in a public conversation about theater with drama critic John Lahr for *Slate* magazine's series "The Breakfast Table: An Email Conversation about News of the Day." They had just begun their first correspondence on September 10, 2001, when the events of September 11 understandably shifted their conversation in ways neither anticipated. Wilson expresses horror over the events but remains skeptical of what he perceives as a rising drumbeat for war. Wilson articulates a critical citizenship, which is informed by America's domestic and international violent acts against black and brown peoples in the face of this possibility. Given that he was at work on a drama concerned with the devastating impacts of trans-Atlantic slavery, these thoughts were at the forefront of his mind. He writes,

> To understand the politics [of a potential war in retaliation] we need to look at the origins of the war and understand that it is not a war driven by territorial disputes and fought by standing armies but hatred for our arrogant display of power and our seeming callous indifference to the rest of the world's humanity. Then I think we can, as you say, begin to address "the deeper problems that made for this fanatic hate." In order for something stronger to emerge from the ashes it is going to take a greater understanding of what was there in the first place. ("The Breakfast Table")

Here Wilson calls on the nation to reflect on its own arrogant display of power and "seeming callous indifference to the rest of the world's humanity." In this moment, the ruptures caused by September 11 reveal larger ruptures of state-sanctioned violence done in America's name, of which slavery looms large.

Wilson's elevation of the history of slavery and its lingering impacts against the backdrop of September 11 demonstrates his practice of critical citizenship that is very much bound up in the play itself. This might explain the ambivalent reception the Broadway performances of *Gem of the Ocean* received to such an extent that it closed earlier than anticipated. In her review of the play, Constance Kathryn Zaytoun suggests that the largely middle-class Broadway audiences likely experienced alienation during the play. She argues, "It [the representation of Middle passage in the play] may have been what confused and alienated so many audience members, unwilling to admit their culpability in the collective history being enacted. Wilson insists that we confront our past and relive it for ourselves, no matter what our race—in Aunt Ester's words 'to live right and die right'" (717). Conceivably, *Gem of the Ocean* produced a rupture that exposed an uncomfortable history, which audiences resisted grappling with, especially in light of the demands for national unity as the country was preparing to invade Iraq in a move erroneously framed as a response to the September 11 attacks. *Gem of the Ocean* presents a radical and arguably alienating critique of America's history of racial terror and its resistance to granting black subjects their rightful citizenship in the postslavery era. We see characters working through various states of unfreedom to attain a sense of self-definition and to write themselves into American narratives and Western landscapes that minimize their historical imprint. Through the fugitive acts of constructing a wall around Aunt Ester's home, recontextualizing slave era artifacts, and charting out black geographies that document black experience, the subjects of *Gem* offer new methods of narrativizing the history of slavery. These critical articulations of freedom and citizenship work alongside Wilson's refiguring of mourning, which adds another layer to *Gem*'s complex representation of slavery.

RACIAL MELANCHOLIA AND RADICAL MOURNING

As I have shown, through various fugitive acts, *Gem of the Ocean*'s characters negotiate feelings of unfreedom and denial of civic membership via the ethos of marronage. In doing so, they reveal how this disenfranchisement communicates a devaluing of black life. In this section, I consider, then, how mourning also becomes a fugitive act in this drama because the act of mourning highlights the unresolved grief of slavery and elevates black suffering. In a June 2015 *New York Times* article following the murders of nine parishioners of Mother Emanuel A. M. E. Church, Charleston, South Carolina, Claudia Rankine writes, "The condition of black life is one of mourning." Citing the history of racial violence against black Americans as well as the endless loop of unresolved grief over deaths at the hands of police who often walk away with impunity, Rankine explains that through mourning and grief, we make legible the historic and pervasive devaluation of black life. Mourning in *Gem of the Ocean* carries a similar political context in that Wilson does more than just commemorate the losses caused by trans-Atlantic slavery. He revises familiar notions of loss and refuses a static narrative of grief and powerlessness. Wilson also resists objectification of black bodies tortured in the Middle Passage and instead presents them as bones, similar to his approach in *Joe Turner*.

We can read these interventions as fugitive acts in their countering of state-sanctioned devaluation of black life by making prominent black mourning.

The ritual of remembrance that takes place on each journey to the City of Bones functions as a constant reminder of the pain and loss that occurred in the Middle Passage. However, this act should not be read as an unproductive dwelling in the trauma of this experience. Rather, these returns are productively read through the lens of what David Eng and Shinhee Han describe as "racial melancholia." Responding to and building on Sigmund Freud's "Mourning and Melancholia," Eng and Han push against Freud's pathologization of melancholia (what he describes as the unending process of grief) and his elevation mourning (what he sees as a more normalized grief process that has an end). To this, Eng and Han express that for minoritized groups, melancholia functions in a much more complex way. They argue that the loss that comes as a result of unrealized inclusion in America for those who are racial minorities is ongoing and is manifest in a series of "failed and unresolved integrations" (670). In the case of the Middle Passage, because the US has yet to formally apologize for slavery and because the magnitude of loss of those who died in the journey from Africa to the West can never be fully known, racial melancholia extends beyond failed integration to losses that can never truly be recovered and whose perpetrators have never truly been held accountable.

Saidiya Hartman in *Lose Your Mother: A Journey Along the Atlantic Slave Route* captures some of the incompleteness that comes as a result of trying to grapple with the minimally documented and obscure histories of the trans-Atlantic slave trade. In light of her difficulty in obtaining information and testimonies, she writes,

> Was the experience of slavery best represented by all the stories I would never know? Were gaps and silences and empty rooms the substance of my history? If ruin was my sole inheritance and the only certainty the impossibility of recovering the stories of the enslaved, did this make my history tantamount to mourning? Or worse, was it a melancholia I would never be able to overcome? (16)

Hartman's series of questions represent the impact of the gaps and silences surrounding the trans-Atlantic slave trade. They also demonstrate the unresolved pain that persists in the black psyche in the context of this history. Although she tells a personal story, it reflects a collective anguish. August Wilson echoes this when he tells an interviewer that the Middle Passage is the largest unmarked graveyard in the world (Dezell 255). Aunt Ester's metaphorical travel to the City of Bones provides a means of marking this graveyard. It also constitutes a fugitive act of psychological escape from the untenable reality of her present to a space outside of time and place where she can remember her ancestors, affirm the value of black life, and support those in pain. She transforms the experience of loss into an experience of healing. Those seeking restoration come to get their souls washed in the waters of the Middle Passage. So, rather than this space representing traumatic experience, which one would endeavor to forget, Aunt Ester reconfigures it as a place that facilitates healing and a balm to those in pain.

Each trip to the City of Bones provides the opportunity for Aunt Ester to perform mourning and negate efforts by enslavers to render enslaved subjects as socially dead. The act of remembering functions in opposition to social death, and it offers a perspective largely unaccounted for in American history. As Aunt Ester prepares Citizen for the journey to the City of Bones, she helps him visualize it. She tells him, "I seen it. I been there, Mr. Citizen. My mother live there. I got an aunt and three uncles live down there in that city made of bones" (54). Notably, Aunt Ester describes her mother, aunt, and uncles as still alive in the City of Bones. Imagining her ancestors as living beings allows Aunt Ester to subvert notions of loss. Unlike traditional notions of melancholia that are portrayed in pathological terms, Aunt Ester's melancholy keeps her ancestors alive in the imagination. She does not allow the finality of death to dictate her engagement with her ancestors.

Aunt Ester's politics of mourning also link her to a past that slavery attempted to sever. Her refusal to allow that past to be severed gets articulated in her theorizing about the City of Bones and reflections on subsequent experiences of loss that she experienced in slavery. She illuminates,

> That's the center of the world. In time it will all come to light. The people made a kingdom out of nothing. . . . The people got a burning tongue, Mr. Citizen. Their mouths are on fire with song. That water can't put it out. That song is powerful. . . . I came across that ocean, Mr. Citizen. I cried. I had lost everything. Everything I had ever known in this life I lost that. I cried a [sic] ocean of tears. . . . The only thing I had was the stars. I say well I got something. I wanted to hold on to them so I started naming them. I named them after my children. I say there go Seefus and that's Jasper and that's Cecilia, and that big one over there that's Junebug. (55)

Positioning the City of Bones (i.e., The Middle Passage) as the "center of the world," Aunt Ester marks the trans-Atlantic slave trade as a turning point of modernity that undergirds nations across the world whose wealth and development is owed to and bound up in slavery. In this way, Aunt Ester centers black experience and the abuse and exploitation of black subjects as meaningful to notions of place, thereby offering them a radically new kind of orientation to the world.

Calling upon song as an act of memory and storytelling, Aunt Ester describes the inhabitants of the City of Bones as having mouths on fire with song that no water can extinguish. Here, she offers a direct response to the concept of social death that Orlando Patterson puts forward in his seminal work, *Slavery and Social Death*. He argues, "The definition of the slave, however, recruited, is a socially dead person." He then elucidates the consequences of this dehumanization for kinship relations of the enslaved:

> Not only was the enslaved denied all claims on, and obligations to, his parents and living blood relations, but, by extension, all such claims and obligations on his more remote ancestors and on his descendants. He was truly a genealogical isolate. Formally isolated in his social relations with those who lived, he was also culturally isolated from the cultural heritage of his ancestors. (5)

By aiming to sever familial connections, the objective of enslavers was to isolate enslaved subjects and deny them access to a past that would confirm their personhood and their capacity for affect. When Aunt Ester describes her experience of loss, particularly the tears she shed as each family member is taken from her by the brutality of the slave system, she speaks back to efforts to negate her ties to her family. Beyond her reframing of the geography of the Atlantic Ocean, she envisions her children as cosmic bodies instantiated by stars after which she names them. The journey to the City of Bones raises up possibilities for community and history for enslaved subjects and their descendants in ways that counter the ongoing devaluation of black life in the present of the drama.

Aunt Ester's affirmation of genealogical bonds can be effectively read in relation to Joseph Roach's genealogies of performance. The song of her ancestors that Aunt Ester proclaims cannot be put out by fire but persists across time, represents the voices of those rendered nameless and subsumed in the Atlantic. Aunt Ester also sings the song of her mother, thereby keeping her song alive in the present. These performance genealogies function as countermemories or, to align with the focus of this chapter, fugitive acts that subvert efforts to suppress the histories of the enslaved and to sever their familial relation. The ritual of performance here and in Aunt Ester's continual return to it serves as an embodiment of memory.

The drama works to counter the psychological damage inherent in the social death of enslavement, yet it problematizes representations of bodily pain that often go unregistered for black subjects.[9] By presenting enslaved subjects who were brutalized in the Middle Passage as bones, Wilson denies an objectifying gaze that reproduces familiar imagery of abject and abused black enslaved subjects. In this way, Wilson refuses to perpetuate imagery of abused black bodies. Saidiya Hartman gives insight into Wilson's choice and how the dissemination of such images can have a desensitizing effect. In explaining her decision not to reproduce the violent spectacle of Frederick Douglass's description of his Aunt Hester being beaten, Hartman notes the casualness with which imagery of ravaged bodies of enslaved subjects are circulated. Of such imagery, she explains:

> Rather than inciting indignation, too often they immure us to pain by virtue of their familiarity—the oft-repeated or restored character of these accounts and our distance from them are signaled by the theatrical language usually resorted to in describing these instances—and especially because they reinforce the spectacular character of black suffering. . . . At issue here is the precariousness of empathy and the uncertain line between witness and spectator. (2–3)

Hartman highlights the numbing impact of being repeatedly exposed to brutalized black bodies in representations of slavery. What is often lost is a true measure of the cumulative effect of this world-destroying experience on those oppressed within this system. The abstraction of abused black bodies as bones in *Gem of the Ocean* militates against the impulse to deploy this familiar imagery.

Wilson troubles the line between witness and spectator by offering an alternative spectacle with this opulent City of Bones that stands in as a representation of the millions lost in the Middle Passage. Rather than emphasize the devastating scene of the slave ship, Wilson offers an unanticipated image of beauty. When Citizen nears the end of his journey to the City of Bones and finally witnesses this place, he remarks, "There it is! It's made of bones! All the buildings and everything. Head bones and leg bones and rib bones. The

---

9. Judith Butler sheds light: "What is real? Whose lives are real? How might reality be remade? Those who are unreal have, in a sense already suffered the violence of derealization. What, then is the relation between violence and those lives considered as 'unreal'? . . . They cannot be mourned because they are always already lost or, rather, never 'were,' and they must be killed, since they seem to live on, stubbornly, in this state of deadness" (*Precarious Life* 33). This derealization is certainly prevalent for minoritized groups. For the formerly enslaved and their descendants, the violence of derealization occurs across time.

streets look like silver. The trees are made of bones" (71). The audience has to imagine Citizen's vision and this collaborative act moves the audience into a more active stance as they collectively imagine Wilson's vision of the Middle Passage. This intervention refuses objectification of black bodies and forces audiences to see those brutalized as subjects. Wilson's choice holds particular significance when we consider how spectacles of black suffering in the slave era have historically been sites of pleasure for white audiences.[10] I do not want to suggest, however, that Wilson minimizes the painful experience of the Middle Passage or even that he desires to obscure documented historical experience. Rather, the use of bones, in addition to their countering the spectacle of black suffering, renarrativizes the Middle Passage as a site of "black subjectivity and human terror, black resistance, and in some cases, black possession" (xi), to return to McKittrick's instructive framing.

We can even see Wilson's radical depiction of mourning at the moment of Solly Two Kings's death. Near the conclusion of the drama, Ceasar Wilkes shoots and kills Solly in retaliation for setting fire to the mill. However, before he pursues Solly, Ceasar attempts to arrest Aunt Ester for what he describes as aiding and abetting "Alfred Jackson [Solly Two Kings's given name], a fugitive of the law" (83). Solly ends the drama as a fugitive not unlike his status during slavery. In his eulogy for Solly, Eli declares, "Solly never did find his freedom" (87). For Solly, and arguably the majority of the black subjects living in the drama's early twentieth-century present, freedom is elusive, something of which one remains in constant search. Hence, the drama ends with the central premise upon which it rests—that emancipation has not yet been fulfilled for black Americans.

To defy a system that refuses to recognize your personhood and citizenship rights, as Solly does, means to remain a fugitive. We see this reinforced with Citizen's act at the end of the drama. As Aunt Ester, Eli, and Black Mary commence singing in preparation for Solly's burial, Citizen elects to honor Solly in a more forceful way. He exchanges his coat for Solly's, takes up his stick, and it is suggested that he intends to continue Solly's work, namely returning to Alabama to safely escort Solly's sister Eliza to the North.[11] We

---

10. See Saidiya Hartman's *Scenes of Subjection: Terror, Slavery, and Self-Making in Nineteenth-Century America*.

11. In many ways, this reflects Joseph Roach's notion of surrogation in black performance. He explains, "In the life of a community, the process of surrogation does not begin or end but continues as actual or perceived vacancies occur in the network of relations that constitutes the social fabric" (2). He also notes that because memory is selective and largely imaginative, it rarely succeeds. However, in that process, he argues, emerges the invention of new forms and ways of understanding the past. We can conclude then that, although inspired by Solly, Citizen will chart a different course that explores new possibilities for resistance.

must note that Citizen, too, is a fugitive as Ceasar intends to arrest him as well. The play's ending denies closure, as it is reflective of the definition of marronage as running counter to the idea of fixed, determinate endings (Roberts 173). This moment instead shows the fugitive Citizen taking up Solly's search for freedom. In this sense, mourning takes on a radical context given that Citizen's act of mourning is the work of freedom.

Gem of the Ocean is often rightly read as a commemorative text,[12] but it should also be understood as a comment on the conditions of unfreedom for black Americans, which was initiated in the aftermath of slavery and arguably continues into the present day. The drama should also be read as a demonstration of the practices of survival enacted by black Americans and their efforts to attain a modicum of freedom in a hostile nation. These efforts toward freedom constitute fugitive acts, which serve to critique the nation while rewriting its narratives in order to make visible black subjectivity and experience. In the refuge that is Aunt Ester's home as well as in the counterarchival work of memorializing material histories of slavery, the deployment of mourning as a practice of freedom, and the reclaiming of geographical space and refusing to visually exploit the brutality of the Middle Passage, *Gem of the Ocean* makes critical interventions in the ways we comprehend slavery's continued resonance across time. In the chapter that follows, I intend to build on my analysis of Wilson's interrogation of visual practices of representing slavery in order to think about how Lydia Diamond and Branden Jacobs-Jenkins perform this critical work in their dramas *Harriet Jacobs: A Play* and *An Octoroon*, respectively. I analyze performances of whiteness that occur within both dramas and how this strategy directly confronts epistemologies of race that have been advanced since the slave era, particularly via blackface minstrelsy and other denigrating imagery of blackness that were meant to distinguish it from whiteness. I consider the significance of Diamond and Jacobs-Jenkins returning to the site of slavery to grapple with issues of racial representation, social constructions of race, and their implications for black subjects.

---

12. See Soyica Colbert's *The African American Theatrical Body* and Elizabeth Pittman's "Voicing the 'Law of the Sea': Commemoration and Cultural Nationalism in August Wilson's *Gem of the Ocean*."

CHAPTER 3

Performing Escape

THE FIGURE CATO of William Wells Brown's *The Escape; Or a Leap for Freedom* performs a supremely radical act of transformation when he surreptitiously takes his enslaver's garments and dresses as him in order to escape to freedom. Cato recounts how he switched clothes with his enslaver and performed his new role so successfully that it resulted in him being able to escape enslavement. In a disguise so convincing it causes even him to question his own image, he declares, "Well now it is me an' I em [*sic*] a free man" (40). Cato, in being able to convincingly embody his enslaver and "pass" as him, reveals the blurred nature of the color line.[1] Cato also exploits ambiguities of racial identification to attain freedom from a system that so arbitrarily deems him as intellectually inferior. Daphne Brooks reads Cato's cunning reversal as staging "the spectacle of a fugitive asserting his subjectivity through the tools of performance and using those same tools to mock and destabilize the subjectivity of the ruling class" (2). Moreover, she argues that Cato's performance can be read as an ur-text for a larger history of early black performance

---

1. In his reading of whiteness in *The Escape*, John Ernest argues that William Wells Brown's drama reflects the instability of whiteness as a category. He writes: "For in various ways and at various cultural levels, white Americans revealed in their political, economic, gender, religious, and aesthetic discourses the extent of their awareness that their whiteness was inextricably linked to blackness and that the racial markers white and black implied boundaries long since crossed" (1114).

that speaks to how "African Americans rehearsed methods to transform the notion of ontological dislocation into resistant performance so as to become the agents of their own liberation" (3). Given that this book is concerned with how contemporary black drama grapples with the unfinished business of slavery and the limits of emancipation, I want to consider how Brooks's analysis here resonates in contemporary dramatic work where black actors perform as white characters to achieve representational liberation even as the specter of slavery haunts their performances. To recall my articulation of performances of fugitivity stated earlier in this book, one particular dimension that emerges in the performative escape Cato inspires is how black performers endeavor to artfully escape objectification.[2] In this chapter, I consider fugitivity in the contexts of artistic expression and racial representation, particularly their implications for how we understand black subjectivity. Two dramas, Lydia Diamond's *Harriet Jacobs: A Play* (2008) and Branden Jacobs-Jenkins's *An Octoroon* (2014), engage the aforementioned subjects by featuring performances of whiteness by black characters at the site of slavery.[3] Doing so calls up genealogies of black minstrel performance as well as similarly transgressive performances of whiteness that have equally storied histories. Performances of whiteness enable black subjects to challenge confining racial constructions and ironically forward more expansive representations of blackness.

In *Whiting Up: Whiteface Minstrels and Stage Europeans in African American Performance*, Marvin McAllister offers valuable context for the performances of whiteness that Lydia Diamond and Branden Jacobs-Jenkins forward. McAllister traces a tradition of performing whiteness throughout the nineteenth and twentieth centuries with a look toward the future continuation of this performance. He identifies "whiteface minstrelsy" as extratheatrical, social performance where people of African descent appropriate white-identified gestures, dialect, and so on often to satirize, parody, and interrogate authoritative representations of whiteness. Conversely, he defines "stage Europeans" as black actors appropriating white dramatic characters initially crafted by white dramatists. Such performances emphasize vocal manifestations of whiteness and often rely on visual effects such as whiteface paint and blonde wigs (1). McAllister ends his work by contemplating the possibility of this kind

---

2. I reference here the definition of fugitivity that James Edward Ford offers: A "critical category for examining *the artful escape of objectification*, whether said objectification occurs through racialized aesthetic framing, commodification, or liberal juridico-political discipline" (110).

3. With the terminology "performances of whiteness" (as opposed to "whiteface"), I take my cue from Faedra Carpenter, who is careful to use this framing to avoid prompting readers to make easy associations with blackface minstrelsy or to suggest that these strategies (blackface and whiteface) function analogously.

of performance to expand representational opportunities for actors of all colors; yet, he wonders if, in the present era, these kinds of performances have run their course. Both produced in the twenty-first century, Lydia Diamond's *Harriet Jacobs* and Branden Jacobs-Jenkins's *An Octoroon* answer the question of whether or not these performances have been exhausted with an emphatic "no." The staging of performances of whiteness at the site of slavery in the contemporary moment demonstrates that this critical work is continuing, and it adds new dimension to how we understand the uses of this performance. Diamond's and Jacobs-Jenkins's new approaches to performing whiteness speak to the shifting ways black creatives are exploring issues of racial representation in performance as well as the effects of performing whiteness in the contemporary era.

By formally staging black actors performing as white characters, while also engaging in parody to challenge perceptions of racial difference, *Harriet Jacobs* and *An Octoroon* utilize performances of whiteness in ways that are racially deconstructive. I contend that the fugitive performances of whiteness in both dramas allow Diamond and Jacobs-Jenkins to offer artistically experimental and transgressive performances as well as engage in a multileveled critique that challenges the arbitrary nature of racial identification that undergirded the slave system. These performances also signal how the perpetuation of racial hierarchies borne of the slave era continue to disadvantage black subjects in the present. The suspension of racial boundaries in these dramas also facilitates a critique of historical discourses of slavery that often suppress black subjectivity. In Diamond's and Jacobs-Jenkins's dramas, black actors and characters perform both literal and figurative escape as a means to elude objectification. These performative escapes manifest not only in the performance of whiteness, but also in enactments of code-switching, disruptions of time, and direct address to the audience. Through subversive performance, Diamond and Jacobs-Jenkins strike at the very heart of the racial logics (or illogics) of slavery to reveal all the ways many discourses of slavery misrepresent black subjectivity and advance problematic conceptions of blackness that resonate in the present.

PERFORMING WHITENESS AT THE SITE OF SLAVERY

Given that the performance trope of blackface minstrelsy prevailed as a caricature of black subjects and that this performance mode was instantiated during slavery, it is unsurprising that contemporary dramatists would direct their focus to this history of performance as they critique the institution of slavery. Presented with varied intentions and methods, blackface has been largely understood as a profitable means to affirm white racial purity and obscure the experience of suffering in slavery.[4] Even though black performers would go on to manipulate the practice of minstrelsy for their own ends (often using it to advance their careers while subversively undermining its racist roots), it remains undeniable that minstrelsy produced copious amounts of demeaning imagery of black subjects that continues to haunt American performance and culture. In confronting the long and consequential history of blackface minstrelsy in their depictions of slavery, Lydia Diamond and Branden Jacobs-Jenkins turn to performances of whiteness as a means to deepen contemporary critical engagement with slavery via performance. In so doing, both playwrights elevate the history of black actors performing whiteness to performatively free themselves from the confines of racial representation while also critiquing racial hierarchies.[5]

Early performances of whiteness illuminate how black subjects gleaned power even as they contended with the subjection of enslavement. Marvin McAllister documents how enslaved subjects assumed whiteness and performed white privilege in semiprivate spaces such as cakewalks and country dances; he also examines how they performed whiteness publicly in Sunday promenades where they would showcase their fashionable garments in places such as Charleston, South Carolina, and New York City. He argues, "Early African American whiteface spectacles were less about ridiculing whiteness and more about showcasing black style, forging communal identity, asserting representational freedom, and training American Negroes for emancipation" (20). Ironically, it is through the performance of whiteness that black subjects are able to assert affirming senses of selfhood and freedom. In this way whiteness functions as a backdrop that militates against the denigrating imagery of "authentic" blackness to reveal a blackness with greater representational possibilities. To return to William Wells Brown's Cato and his performative escape into whiteness, Cato exploits his enslaver's paternalistic need to shape

---

4. See Eric Lott's *Love and Theft: Blackface Minstrelsy and the American Working Class* and Saidiya Hartman's *Scenes of Subjection: Terror, Slavery, and Self-Making in Nineteenth-Century America*.

5. We see similar interventions in works like Lin-Manuel Miranda's *Hamilton*. By using a black and Latinx cast, he writes minoritized bodies onto an historical narrative that has excluded them in many respects. The musical's artistic director, Oskar Eustis, asserts, "By telling the story of the founding of the country through the eyes of a bastard, immigrant orphan, told entirely by people of color, he [Miranda] is saying, 'This is our country. We get to lay claim to it'" (Mead). Diamond and Jacobs-Jenkins's interventions depart a bit, however, from Manuel's project. In staging enslaved subjects and featuring the subject while performing whiteness, they directly address underlying myths of race that undergird the color line.

Cato into his own image (he has Cato work as an apprentice in his dental practice and serve as his domestic assistant). Cato ultimately performs as a replica of his enslaver, which enables his freedom.[6] Cato's outmaneuvering of his enslaver reveals another liberatory dimension of performing whiteness—challenging the stability of the color line. Performing whiteness has the capacity to prompt "reconsiderations or reconstructions of what whiteness and blackness, as well as other identity markers such as class and gender, can potentially signify for artist and audience" (McAllister 5–6). To wit, Ellen and William Craft's escape to freedom nicely demonstrates how performing whiteness can work alongside the troubling of other identity markers such as gender. Dressed as a male planter and performing as disabled to avoid having to sign her own name, which she was unable to do, Ellen Craft performed as a white man to free herself from slavery (*Conjugal Union*, Reid-Pharr 58). Craft at once undermines the rigidity of race and gender in order to attain freedom. She simultaneously draws upon the freedom of whiteness and maleness to free herself. This act contests these categories to reveal their arbitrary nature.

Destabilizing the very foundations upon which racial hierarchies are constructed holds special significance for black subjects who often languish on the lower rungs of such hierarchies. In the era of slavery, we see black subjects who are perceived as property seize the "property" of whiteness as a means to define and free themselves in a figurative and sometimes literal sense. Across time, we can see permutations of such performances for similar ends where black performers utilize the performance of whiteness to illuminate the flawed logic of racial categories and the sustained impact it has had on black social and economic mobility.

Performing whiteness figuratively claims the property of whiteness and inscribes it onto the black body in direct response to how whiteness has functioned as a mechanism of exclusion. The transformation of whiteness into property reinforced the color line and cut off racial minorities from opportunity. Cheryl Harris in "Whiteness as Property" explains,

> Slavery as a system of property facilitated the merger of white identity and property. Because the system of slavery was contingent on and conflated with racial identity, it became crucial to be "white," to be identified as white, to have the property of being white. Whiteness was the characteristic, the attribute, the property of free human beings. (1721)

---

6. See Marvin McAlister's *Whiting Up* (21) for an extended discussion of the paternalism underlying white enslavers desiring to remake the enslaved in their image.

Harris identifies not only whiteness's exclusionary power but also its freeing capabilities. To possess whiteness meant one possessed freedom. Today, whiteness continues to grant individuals a sense of belonging and community in America. Judith Butler explains the contemporary practices of "doing whiteness" that continue to operate in American culture: "Understood as the sometimes explicit power to define the boundaries of kinship, community, and nation, whiteness inflects all those frameworks within which certain lives are made to matter less than others" ("What's Wrong"). By claiming the power of whiteness to define social boundaries and parameters of human value, black subjects make themselves legible in a world that often relegates them to the margins. This act also carries an economy of use, to return to Harris's metaphor of whiteness as property. In the performance of whiteness, black subjects actively define themselves outside of commoditized tropes of blackness to reveal how the *currency* of whiteness attains value when juxtaposed against the *product* of blackness.[7]

We should not, however, read the performance of whiteness as simply a reversal of blackface minstrelsy, but as a critique of the very foundations upon which whiteness was constructed. Continuing the work of Marvin McAllister, Faedra Carpenter's *Coloring Whiteness: Acts of Critique in Black Performance* considers performative and dramaturgical strategies of making whiteness "strange" and revealing it as "a social, political, and economic construct" (3). The notion of making whiteness "strange" through black performance also speaks to Daphne Brooks's concept of "Afro-alienation." Brooks explains that black performers of the late nineteenth and early twentieth centuries used strategies of Afro-alienation to defamiliarize the spectacle of their own bodies, thereby yielding alternative racial and gender epistemologies. "By using performance tactics to signify on the social, cultural, and ideological machinery that circumscribes African Americans, they intervene in the spectacular and systemic representational abjection of black peoples" (Brooks 5). The strategy of Afro-alienation facilitates the performance of escape that we see in enactments of whiteness. Performing whiteness directly counters the representational abjection of black subjects and troubles the objectifying white gaze. Although her work focuses on nineteenth-century and early twentieth-century black performance, Brooks's notion of Afro-alienation enables a reading of transgressive acts occurring in Diamond's and Jacobs-Jenkins's dramas beyond performances of whiteness. These strategies emerge in the Brechtian alienation effects upon which Brooks signifies, such as direct address to the

---

7. See Fred Moten's *In the Break* for a rich analysis on the imbrications of capital and blackness dating back to slavery and extending into subsequent modes of black expressive culture.

audience and the disruption of climactic scenes in a meta-theatrical manner. We can also see this in switches that occur in both dramas whether it be in the form of linguistic code or time. Through these effects, Diamond and Jacobs-Jenkins forward new epistemologies of race, gender, and slavery because they cause audiences to question the reliability of historical narratives in offering a full picture of slavery and black humanity.

DEFAMILIARIZING SLAVERY AND RACE IN *HARRIET JACOBS: A PLAY*

In the front matter of the drama *Harriet Jacobs: A Play,* playwright Lydia Diamond asks audiences to free her, the narrative she has produced, and the subjects featured in the narrative from preconceived notions of enslaved experience. She requests that audiences "live in the present I've tried to create" (xv) and to resist dwelling only in the pain of slavery. Instead, she asks audiences to join her in celebrating the "humanity that lived between and around the pain" (xv–xvi). Diamond's radical move aims to reorient audiences' affective understandings of slavery away from familiar tropes of abject and abused black bodies, and toward less predictable and more complicated representations of slavery and blackness. In the process, she also attempts to account for the silences and omissions with which a number of artists and thinkers, especially those writing within the neo-slave narrative tradition, have endeavored to grapple. In their forward to *Harriet Jacobs: A Play,* Megan Sandberg-Zakian and Jean Fagan Yellin assert, "Diamond's text, like Jacobs's, asks us to consider all the ways we *don't* understand history, all the ways we have become comfortable with one kind of narrative of slavery and, by extension, with one kind of narrative about race, class, gender, power, and privilege" (xii). Diamond's critical project, then, functions as a way to trouble slavery's inherently troubling narrative in order to explore the productive possibilities in depicting this history.

Presented approximately five years after August Wilson's *Gem of the Ocean, Harriet Jacobs: A Play* constitutes one of the earlier dramas within the growing body of contemporary dramas featuring slavery; however, few critical analyses of this play exist.[8] Because of its use of experimentation and its adaptation of Jacobs's iconic narrative, this play should be understood as a

---

8. At the time of this writing, the only scholarly treatment that exists of this play is Ruby Berryman's "Distilling Genocide into Drama: Adaptation of Holocaust and Slave Narratives to the Stage." While this article offers an insightful reading of the play, it does not deal in detail with Diamond's innovative representations of race and Jacobs's story.

prominent work ushering in an era of dramas that reimagine slavery in radical ways. In my analysis of this drama, I consider how Diamond produces performances of fugitivity in her vigilance against rendering an objectifying presentation of slavery as she depicts the fugitive Harriet Jacobs. These performances of fugitivity manifest in a number of performative escapes, largely enabled by Diamond's upending of racial difference as a foundation for slavery. Diamond's work calls for an all-black cast, and these cast members also play white characters in the drama. The performance of whiteness in the drama creates representational room for a defamiliarized depiction of Jacobs and her experience. Other performative escapes occur in the drama such as code-switching and the representation of the garret space as a quintessential fugitive site that makes freedom for Jacobs possible. My analysis of *Harriet Jacobs* is also informed by Diamond's engagement with issues of race and politics during the time in which the drama was developed. Diamond wrote and presented the play during the lead-up to the election of the US's first black president, Barack Obama. Considering this cultural backdrop, I will analyze how Diamond infuses her presentation of Jacobs's narrative with contemporary political conversations about race and cultural progress. In my discussion of this work, I will draw upon the script of the drama, Diamond's public writing on the 2008 election, and notable theatrical productions of the drama presented between 2008 and 2010.

Commissioned and premiered in 2008 by Steppenwolf Theatre Company as part of their Steppenwolf for Young Adults programming, *Harriet Jacobs: A Play* adapts Harriet Jacobs's *Incidents in the Life of a Slave Girl*, focusing on the years leading up to her escape. It is a two-act play that features a young Harriet (as she is so-named in the drama), who is an avid reader and a spirited individual. She often moves between the space of her grandmother's home and the plantation. Also, she falls in love with a young man named Tom, a carpenter and enslaved man on a neighboring plantation, whom Jacobs also references in her narrative. Layered onto more benign scenes from Harriet's life are monologues from other enslaved subjects who detail their experiences of the brutality within the slave system. Harriet refers to the interludes where enslaved characters recount the horrors they experienced in slavery as "stories that never stop." By framing these narratives as "stories that never stop," Diamond signals the haunting aspect of this history and gestures to its contemporary relevance. "Stories that never stop" also call up the unfinished, elusive, and uncontainable narratives that compose slavery's yet-to-be-told archive. This multifaceted drama also includes key revisions of names. Diamond unmasks the figures for whom Jacobs used pseudonyms to protect their identities including her own. She restores Harriet Jacobs's name (as opposed to referring to her as Linda Brent) and others. Instead of Dr. Flint, she uses the name Dr. Norcom. Diamond also uses the real names of the father of Jacobs's children—Samuel Treadwell Sawyer, and her children—Joseph and Louisa.

Diamond's defamiliarizing of Harriet Jacobs's iconic narrative also came at a time when the nation was entering an *unfamiliar* period with its first black President. In fact, Diamond notes that she wrote *Harriet Jacobs: A Play* during the 2007 Democratic primary elections and presented the drama in 2008, the year of President Obama's election, stating that this historic moment deeply influenced her approach to presenting issues of race on stage. She explains, "It leveled me. . . . It really asked that I step it up in a really profound way. The conversation [about race], for me, felt more urgent but had to be more sophisticated than it had ever been" (Myers). Diamond ultimately channels this urgency into her drama about Jacobs, using slavery as a site to upend conceptions of this history as well as conceptions of race in the present.

In choosing the site of slavery to have what she calls a more sophisticated conversation about race, Diamond confronts the logics undergirding the slave system and the damaging perpetuation of such logics. The performance of whiteness through her utilization of an all-black cast facilitates her critique. Having black actors perform as enslavers destabilizes notions of racial difference and certainly upends familiar conceptions of slavery. Diamond explicitly states in the stage directions for the play:

> It is imperative that all cast members are black. All "White" characters are represented by Black ensemble members, donning skeletal white hoopskirts, bonnets, top hats, and the like. It is important that some theatrical gesture (for example, putting on gloves or white skirts onstage) accompany the transforming of the ensemble members into "White" characters. (2)

The practice of putting on whiteness that Diamond describes is a performance of what Faedra Carpenter calls "nonconforming whiteface," in which characters imitate corporeal whiteness solely through props, symbolic attire, or other objects associated with the actor's body (see figure 3) (24). Moreover, by placing the word *White* in scare quotes, Diamond directly challenges the politics of racial categorization. But her controversial demand that black actors portray white characters runs the risk of obscuring those who perpetuate this system, thereby limiting their accountability. Nevertheless, Diamond's radical approach to casting works to compel audiences to question not only what they

FIGURE 3. Genevieve VenJohnson and Leslie Ann Sheppard as two "White" women in Steppenwolf Theatre Company's 2008 production. Used with permission from Steppenwolf Theatre, Chicago, IL.

know about slavery but also the underlying racial myths that sustained the institution. That is, as audiences imagine enslavers via black actors, the logics of the color line become undone.

Here, the black body becomes a medium with which to articulate new narratives about enslaved experience. Certainly, Western culture has objectified and overdetermined the black body, which Harvey Young calls attention to when he terms the black body as a "second body," an abstracted and imagined figure that shadows or doubles the real one (7). This "second body" is highly (mis)recognized yet structures much of black experience (Young 10). Diamond utilizes this strategy of cross-racial casting to cite slavery's role in constructing arbitrary racial categories and to call attention to how the legacies of these constructions bear out in our present. When we consider this choice in light of the fact that Diamond is writing in the lead-up to Barack Obama's 2008 election, we can also see the casting choice as a contestation of premature declarations of the US being a postracial society because a black man is a viable candidate for president. Conversely, Brandi Catanese cites Obama's election and the response to it as evidence of the need to resist rhetoric of "transcending race," a formulation which she suggests actually works to facilitate a devaluation of blackness (22). She argues that instead we should see figures like Obama in the context of racial transgression where his public speeches about race relations in America require that audiences deal with the subject matter from a race-conscious perspective rather than a color-blind/transcendent one. Such performances, Catanese suggests, foreground the possibility of black performance as a transformative practice within American culture (31).

Catanese's framing provides a valuable heuristic through which to read Diamond's all-black casting choice. Indeed, Diamond's casting guidance refuses racial transcendence (or postraciality) in favor of racial transgression. Diamond structures a set of conditions where blackness remains present even as it transgresses the spaces of whiteness on the plantation. This casting choice transgresses the boundary of the color line to remind audiences of the performative aspects of race and how maintaining an investment in racial distinctions obscures an understanding of our shared humanity.

The play's effort to challenge constructions of race and the injustices brought on by them also reflects Jacobs's own commentary on the arbitrary nature of racial categories in *Incidents*. Jacobs notes that her parents were considered mulattoes as a result of their mixed ancestry and that her uncle Benjamin was nearly white, having "inherited the complexion [her] grandmother had derived from Anglo-Saxon ancestors" (10). These descriptions work to demystify race as the basis for slavery. They also advance a characterization of slavery as irrational. Jacobs notes two girls playing together—one enslaved and one her mistress. The children also happened to be sisters by virtue of slavery's "monstrous intimacies."[9] Jacobs writes, "When I saw them embracing each other, and heard their joyous laughter, I turned sadly away from the lovely sight. I foresaw the inevitable blight that would fall on the little slave's heart. I knew how soon her laughter would be changed to sighs" (27–28). In offering these meditations on the entangled relations between the enslaved and their enslavers, Jacobs prefaces her argument against slavery over the false distinctions of race used to justify the system.

Jacobs even more passionately assails racial discrimination once she flees North and experiences this discrimination firsthand. In her chapter entitled "Prejudice against Color," she describes the humiliation of being segregated away from her white counterparts, being denied service when accompanying Mrs. Bruce to dining areas, and suffering public scorn when she resisted her oppression. In reflecting on her experience, she asserts, "Let every colored man and woman do this [reject presumptions of their inferiority], and eventually we shall cease to be trampled underfoot by our oppressors" (138). Thus, even in the "free" North, Jacobs still experiences intense forms of antiblack oppression. The presumptions of black inferiority that sustained slavery and

---

9. See Christina Sharpe's *Monstrous Intimacies*.

the illogic of the color line that structured social relations throughout the nation persisted long after Jacobs made her escape.

Thus, Diamond draws a connecting line from Jacobs's critique of racial essentialisms and segregation to the contemporary moment by upending racial categories with her all-black cast. In a brief monologue in 2012 entitled "The Author's America" written by Diamond for Baltimore, Maryland's Centerstage Theatre, she gives insight into her motivations for this choice. Her monologue focuses on the paradigm shifting potential of Barack Obama's election and how his biracial identity raises awareness of the instability of concrete conceptions of race. She refers to him as "black, biracial, black identified . . . most of the time." It is clear with this meditation that Diamond sees racial identification as slippery at best even as she acknowledges its very real effects on racial politics. In this way, the use of the all-black cast gestures to realities for many who negotiate the space between the static categories of black and white. This reflects the transgression of the color line that Brandi Catanese theorizes. It also recalls the reductive phrases, "acting black" and "acting white," which clearly demarcate race as performative even as many reinforce the legitimacy of these ideas.[10]

But more than just a means of challenging racial boundaries, Diamond's use of an all-black cast also signifies on the history of cross-racial performance during the antebellum era—with William Wells Brown's *The Escape; or, A Leap for Freedom* serving as a seminal text for how black playwrights and performers utilized cross-racial performance in efforts to achieve societal transformation. Additionally, Heather Nathans explains that white actors often played enslaved characters in antebellum slave dramas. Based on the premise of similarity between themselves and dominant audience members, these actors would facilitate empathy and thus an "affinitive politics" that would enable social change (6). Nathans emphasizes the danger of such practices insofar as they had the potential to limit spectators from engaging with the actual lived experience of enslaved subjects. Instead, the spectator risks substituting himself for the enslaved, which produces a tenuous empathy that could result in the exploitation of black pain (6). Considering this history, Diamond cleverly overturns the standards of the antebellum sentimentality in her drama. By offering only black actors for multiracial audiences with whom to relate and perhaps empathize, Diamond breaks down the assumption that affinitive politics can only be cultivated through racial sameness.

---

10. See McAllister and Carpenter.

Diamond also frees up her black characters by giving them greater representational room through their acts of "whiting up." Ironically, it is through performances of whiteness that black subjects are able to assert affirming senses of selfhood and freedom. In this way, whiteness functions as a backdrop that militates against the denigrating imagery of "authentic" blackness and presents a blackness with greater representational possibilities. Actors in the play have noted the latitude and signifying potential that whiting up offers. For instance, actors in Central Square Theatre's (Cambridge, MA) production appreciated the opportunity to expand their skills by performing as white characters. One actress, Obehi Janice, saw her act of putting on whiteness as symbolic of "tapping into white privilege" (or the mimicking of white social ease in which white subjects fluidly move in the society without laboring over how their bodies are perceived in public space). Another actor, Sheldon Best, who played Tom, suggests that the disrupting nature of black actors playing slave owners is effective because we are so familiar with slavery's white versus black antagonisms that we have become inured to the image of a white man attacking a black person (Haverson). Here the actors see their performances of whiteness as opening up possibilities for actors as well as for audiences in challenging racial identification. Furthermore, Diamond's call for black actors to white up in *Harriet Jacobs* allows her to redirect audiences' attention away from familiar and prescriptive racial paradigms and toward an understanding of race-based systems of domination such as chattel slavery as grounded in surreal concepts and conditions that should always feel unfamiliar and discomforting. The performance of whiteness in the play thus facilitates escape in multiple ways. For black performers, it becomes a means to create greater representational room for black subjectivity that demurs the confines of black/white binaries. Moreover, the performance of whiteness in the play functions as a figurative, albeit momentary, escape for audiences from racial hierarchies that are harmful to black subjects.

In drawing upon the visual, phenomenological, and symbolic possibilities performance entails, Diamond expands the boundaries of the neo-slave narrative. Particularly, her casting choice functions as a mode of intertextuality where she brings the subject of cross-racial casting practices of the antebellum era in conversation with problems of racial categorization of the present. Because she is doing so in terms of performance, Diamond's strategy enlarges the capacity of the neo-slave narrative in written form because it cannot fully represent and place itself in conversation with such performance histories that Diamond presents. The performance of nonconforming whiteface also enables a deeper exploration of an originary concern of black writers of the neo-slave narrative, which was/is the need to contest "hegemonic racial formations of the state" (Rushdy 99).

Moreover, Diamond's troubling of race has a cumulative effect in that it opens up space to see the entire institution of slavery through a fresh lens. This has particular implications for Diamond's portrayal of Harriet Jacobs. Although the character Harriet Jacobs does not perform as a "white" person in the play, she moves through the drama in complex and unanticipated ways. Diamond harnesses Jacobs's personae and the spirit of her narrative to more deeply depict Jacobs's interior life. Because the text upends basic premises upon which we have understood slavery and race, Jacobs's subjectivity emerges more forcefully. In the following discussion, I consider how Diamond's radical representations of race extend to her depiction of Harriet Jacobs and the slave era. Just as the performance of whiteness constitutes a strategy of Afro-alienation, to recall Daphne Brooks, Diamond relies on other effects such as: a disruption of the form of the slave narrative to reflect the resistant spirit of Harriet Jacobs's work, direct address, code-switching, and unanticipated visual imagery to yield new epistemologies of Jacobs and the slave era.

Harriet Jacobs is perhaps one of the single most significant figures of the slave era, and her narrative has been engaged critically by a multitude of scholars. Angelyn Mitchell argues that *Incidents in the Life of a Slave Girl* is the "ur-narrative" of black womanhood and one that has inspired the majority of neo-slave narratives produced by black women writers. Given her prominence in the discourse on slavery, she has taken on a kind of iconicity, which would seemingly leave her vulnerable to one-dimensional understandings of her life and narrative. Yet, an increasing number of critics and thinkers have offered innovative approaches to understanding Jacobs as a figure and her narrative.[11] Lydia Diamond, too, participates in this effort with her drama featuring Jacobs. Diamond makes clear that her drama developed out of her commitment to staging black women's narratives in fresh ways. Of Jacobs, she writes, "I want Harriet Jacobs to exist, theatrically, alongside Anne Frank and Joan of Arc because she deserves to. Because young and old, we need her" (xv). Additionally, in a preshow symposium for Central Square Theater's 2010 production of the play, she explains that she did not want to reproduce what she calls the same romanticized images of slavery that we've seen and instead to push audiences beyond their "infantilized historical perspective[s] of peo-

---

11. See Nellie McKay and Frances Smith Foster's Edited Collection of *Incidents* for representative scholarship. Also, see Maurice Wallace's *Constructing the Black Masculine: Identity and Ideality in African American Men's Literature and Culture, 1775–1995*, which offers an extended reading of the enslaved figure Luke in *Incidents* and its queer subtexts.

ple of color, particularly black women" ("Harriet Jacobs Symposium"). So, it is with this consciousness that she approaches Jacobs's narrative.

The figure Harriet in the drama serves as a vehicle to forward new epistemologies of slavery and enslaved subjectivity. Early in the drama, Harriet directly addresses the audience and expresses a refusal of the notion that there can be any singular, authoritative account of slavery. When the drama opens, a small shed structure reveals Harriet lying on her stomach and writing "furiously" by candlelight. She then speaks directly to the audience and explains that the story she is about to tell them is not the one that they have heard over time. She moderates their expectations more by causing them to question their own knowledge of slavery, saying, "I promise that you may believe you have heard it, you may believe you know this, and I suggest that it is slightly beyond knowing, because still, I hear the stories, I live the stories, and I do not yet understand" (6). In referring to slavery as "slightly beyond knowing," Harriet speaks directly to Diamond's epistemological project. Diamond seeks to question received epistemologies of slavery and forward new ones that offer more humanized depictions of black subjects.

Diamond's presentation of Harriet Jacobs also complicates form in terms of the slave narrative. Undeniably, the text *Incidents in the Life of a Slave Girl* remains the central medium whereby audiences meet and engage with Harriet Jacobs. By opening the drama with Harriet telling the audience that there are aspects of slavery beyond knowing, Diamond enacts a reversal of the certainty with which most slave narratives are prefaced. Often, they begin with prefatory statements by the author and a white dignitary or set of prominent white men or women (in the case of *Incidents*—Lydia Maria Child) who vouch for the authenticity of the document. Rather than have Harriet assert that the narrative the audience will hear is an authentic one, she does quite the opposite in suggesting that the stories they are about to hear are incomplete. This move positions the drama as a kind of neo-slave narrative in that it captures the spirit of the slave narrative, yet it departs in an effort to advance new epistemologies of this history as well as explore suppressed and unexamined aspects of this history. Diamond's experimentation with form functions as an escape from the text that is not altogether different from Jacobs's own efforts to escape the containment of the strictures of autobiographical form and dominant abolitionist discourse. Michelle Burnham notes the interplay between confession and concealment in *Incidents* and how Jacobs's text amplifies this relationship by demonstrating that "these two operations are mutually implicated in each other, that hiding is always accompanied by exposure, that enclosure always performs an escape. It is this complex relation between concealment and confession that ultimately enables black feminist agency to operate in Harriet Jacobs's narrative" (56). Jacobs's elusive narrative strategies and challenges to form can be felt in Diamond's drama as we see the figure Harriet navigate the precarity that exists between enclosure and escape.

In the drama, Harriet shuttles between the space of her grandmother's home and the planation, which also symbolizes the movement between freedom and captivity. Diamond emphasizes Harriet's liminal status in her character description. She describes her as "an adept and unconscious 'code-switcher,'" someone who is very educated and moves fluidly between more formal language and "casual slave vernacular" (2). Harriet's shifting between two linguistic poles performs both escape and survival. We see her experiencing various kinds of pleasure in her grandmother's home where she interacts with her love interest Tom and engages in playful banter with her grandmother. For instance, when her grandmother enters the opening scene after Harriet's direct address to the audience, she asks Harriet, "Who are you talking to?" (6). Harriet corrects her grammar by saying, "To *whom* am I talking Grandma . . ." Her grandmother then responds, "I'm sure my granddaughter is not tellin' *me* how to speak . . ." to which Harriet replies, "I'm jes' teasing with you" (6). Harriet's teasing of her grandmother depicts a light-hearted and jovial relationship between the two that demonstrates the extent to which her grandmother's home was a refuge and a place where Harriet could be free to laugh.

Although Diamond depicts Harriet's grandmother's home as a place where Harriet can escape the surveillance of the plantation and speak freely, she also shows Harriet navigating more precarious spaces on the plantation. Her grandmother expresses concern about Harriet's independent spirit and intellect. At one point, she admonishes Harriet saying, "Please try not to let that mouth get you in trouble" (9). While it is clear that Harriet's grandmother enjoys her granddaughter's playful chatter, she knows that on the plantation, she would be punished for behaving similarly. We see her fears confirmed in another instance in the drama when her mistress finds Harriet reading a book. Harriet switches into what would be considered a stereotypical dialect of enslaved subjects and apologizes saying, "I'z sorry. Pleeeze may ah go back to mah work?" (26). In this moment, the mistress goes on to tell her that her suitor Tom came to the plantation and asked Dr. Norcorm if he could purchase Harriet. He responded to Tom's gesture by burning the money. Harriet appears to weep upon learning of this; however, when the mistress asks if she is crying, Harriet replies "No ma'am" (29). This sobering moment reveals the limits of the freedom that Harriet's grandmother's home provides and demonstrates how code-switching and emotional masking were not simply evidence of the flexibility of the enslaved in moving between the worlds of the plantation and their interior existences, but also tools that they used to survive. Again, the dynamic of pleasure and pain are magnified here. The interaction between Harriet and her mistress also reveals Diamond's attempt to present black emotional life with greater depth as well as show the pervasive regulation of the emotional life of the enslaved.[12]

Diamond also uncovers aspects of Harriet Jacobs's inner life by depicting her in moments where she escapes the daily operations of the plantation to be alone. This allows us to see Harriet as a dynamic individual who envisions the world in unconventional ways. The drama depicts Harriet as often sneaking away to read books that are tucked in her pockets. She explains to her audience, "Lost in the pages of a book, I travel into exciting lands and become princesses and fair maidens. They always *fair*, but in my mind they look jes' like me" (25). Here, Harriet utilizes her imagination to transport herself away from the realities of her life and into spaces where she is a princess or fair maiden. Reimagining them in her image is one way that Harriet refuses to accept her current reality as her only possibility. She enacts a similar strategy in her description of the cotton field. She addresses the audience, "If you have not seen a cotton field, when the cotton is almost ready for picking, you have missed one of the most beautiful sights God has given us" (12). She then expresses that she likes to "kneel in the middle of an open field so the cotton is just below my eyes. For as far as you can see it looks like a soft blanket or maybe even heaven" (12). Because cotton functioned as a source of physical pain for the enslaved, and in many cases, served as the product necessitating their captivity, it is difficult to imagine an enslaved person finding beauty in this sight. However, through Harriet's bold vision, audiences must expand their conceptions of enslaved persons' relation to this crop and to the land itself. In essence, Harriet constructs a *sight of memory*[13] that reframes how we have visualized slavery.[14]

It is important to note that Harriet's representation of the cotton field is markedly different from the one Harriet Jacobs offers in *Incidents*. At a number of moments in *Incidents*, Harriet Jacobs utilizes imagery of cotton to con-

---

12. See Hartman's *Scenes of Subjection*.
13. In *Demonic Grounds: Black Women and the Cartographies of Struggle*, Katherine McKittrick employs this turn of phrase to mean returning to slavery's painful places and seeing these traumatic moments again (33). My use of the phrase the "sight of memory" encompasses both the return and the production of a new image once that return takes place.
14. I concur with Megan Sandberg-Zakian and Jean Fagan Yellin that in depicting the cotton field in this way serves to disrupt audiences' associations of cotton and slavery, and to challenge them to think beyond those frameworks. They write, "While we might once have felt familiar, even comfortable, with the cotton field as a symbol of slavery, we are now experiencing the same image as unfamiliar, uncomfortable, unknown" (xii).

vey slavery's brutality. She recalls a young enslaved man named James being placed between the screws of a cotton gin as punishment for attempting to escape. She describes the arduous labor of farming a cotton plantation and laments, "These God-breathing machines [enslaved persons] are no more, in the sight of their masters, than the cotton they plant, or the horses they tend" (12). Jacobs features cotton in order to revise the perception of it at the time as an innocuous source of white American prosperity and instead highlights the material consequences of its production on the bodies of black subjects. Diamond's radical representation of cotton, which stands in sharp distinction to Jacobs's, illustrates the extent to which Diamond attempts to render familiar imagery of slavery as unfamiliar. To be sure, she does not allow the single image of the beauty of the cotton field to stand. She intermingles the beauty of the cotton field with a reminder of the cotton field as a site of extreme labor and violence, as reflective of Jacobs's rendering of it. Immediately following Harriet's reenvisioning of the cotton field, an enslaved character named Harold describes being beaten after he refuses to have public intercourse with a young girl his overseer surreptitiously observes him courting. In that moment, Harriet's vision of the cotton field changes, and she sees images of blood, sweat, and tears drip from the cotton (14). Here pain mixes with pleasure, capturing Jacobs's representations of cotton alongside Diamond's desire to contest the ways slavery placed black subjects at odds with the land.

One final aspect of the drama that is effectively read through the lens of Afro-alienation is Diamond's treatment of the fugitive space of the garret (where Jacobs lays in wait for approximately seven years before traveling North). We can understand Harriet's performance of fugitivity as manifested literally through the presence of the garret. Much in the way that performances of whiteness in the drama challenge logics of race to make space for more complex representations of race and black subjectivity, the staging of the surreal experience of the garret deepens audience understandings of Jacobs's precarious suspension between freedom and captivity. Diamond materializes this nine-foot-long and seven-foot-wide space for audiences and deploys it as a metaphor for Jacobs's position as a liminal figure, a literate enslaved woman existing for years as both free and unfree and working to balance telling the story of her life with those of many other enslaved subjects whose stories would have been lost to public hearing, but for her courageous act of exposing the institution.

The garret has come to represent a powerful metaphor for black life both during and after slavery. This metaphor captures not only the ways that black Americans were often caught between worlds—balancing conditions of freedom and unfreedom whether on plantations or in spaces beyond slavery—but it also represents how black subjects post slavery often disrupt various myths about America and issues of citizenship. Hortense Spillers engages Jacobs in this sense and theorizes, "We might interpret the whole career of African-Americans, a decisive factor in national political life since the mid-seventeenth century, in light of the *intervening, intruding* tale, or the tale like Brent's 'garret space'—'between the lines,' which are already inscribed as a *metaphor* of social and cultural management" (79). When we consider Diamond's ultimate project of intervening on familiar or comfortable understandings of the history of slavery, then the staging of the garret encapsulates her efforts. Diamond explores this space and its multiple utilities in speaking to the various paradoxes and modes of resistance that characterize black subjectivity, past and present.

Moreover, the staging of the garret gives the audience another window into Jacobs's interior life, particularly as it relates to the trauma undergirding her narrative. Although she clearly has been resilient enough to survive her experience and share it with audiences, we must not overlook Jacobs as a victim of trauma. Diamond creates the possibility for greater exploration of this. It is in the garret space that Harriet hears voices of the enslaved recounting the brutality that they experienced during their enslavement, including an enslaved woman being raped by her enslaver and then beaten by her mistress for giving birth to the child who was a product of that rape (15–16); an enslaved man who carries the guilt of beating other enslaved individuals to death at the direction of the overseer (19–20); and other stories that recount separation from children and various family members. These multivoiced narratives of trauma are inspired by the voices Jacobs herself sought to include in her narrative. As their interlocutor, it is inevitable that this trauma, coupled with her own traumatic experience of sexual harassment, would impact her as well.

The inclusion of the multiple experiences of trauma that come to Harriet casts new light on Jacobs's reflection near the end of *Incidents* where she speaks to the impact that witnessing slavery had on her. To recall Jacobs's words,

> It has been painful to me, in many ways, to recall the dreary years I passed in bondage. I would gladly forget them if I could. Yet the retrospection is not altogether without solace; for with those gloomy recollections come tender memories of my good old grandmother, like light, fleecy clouds floating over a dark and troubled sea. (156)

The paradox of memory for Jacobs reminds us that her narrative is as much about trauma as it is about her triumph in escaping slavery. The stories she holds from her experience are ones that she would "gladly forget" if she could. Diamond, then, captures the spirit of this reflection in depicting the stories that continually come to her, primarily when she is alone in the garret.

Along with capturing the conflicting experiences that framed Jacobs's life, Diamond also defamiliarizes the garret to reveal its paradoxes, so as not to depict it as a singularly liberating space or as singularly tortuous. As referenced in chapter 2 and my analysis of how August Wilson recontextualizes historical objects to comment on historical tellings of slavery, Diamond's presentation of the garret can be read through the lens of Bert States and Alice Rayner as well. In the theatrical space, the garret with its fluid possibilities represents not only peril and promise but also narrative possibility. Diamond depicts both the power of Jacobs's position within this space as well as her precarity. In one sense, it is a space where Jacobs could read and sew freely as she notes in her narrative (93). However, the cramped quarters and thin construction leave her vulnerable to the elements, which take a toll on her body. The garret is at once liberating and dangerous. An October 2010 Kansas City Repertory production of the play represents this duality in its representation of the garret space (see figure 4). Joycelyn Buckner describes its staging:

> The long, narrow, triangular cutout space was built into the proscenium high above the stage and hovered just below the eaves of the house. Although the space limited physical movement, it glowed in the light of Jacobs's candle and swelled with the resolve, desperation, and hope reflected in her writing. It was simultaneously a womb- and tomb-like space that the audience (and Jacobs herself) wondered if she would ever succeed in exiting alive. (461–62)

In Diamond's drama, Harriet narrates what it means to occupy the garret and its capacity to function as a womb or as a tomb. She explains that the space is small, "but, even on the worse days, it is bigger than my world outside. This space bigger than my world ever was or ever could be" (54). It is also within this space that she charts out what Megan Sandberg-Zakian and Jean Fagan Yellin in the foreword to the play observe as a neo-utopian vision, one that is romantic about the future rather than the past (*Harriet Jacobs* xi). Harriet explains that in the garret she writes stories about "what I remember, way I want it to be, way I hope it be someday" (56). Diamond's interpretation of Jacobs articulating a hopeful vision in spite of the devastating realities of slavery functions as yet another unanticipated perspective that causes audiences to see Jacobs's work anew.

FIGURE 4. Cheryl Lynn Bruce as Grandma and Nambi Kelly as Harriet Jacobs. Used with permission from Don Ipock via Kansas City Repertory Theatre.

In depicting Jacobs as light-hearted, liminal, and a visionary, Diamond reframes critical elements of her narrative, which add greater depth to her story. She uses the strategy of defamiliarizing the familiar aspects of her character in the hopes of producing a story that enlarges the audience's understanding and moves her beyond previously conceived notions about her life. Diamond's portrayal of Harriet Jacobs aligns with her overarching goal of forwarding a narrative of slavery that emphasizes black humanity alongside the pain. Her racially deconstructive approach to representing whiteness enables a number of subsequent critical moves that offer an unanticipated view of slavery. By placing herself in conversation with her contemporary moment and with cultural conversations about race occurring in tandem with (and arguably occasioned by) the historical election of President Barack Obama, Diamond deftly weaves in a contemporary context to tell a story about the past.

To return to the "Quick Note from the Playwright" that prefaces the print edition of *Harriet Jacobs: A Play*, Diamond forcefully articulates her vision in creating this work. She requests of her audiences,

> Honor, please, the humor in this play, where there is humor. Honor the burgeoning affectations where they exist. The familial love where it lives. Try not to plod through it with a guilty, pained, apologetic, pitying, angry, contemporary sensibility—that's too easy. Let it live, please, from moment to moment, from laughs to tears, as we live life, walking through the murk of our personal and societal contradictions. We owe it to Ms. Jacobs. We owe it to the ancestors. (xvi)

Asking that audiences "let it live" and allow for possibility and surprise (in spite of the ways the nature of this history seemingly forecloses these options) *frees* Diamond and the subjects of her work, which enables them to go beyond the boundaries of the expected and to offer a fuller picture of slavery. "Let it live" is a request for us to see slavery as fluid, to recognize that we constantly need to adjust what we think we understand about the institution in order to make room for new insights and understandings. She wants audiences to be open to this process and to allow the enslaved subjects who populate her drama the freedom of possibility often denied them in life.

CONJURING WHITENESS IN BRANDEN JACOBS-JENKINS'S *AN OCTOROON*

The quest for representational freedom gets amplified in Branden Jacobs-Jenkins's *An Octoroon,* in which he draws on performances of whiteness as a means to escape the confining racial boundaries of American theater and culture at large. Although *An Octoroon* is not Jacobs-Jenkins's first foray into cross-racial performance, blackface minstrelsy, and other kinds of play with the subject of race,[15] it is his only drama to situate issues of racial representation firmly in the slave past. Perhaps this is merely a product of his direct engagement with Dion Boucicault's antebellum drama *The Octoroon*; however, his interrogation of racial categorization against the backdrop of slavery becomes meaningful for how we contextualize problems of racial representation in American performance. The problematic ways that race is rendered on the American stage has been an ongoing query for Jacobs-Jenkins. Three of his plays (*Neighbors* [2010], *Appropriate* [2014], and *An Octoroon* [2014]—all of which he identifies as related but not necessarily a trilogy) pursue questions related to "representations of blackness and how to represent social constructs on stage that are so tied to a specific culture of a nation," Jacobs-Jenkins explains in an interview with Eliza Bent. These plays also stem from Jacobs-Jenkins's curiosity about how blackness on stage works. He says, "It's just a thing that has always confused me. I don't know what anyone is talking about when they talk about black theatre, black drama, black actors. I don't know. No one walks around saying white theatre or white actors" (Bent). What Jacobs-Jenkins speaks to here is a tendency to make whiteness normative in American theater. By producing performances of whiteness onstage, Jacobs-Jenkins engages in the practice of "making whiteness strange," as Faedra Carpenter would have it. The escape into whiteness also facilitates some degree of representational freedom for his black actors and characters because it actively deconstructs race as a concept to reveal its confining parameters.

First staged in 2014 at SoHo Rep in Brooklyn, New York, *An Octoroon* dramatizes the crisis of racial misrepresentation, propagated initially by minstrel performance. The play exposes how such misrepresentations have formed the basis for cultural exclusion of black subjects in America. Just as whiteness demarcated the free versus the enslaved, minstrel performance buttressed those efforts by defining blackness in denigrating terms that stood in sharp contrast to conceptions of whiteness. E. Patrick Johnson explains, "When white Americans essentialize blackness, for example, they often do so in ways that maintain 'whiteness' as the master trope of purity, supremacy, and entitlement, as a ubiquitous, fixed, unifying signifier that seems invisible"

---

15. Jacobs-Jenkins playfully describes his early explorations of the historical legacies of blackface minstrelsy. He tells Eliza Bent, "Then [exact time/dates not offered] I started making more work and started playing around with blackface. I think I was trying to explore the idea of minstrelsy and its limits, so I did this series of performance where I'd wear blackface and like a [sic] really expensive clothes—like a $400 pair of jeans—and do these clown bits to pop songs."

(4). Branden Jacobs-Jenkins's incorporation of performances of whiteness and histories of minstrelsy into his dramas responds to the legacies of blackface minstrelsy and its production of confining and essentializing identity frameworks for black Americans as a way to reinforce whiteness. The specter of blackface minstrelsy continues to haunt contemporary American performance cultures and contributes to the ongoing perpetuation of pernicious fictions of racial difference. In his inversion of the spectacle of blackface via performances of whiteness, Branden Jacobs-Jenkins boldly takes on these legacies.[16] By performing whiteness at the site of slavery, Jacobs-Jenkins confronts this haunting by critiquing slavery's damaging formation of tropes of blackness. He also explores black interiority as a counter to the historical and theatrical construction of black subjects as one-dimensional. Although he stays fairly close to Boucicault's drama, he makes meaningful interventions that allow black subjects to escape objectification.

In order to understand the subtext of *An Octoroon*, it is essential to be familiar with its predecessor—Dion Boucicault's 1859 play *The Octoroon*. Both dramas weave together intricate narratives that border on the fantastic. Boucicault's drama is unique in that it was the first drama to employ the daguerreotype. At the time, photography was a relatively new technology.[17] Also, because he was Irish, Boucicault's drama presents American cultural issues from the critical distance of an interested observer. The cultural milieu at the time of the play's premiere was one of crisis in America. Audiences were likely attracted to the play's engagement with visual politics because Americans were working to develop methods of racial recognition in response to the numerous racially ambiguous enslaved individuals born out of the systemic rape of black women by white men. The play also premiered just two days after John Brown was hung for coordinating a raid on Harper's Ferry, West Virginia, signaling the growing national tensions over the institution of slavery (Sellar).

At the center of Boucicault's narrative is Zoe, the titular figure and love interest of George Peyton, who is the nephew of the now-deceased enslaver of Terrebone Plantation in Louisiana. George has returned from France to help Mrs. Peyton sort through the business of managing the Peyton estate. However, they learn that the place is bankrupt and, saving for one significant debtor who has yet to pay, they are preparing to sell the property (including

---

16. Glenda Carpio cites theatrical instances (such as Ntozake Shange's *Spell 7*) where playwrights have attempted to "exorcise the demon" of the specter of minstrel, but maintains that this demon continues to haunt the stage as a specter (206).

17. See Adam Sonstegard's "Performing Remediation: The Minstrel, The Camera, and *The Octoroon*" for extended conversation on Boucicault's innovative use of the new technology of the camera for his nineteenth-century audiences.

the enslaved) in order to settle the affairs of the estate. Multiple narratives circulate around this larger one. Dora Sunnyside of Sunnyside Plantation also loves George and desires to marry him, which would have the added benefit of giving him access to her family fortune and save Terrebone. Jacob M'Closky, the incompetent overseer and bookkeeper who aided the family into its ruin, serves as the drama's villain. He desires to purchase the plantation and the enslaved individuals who inhabit it, which would include Zoe, in whom he has a romantic interest. He ultimately kills a young enslaved boy, Paul, to get papers that will ensure that the Peyton family does not learn of their debtor's willingness to pay.

The iconic auction block scene brings this drama to a head. At the auction, M'Closky purchases Zoe to everyone's doom. However, by fortunate happenstance, Pete, an enslaved man, discovers the photograph that captures M'Closky's murder of Paul, thus solving the mystery of his death. Zoe, unaware of M'Closky's undoing, secures poison and kills herself to avoid becoming M'Closky's property and to end her despair over being unable to marry George due to her racial identity. The play also includes a host of other characters, namely, Salem Scudder, the current overseer of Terrebone and photographer. He introduces the camera into the drama. There is also Wahnotee, a Native American character and friend to Paul. Enslaved individuals Pete, Minnie, and Dido enter various scenes. Pete and Paul constitute minstrel figures that provide comic relief. The actors for the drama were white actors in blackface paint with the exception of Boucicault's wife Agnes Robertson who played Zoe without blackface paint.

Even though *The Octoroon* takes an antislavery stance in its portrayal of the devastating effects of slavery on the enslaved and all those bound up in the institution, the promotion of racial caricatures undermines its goal of producing a sympathetic portrait of black subjects. Saidiya Hartman critiques the drama, asserting that *The Octoroon* with its blackface minstrelsy participated in the culture of denigrating performance that transformed black suffering into wholesome pleasures (32). Branden Jacobs-Jenkins, however, deftly presents the drama in a way that does not obscure but instead reveals black suffering. Drawing on my observations from the June 6, 2014, SoHo Rep production that I accessed via the Theatre on Film and Tape archives of the New York Public Library and production materials from the Woolly Mammoth Theatre Company in my analysis of *An Octoroon*, I will consider how the play stages Afro-alienation via a number of performance strategies (most chiefly the performance of whiteness) and textual revisions. Primarily, I will examine how the performance of whiteness enables a form of escape for the drama's troubled protagonist, BJJ. This performative escape, I argue, makes possible

Jacobs-Jenkins's other theatrical interventions into Boucicault's drama. Jacobs-Jenkins's use of humor, his conjuring of Br'er Rabbit and the trickster figure, as well as the time-switching and code-switching that facilitates the escape of objectification for the drama's black subjects, all disrupt Boucicault's original to offer another vantage point on the melodrama. I will also analyze Jacobs-Jenkins's most significant disruption of the form of Boucicault's melodrama with his revision of the sensation scene, which works to express black suffering borne out of the legacies of the slave era. These collective acts perform escape as they create greater representational space for black subjects, a central objective in Jacobs-Jenkins's larger theatrical project.

At the outset, Jacobs-Jenkins's reveals his intention to interrogate the devastating effects of totalizing representations of blackness with his altering of Boucicault's title. Switching from the definite article "the" to the indefinite one "an" serves as the first of many critical departures that allow us to see the original in a new light. The use of the article "an" implicitly rejects the notion that there is a singular and definitive account of black experience. In this turn away from the notion that somehow racial authenticity can be represented, Jacobs-Jenkins clears space to offer a more complex rendering of race on stage.

The center of *An Octoroon* is not Zoe, the enslaved tragic mulatto, but a playwright named BJJ, whose name we can assume gestures to the playwright himself. The play opens with BJJ lamenting the politics of race in American theater, particularly his frustrations at being labeled a "black playwright" and at the perpetuation of reductive views of blackness in American drama. After white actors reject participation in his version of Boucicault's play (an interesting bit of meta-theater), BJJ proceeds to put on whiteface paint to play the white roles. He plays both the hero (George Peyton) and the villain (Jacob M'Closky). The play also exhumes Dion Boucicault, who serves as an alter-ego to BJJ. Early in the play, they exchange a series of "fuck-yous" that humorously set the tone for the drama. The actor playing Boucicault also dons redface to play the Native American character, Wahnotee. (Boucicault also played Wahnotee in redface in *The Octoroon*.)

The drama stages BJJ as an alienated figure at the outset. As the play opens, he enters an empty stage and is mostly nude, exposed and somewhat despairing. He is also having a veritable identity crisis, or what he jokingly refers to as "low-grade depression" (7). This opening scene reveals BJJ as an ambivalent figure, who is alienated by the theater world's tendency toward racial stereotyping, yet appreciative of theater's possibility as a space of connection. He demonstrates as much in his confession-like opening: "Hi everyone. I'm a 'black playwright.' I don't know exactly what that means," he announces (7). By referring to himself in this way, he challenges perceptions of his identity and the kind of work he is expected to do. In this way, he reflects the ethos of theater practitioners such as Suzan-Lori Parks who reject reductive and essentialist analyses of black dramas. Parks excoriates these efforts as "a fucked up trap to reduce us to only one way of being. We should endeavor to show the world and ourselves our beautiful and powerfully infinite variety" ("Equation" *The America Play* 22). Determined to avoid the trap, BJJ decides to perform his way out of it. In the conversation with his therapist that he relays for the audience, he identifies Dion Boucicault as a professional role model and decides to enact a drama in the spirit of his successful play, *The Octoroon*. By drawing on Boucicault's own creative freedom and his racial crossing to play nonwhite characters, BJJ performatively, albeit temporarily, escapes the trap, thereby enacting a fugitive performance.

The lenses of W. E. B. Du Bois's double consciousness and Daphne Brooks's Afro-alienation (referenced earlier in this chapter) allow us to more effectively read the deep ambivalence BJJ expresses about theater and his attempt to escape being objectified as a black playwright. Because Branden Jacobs-Jenkins mentions Brecht directly in the text of *An Octoroon,* I want to explore in greater detail how Brooks's concept adapts Brechtian theories of theatrical alienation to speak to specific aspects of black performance in which Jacobs-Jenkins is most certainly participating. Although much further removed in time, BJJ's attempts to carve out greater creative space for himself in the theater are not altogether distant from the efforts of early black performers to negotiate double-consciousness and the traumas of self-fragmentation resulting from captivity and subjugation. Daphne Brooks reflects on the interconnectedness of double-consciousness and Afro-alienation. She writes,

> In Afro-alienation, the "strange" situation of "looking at one's self through the eyes of others" evolves into what Brechtian feminist Elin Diamond describes as the enlivened position of "'looking at being looked at ness.'" Calling attention to the hypervisibility and cultural constructions of blackness in transatlantic culture, the historical agents in this book [*Bodies in Dissent*] rehearsed ways to render racial categories "strange" and to thus "disturb" cultural perceptions of identity formation. (5)

An Octoroon demonstrates that the rehearsal of methods to trouble racial categories and perceptions remains an ongoing critical project in black performance. My analysis of *An Octoroon* draws upon Du Bois's and Brooks's theories to uncover the motivating factors and means that drive the performance of escape in the drama.

BJJ's performance of whiteness in *An Octoroon* is very much intertwined with blackness and functions as the drama's most consequential Afro-alienation effect. In the prologue of the drama, he puts on whiteface paint as a "loud, vulgar, bass-heavy, hypermasculine hip-hop track" plays on a loop (9). (In the SoHo Rep production I viewed, the track was "Fuckin' Problems" by 2 Chainz and Drake.) He then launches into an increasingly tense monologue that details his grievance with racial essentialism and how it has suffocated him. The audience must balance his speech with the image before them. Having the hip hop song playing in the background as BJJ is putting on the white paint serves as a layer that keeps blackness visible because hip-hop functions as a modern expression of black culture. This act can also be read through Faedra Carpenter's term "naturalized whiteface," which she defines as

> the intentional process of "whitening up" through artistic intervention, elaborate makeup, plastic surgery, or medical technology. These transformations may not result in a realistic or aesthetically pleasing countenance, but they suggest a deliberate effort to acquire the phenotypical markers and cultural capital frequently associated with whiteness. (24)

In BJJ's performance of the "whitening up" process, the audience must hold a singular image the black man they have been introduced to alongside the white characters into which the playwright transforms. BJJ renders whiteness "strange" and does not aim for a realistic presentation of whiteness. Rather, his performance of whiteness serves primarily to give him access to the cultural capital of whiteness—in this case, the creative freedom to experiment in performance and not be bound by demands of racial authenticity.

Associated materials for productions of the drama provide greater depth into how the performance of whiteness should be perceived by the audience. An image from the 2018 Stage West Theatre (Fort Worth, TX) production features a black subject in the center with a paintbrush in his hand and a streak of white paint across his face (see figure 5).

The actor stands in the center of the image, staring defiantly into the camera. The white paint symbolizes the enactment of power over Boucicault's drama, retelling it from the vantage points of those caricatured within it. Just as the hip-hop track keeps blackness visible in BJJ's whitening up process, this image keeps the character's black skin visible while the optic whiteness of the paint communicates the idea of whiteness as an artificial construction or even the notion that whiteness cannot be read visually without blackness. *An Octoroon* does not seek to imitate whiteness, but to possess it, revise it, and

FIGURE 5. Production image for *An Octoroon*. Used with permission from Evan Michael Woods via Stage West Theatre.

reduce its power. Because the performance of whiteness occurs throughout and underlies the defiant spirit of the drama, I will return to it at relevant moments in my analysis.

The performance of whiteness initiates the larger antirealist interventions Branden Jacobs-Jenkins makes into Boucicault's drama. In the spirit of Brechtian theater, *An Octoroon* functions in opposition to the classic melodrama. Whereas the melodrama advances moral binaries and aims to produce emotional responses for the audience, Jacobs-Jenkins's drama resists empathy or the possibility of being seduced by a performance. He utilizes distancing mechanisms such as the direct address with which he opens the drama and other disruptions that call attention to the play as a production rather than a facsimile of the slave era. Melodramatic tableaux are disrupted, cotton balls fill the stage to represent the plantation, and at one point, BJJ and the "playwright" Dion Boucicault break to discuss just how to effectively stage a scene.[18]

Perhaps the most disarming element of the play is the presence of an actor playing the role of Br'er Rabbit. Gesturing to the iconic trickster figure in folktales, Br'er Rabbit represents an enduring legacy of black humor and cunning even in the midst of extreme oppression. Act 2 describes Br'er Rabbit randomly wandering through a scene. He disrupts various tableaux, and we later learn via the stage directions that Br'er Rabbit could even be played by Jacobs-Jenkins himself quietly reminding the audience of his presence. In fact, in the premiere of *An Octoroon* at SoHo Rep, Jacobs-Jenkins dressed up as Br'er Rabbit, something that reviewers described as surreal.[19] Jacobs-Jenkins, by altering the original drama and challenging conceptions of race in irreverent and unconventional ways, functions as the ultimate trickster figure in this drama.

Through Br'er Rabbit, Jacobs-Jenkins reveals his indebtedness to black humor and satire, which both critiqued the outrageousness of the peculiar institution of slavery. By exhuming Boucicault and Br'er Rabbit, Jacobs-Jenkins employs the *aesthetics of the conjure,* a term Glenda Carpio coins in her analysis of black humor. This term refers to conjuring as an act performed by contemporary artists and performers to summon up the past and bring it to life in a way that makes it bigger than life (15). She analyzes this in the context of Suzan-Lori Parks's work and her exhumation of Abraham Lincoln in *The America Play* and *Topdog/Underdog,* and argues of black humor in general that it is more than simply a coping mechanism, but is a "bountiful source of creativity and pleasure and an energetic mode of social and political critique" (7). We can think about this similarly with Jacobs-Jenkins's conjuring of Boucicault where he brings forth the historical figure as both a figure of admiration and a reflection of the various absurdities promoted in slavery. The play functions as both an extremely creative work and a form of social critique.

Moreover, *An Octoroon* participates in the genre of satire, a more elaborate and critical form of black humor often delivered in the medium of the novel. Daryl Dickson-Carr in his analysis of African American satire notes, "African American satire's earliest purpose in both oral and written form was to

---

18. See Verna Foster's "Meta-Melodrama: Brandon Jacobs-Jenkins Appropriates Dion Boucicault's *The Octoroon*" for a complementary discussion on Jacobs-Jenkins's disruption of the melodrama.

19. In his review of the play, Ben Brantley notes the "play" of Jacobs-Jenkins dressing up a Br'er Rabbit, which also resembles a Beatrix Potter-style rabbit. Brantley observes that the drama repeatedly calls attention to its own artifice.

lampoon the (il)logic of chattel slavery and racism itself" (3). Jacobs-Jenkins joins this history by satirizing the era of African American satire's very roots.[20]

The black enslaved women, Minnie and Dido, drive much of the drama's humor. In the original drama, their roles are minimal; however, Jacobs-Jenkins elevates them here as key interlocutors for him as he complicates conceptions of black identity. He presents Minnie and Dido as incongruous with the era by having them speak in twenty-first-century hip-hop slang. They exchange gossip about various slaves. For instance, Minnie shares with Dido, "Oh, you know, Chris was messin' with Trisha over in the sugar mill for a li'l bit an' I met him and Darnell through her at a slave mixer over by the river before she dumped him because, you know, she couldn't deal with the long distance" (18). Jacobs-Jenkins defamiliarizes these characters by showing them as relatively resigned to their lives as slaves and very pragmatic about how they will survive the system. Far from feeling defeated about their situations, they speak with startling clarity about the circumstances of their lives and the situations of those around them.

Minnie and Dido's contemporary speech also serves to intervene in the temporal linearity of the drama, which represents another strategy that Jacobs-Jenkins uses to rewrite Boucicault's text. The disruption of time also signals that the complexity of enslaved experience cannot be accounted for in standard, authoritative linear time trajectories.[21] Because Minnie and Dido have psychically escaped their circumstances by maintaining humor in the face of extreme adversity, they also exist outside of the drama in a kind of "fugitive time" reminiscent of how time is rendered in dramas such as George C. Wolfe's *The Colored Museum*. To return to my definition of fugitive time, it is both a temporal accounting for the fluidity of black fugitivity from the slave era to the present, and it is a practice of freedom. It represents time as both suspended and atemporal/outside of time with the fugitive in perpetual motion. In this sense, time contracts or expands depending on the limits of one's freedom. The condition of enslavement, as many slave narratives demonstrate, was never one of absolute subjection. Fugitive time represents this fluid movement and disrupts structures of power that order time in oppressive ways for racialized subjects. As enslaved women, Minnie and Dido are

---

20. In her discussion of the reimaginings of *Uncle Tom's Cabin* in post-Civil Rights era black performance, Salamishah Tillet asserts that satire is "the perfect genre for black dissent and dissidence in the face of ongoing political invisibility and civic estrangement" (59). Jacobs-Jenkins locates those feelings of invisibility and estrangement within the politics of the theater, which refuses to see BJJ as anything other than a black playwright and has thus estranged him from the art world with which he desires affiliation.

21. See Calvin Warren's "Black Time: Slavery, Metaphysics, and the Logic of Wellness" in *The Psychic Hold of Slavery*.

veritably always "on the clock," but they often spend their time engaging in witty banter and determine the pace of their labor. Their use of contemporary vernacular also allows them to escape static representations of black women in slavery. They are able to elude containment through their resistant performances.

Jacobs-Jenkins's radical experimentation with Minnie and Dido extends beyond their disruptions of time. They also trouble understandings of the violence and abuse that enslaved women endured. When Minnie and Dido learn that they will be sold away from Terrebone Planation, they become very taken with the idea of being purchased by a seaman, Ratts, and living on a ship. Minnie tells Dido, "We gotta get bought by him, girl! Imagine if we lived on a steamboat, coasting up and down the river, looking fly, wind whipping at our hair and our slave tunics and shit, and we surrounded by all these fine muscle-y boat niggas who ain't been wit a woman in years" (42). This depiction is certainly startling considering what we know about the trauma of the auction block. It also could be read as offensive since it diminishes the realities of rape that enslaved women and girls endured. Darryl Dickson-Carr observes satire's penchant for being iconoclastic, offensive, and sexist (5). Although Jacobs-Jenkins offers other portrayals of Minnie and Dido that are more sympathetic (which I will discuss momentarily), the infusion of humor in sexual violence not only disturbs notions of black women's victimization but is also profoundly disturbing.

Even as he forwards a troubling portrayal of Minnie and Dido with regard to their sexual lives, Jacobs-Jenkins also offers more expansive representations of black experience across the drama. He challenges conventional understandings of the subjectivities and interior lives of enslaved individuals as well as familiar perceptions of their modes of expression. He does this most effectively with Pete, who, in keeping with the original drama, is played by a non-black actor in blackface. Pete represents the specter of blackface minstrelsy that continues to haunt the American stage. In his depiction of Pete, Jacobs-Jenkins confronts this specter and critiques the perpetuation of myths about black speech and expression that continue to confine black playwrights and actors today.

Dion Boucicault presents Pete as a classic minstrel and form of comic relief. He uses heavy dialect to depict the speech of the enslaved. Early in *The Octoroon*, Pete is chasing slave children who are eating bananas. Pete cries out: "Hey! laws a massy! why, clar out! drop dat banana! I'll murder this yer crowd. . . . Dem little niggers is a judgment upon dis generation" (22). From the stealing of bananas, which aligns the children with criminality and monkeys to Pete's pronounced dialect, Boucicault presents a demeaning caricature of the enslaved that seemingly is at odds with his supposed critique of slavery through the plight of Zoe. In his version, Jacobs-Jenkins addresses the problematic depiction, particularly with regard to the dialect, by stating in the stage directions: "I'm just going to say this right now so we can get it over with: I don't know what a real slave sounded like. And neither do you" (17).[22] Here he challenges the notion that one has the capacity to represent slavery with true authenticity.

Alternately, Jacobs-Jenkins presents Pete in *An Octoroon* as a code-switching trickster who outwits his owner, thereby exposing Pete's behavior for what it is—a performance. Pete effectively performs an Afro-alienation effect in overturning perceptions of him as comic relief and revealing in moments his interiority. In act 2, Minnie and Dido are engaged in banter about life on the plantation when Pete approaches, speaking in a fairly standard version of American English, saying, "I see you finished fruit duty already, Minnie. Good job. You settling in all right?" (19). However, when Dora Sunnyside and George Peyton enter the scene, Pete immediately slips into his act, slapping Minnie's hand and telling her, "Hay! Hay! Drop dad banana fo' I murdah you!" (19). To this, Dido reassures a shocked Minnie: "He do this every morning. You'll get used to it" (20). What Dido references is Pete's ongoing code-switching performance when he is in the presence of white subjects. Much like the code-switching that takes place in Lydia Diamond's *Harriet Jacobs*, for Pete, these linguistic transitions function most specifically as an act of survival, where he feels he must perform a role of subservience to not appear dangerous to his enslaver. In the auction block scene, however, we get a glimpse into Pete's interior life when he drops his act and declares, "I'm tired of being a slave" (44). In showing Pete from both perspectives, Jacobs-Jenkins takes a character used as comic relief in Boucicault's work to show a much more complex figure who uses performance as a self-sustaining mechanism. Moreover, Jacobs-Jenkins goes further by showing how early instantiations of blackness on the minstrel stage, perpetuated throughout slavery and beyond, continue to impact the lived experiences of black Americans today. The auction block and sensation scenes depict the effects of legacies of racial misrepresentation with a decidedly somber tone that serves as a jarring contrast to the humor.

---

22. Although it is clear that Jacobs-Jenkins is questioning the potential of depicting slavery with any degree of authenticity, it is important to recognize the work of the WPA and the Library of Congress in collecting audio and textual accounts of formerly enslaved persons via the online database "Voices from the Days of Slavery" located here: https://memory.loc.gov/ammem/collections/voices/

FIGURE 6. Auction block scene with Ryan Woods as George Peyton/Jacob M'Closky. Used with permission from Evan Michael Woods via Stage West Theatre, Fort Worth, TX.

As *An Octoroon* develops, we see a progressive breaking down of the drama's efforts to conform to the spirit of the original. The humor becomes more forceful in its critique, and these competing influences converge in the auction block and sensation scenes. In the auction block scene, Jacobs-Jenkins stages a confrontation between George Peyton and Jacob M'Closky (both of whom are performed by BJJ in whiteface paint). The optics of this scene communicate BJJ's internal conflict rather than the external one he attempts to stage. At the moment where M'Closky is about to purchase Zoe, the two men scuffle. Given that BJJ is performing as both men, he is literally fighting with himself (see figure 6). This moment reflects the Du Boisian notion of double-consciousness where we literally see two warring souls in one dark body. BJJ reflects the black subject Du Bois describes who must reconcile how white society has defined him vs. how he defines himself. All of these issues come together in this climactic moment, which is followed by a larger commentary on the danger of racial essentialism.

The sensation scene immediately follows BJJ's performance of double consciousness. A key component of most melodramas, the sensation scene served as a moment of revelation and an articulation of certain truths that the drama desired to communicate. Linda Williams describes it in this way:

> The theatrical function of melodrama's big sensation scenes was to be able to put forth a moral truth in gesture and to picture what could not be fully spoken in words.... Usually, the unspeakable truth revealed in the sensation scene is the revelation of who is the true villain, who the innocent victim. The revelation occurs as a spectacular, moving sensation—that is, it is felt as sensation and not simply registered as ratiocination in the cause-effect logic of narrative—because it shifts to a different register of signification, often bypassing language altogether. (52)

Producing this moment causes a crisis for BJJ, and he breaks from character to work with the playwright, Dion Boucicault, to determine just how to stage the scene. BJJ first laments that he doesn't have enough white men to effectively present the moral of the show and its universal themes. After brainstorming, he and the playwright determine that the image of Paul's murder (the original sensation scene in *The Octoroon*) does not constitute enough of a sensation in modern times because photography has become cliché to twenty-first-century audiences. BJJ explains, "We've gotten so used to photos and photographic images that we've basically learned how to fake them, so the kind of justice around which this whole thing hangs is actually a little dated" (50). They contemplate a number of options including setting the actual theater on fire. They eventually settle on a lynching photograph projected onto a back wall where they perform the remainder of the act in the light of the projection. Through this moment, the moral truth of the play emerges.

Using the updated technology of screen projection, Jacobs-Jenkins manages to create a sensation for contemporary audiences that shocks them into awareness about the tragic legacy of slavery through dehumanization of black people. A common sentiment in the critical reviews of the play was that of shock and in some cases horror at the image of the lynching photo being introduced into the play. One reviewer refers to the image as a "horrifying projection," and others comment on its upsetting qualities.[23]

The use of the image communicates how the devastating depictions on the minstrel stage had real implications for blacks beyond emancipation. In essence, the dehumanizing spectacle of the nineteenth-century minstrel stage transforms into the early twentieth-century theater of lynching. The villains in the tragedy of the lynching spectacle included: those who committed the

---

23. Reviewers are unified in their remarks about the image of a lynching projected at the end of the Soho Rep production. Elisabeth Vincentelli refers to it as a "horrifying projection." Also, Jacobs-Jenkins explores the reverberations across time of lynching photography in his play *Appropriate*.

crime, those who looked on at these acts as entertainment, and the society that chose not to punish these transgressions—an ultimate statement of devaluing black life. The use of the lynching photo also serves as a reminder that black bodies were objectified well beyond humorous derision. In the postlynching event, their body parts were passed around as souvenirs. Harvey Young provides greater context in his analysis of the use of the lynched black body after the event, arguing that the black body functioned as a souvenir, a fetish, and a performance remain. He explains, "Lynching objectified the bodies and rendered them permanently still." Lynching souvenirs commodified the black body turning it into a "screen upon which another meaning can be projected" (176). Young also asserts that the use of the black body as souvenir not only had the effect of dehumanizing the individual but erasing the individual from history altogether. In this moment, Branden Jacobs-Jenkins writes this body into history via performance while also confronting audiences with his moral truth, which not only indicts M'Closky, the proverbial villain, but also the society in their complicity in viewing black suffering as entertainment.

The shocking moment of revelation in the sensation scene presents a humanized and vulnerable black subject that stands in stark contrast to the comic spectacle. This intervention moves the black subject toward a recognition not afforded him/her in the slave era. Minnie and Dido dramatize this in the final scene where they reject the idea that others have the power to define them and that they are someone else's property. When Dido recounts to Minnie that Zoe came to her for poison, she is most disheartened by Zoe referring to her as "mammy." Dido explains to Minnie, "And you know she kept calling me 'Mammy'! And I was like, bitch, what? We are basically the same age!" (56). Clearly upset by the characterization, she forcefully declares to Dido, "I just don't like when people be treating me like I'm some old woman. I am not a mammy! I'm not!" (57). This act of rejecting the mammy figure symbolizes the move toward self-definition, which is the implicit objective of the drama.[24]

Minnie communicates a powerful message in response to Dido's lament over being misnamed when she says, "I know we slaves and eveurthang but you are not your job" (58). Constructing her life as a slave as nothing more than a job rather than a characterization of her identity serves as a compelling ending to this provocative play. She articulates a liberated subjectivity even as she is one of the most marginalized characters in Boucicault's drama.

---

24. In his drama, *Neighbors*, Jacobs-Jenkins explores in greater detail the psychic impact of plantation era stereotypes and depicts black characters grappling with these legacies.

In the original play, Minnie and Dido functioned as nothing more than props whereas Jacobs-Jenkins portrays them with attention to their complex interior lives.

An Octoroon aims to unfix demeaning caricatures that were designed to fix black Americans in time and place by challenging those representations in a number of ways. The performance of whiteness, similar to what we see in Lydia Diamond's *Harriet Jacobs*, facilitates escape from these problematic representations. Both works demonstrate the ongoing critical work of black playwrights and performers in troubling notions of race and representation in order to offer more complicated depictions of black subjects. That they center their work on slavery is meaningful because they directly confront the origins of caricatures of blackness, constructions of race, and their problematic legacies. In the following chapter, I turn to another aspect of unaccounted for enslaved experience, the queer subject. Playwright Robert O'Hara, like Diamond and Jacobs-Jenkins, disrupts familiar understandings of enslaved experience and black identity in his depiction of queer subjects negotiating the aftermath of the slave era.

CHAPTER 4

Fugitive Intimacies

DEEP INTO Harriet Jacobs's *Incidents in the Life of a Slave Girl* she recalls the story of a young enslaved boy named Luke. Passed down to a morally corrupt and bedridden young enslaver, Luke was flogged daily—so much so that he was instructed to wear only a shirt in readiness to be beaten. As his enslaver's mental and physical state worsened, he becomes more intensely cruel. Jacobs writes:

> The fact that he [the enslaver] was entirely dependent on Luke's care, and was obliged to be tended like an infant, instead of inspiring any gratitude or compassion towards his poor slave, seemed only to increase his irritability and cruelty. As he lay there on his bed, a mere degraded wreck of manhood, he took into his head the strangest freaks of despotism; and if Luke hesitated to submit to his orders, the constable was immediately sent for. Some of these freaks were of a nature too filthy to be repeated. When I fled from the house of bondage, I left poor Luke still chained to the bedside of this cruel and disgusting wretch. (149)[1]

---

1. See also Maurice Wallace's *Constructing the Black Masculine: Identity and Ideality in African American Men's Literature and Culture, 1775-1995* for an extended reading of Jacobs's depiction of Luke.

In this moment, Jacobs details (to the extent that she allows herself) what she deems as unspeakable violence committed against Luke, a violence of deeply erotic dimensions as evinced by Jacobs's charged image of Luke chained to his enslaver's bedside and her description of the enslaver's mental state as being corrupted with the "strangest freaks of despotism" so "filthy" that they could not be repeated. We can conclude that in addition to the beatings that Luke endured that he was also being sexually violated. Jacobs, in her account of her own sexual violation via her enslaver's constant harassment, then, aligns with Luke to paint a full picture of slavery and show the extent to which sexual violence was imbricated into the brutality of slavery.

Narratives of slavery, like Jacobs's, are populated with perverse intimacies—the known and unknown intimate horrors of slavery felt across generations that inhere black subjection and subject formation (Sharpe *Monstrous Intimacies* 3). These representations can be traced from the formative experience of Frederick Douglass witnessing his Aunt Hester's sexually layered whippings at the hands of her jealous enslaver to Toni Morrison's contemporary rendering of Paul D's violation where he is made to perform fellatio on his captors while other men are being sodomized on the chain gang. Hortense Spillers coins the term "pornotroping" to describe the captive body in its powerless state, reduced to a thing and vulnerable to various forms of sexual exploitation.[2] This constitutes the primary account we have of sexual intimacy in slavery. Implicit in the accounts of enslaved subjects being denied personhood and a validation of their sentient experiences was the denial of a nonpathologized experience of intimacy. Although brief gestures to pleasure and love interrupt these accounts of violation, the dominant discourse around enslaved sexuality remains pathologized.

I turn to Robert O'Hara's dramas *Insurrection: Holding History* (1996) and *Antebellum* (2009) to consider what becomes possible in the centering of consensual and affirmative intimate relations in the depiction of slavery. In both dramas, O'Hara forwards radical practices of intimacy and troubles the intimate space of the home through enslaved queer subjects negotiating slavery's long shadow. In these dramas, queer subjects find refuge in intimacy and in the deconstruction of normative notions of home. Their acts represent *fugitive intimacies* whereby a modicum of freedom is achieved through pleasure and in the reconceptualization of intimate spaces. Darieck Scott is instructive as to the possibilities of owning pleasure for the enslaved and formerly enslaved in his analysis of Paul D and Sethe's coupling in *Beloved*. He writes:

---

2. See also Alexander Weheliye's *Habeas Viscus: Racializing Assemblages, Biopolitics, and Black Feminist Theories of the Human.*

> Within the bounds of their [Sethe and Paul D's] relationship, they are in control of the logic of the fetish; it is their fetishism. And as with any such fetishism, its surer product is not safety . . . but some form of *pleasure,* however limited, however provisional, however attenuated: the pleasure of authoring choice, the pleasure of role playing, the pleasure of social making. (149; author's emphasis)

Using pleasure and affirming practices of intimacy to claim power over slavery's sexual objectification and inherent violence can be understood as a form of freedom, albeit limited. This chapter considers how fugitive intimacies in *Insurrection* and *Antebellum* make it possible for queer characters to access the freeing possibilities of pleasure, particularly the pleasure of social making. In this sense, I place "social making" in the realm of black social life that militates against active attempts to render black subjects as socially dead.

I do want to note, however, that to imagine sexual pleasure in slavery is certainly a risky proposition. There is a danger in obscuring the many horrors of enslaved experience and minimizing the oppression when attempting to represent pleasure. As we see with Branden Jacobs-Jenkins's *An Octoroon,* which I discussed in chapter 3, treating the subject of sexual pleasure for black subjects at a time when sexual violence so thoroughly subjugated them has the potential of making victims appear complicit in their sexual exploitation. Hortense Spillers illuminates,

> Whether or not the captive female and/or her sexual oppressor derived "pleasure" from their seductions and couplings is not a question we can politely ask. Whether or not "pleasure" is possible at all under conditions that I would aver as non-freedom for both or either of these parties has not been settled. Indeed, we could go so far as to entertain the very real possibility that "sexuality" a term of implied relationship and desire, is dubiously appropriate, manageable, or accurate to any of the familial arrangements under a system of enslavement, from the master's family to the captive enclave. Under these arrangements, the customary lexis of sexuality, including "reproduction," "motherhood," "pleasure," and "desire" are thrown into unrelieved crisis. (76)

For Spillers, our conventional understandings of sexuality, pleasure, and desire are upended against the backdrop of slavery. That the very question of sexual pleasure is *not a polite one to ask* indicates the extent to which these issues are charged and overflowing with traumatic instability. Saidiya Hartman also interrogates pleasure in slavery, revealing it to be primarily a site of terror.

Enslavers forced the enslaved to feign affects of pleasure in order to obscure the horrors of their everyday existences. Hartman also notes that the antebellum minstrel stage largely transformed suffering into wholesome pleasures. Thus, the claiming of pleasure in black creative work about slavery is a radical act that gives the enslaved agency over their pleasure and complicates their identities by depicting them as sexual subjects.

Pleasure in O'Hara's work calls up the history of black sexual suffering while also showing queer subjects claiming pleasure, which constitutes a refusal to be defined by their oppression. Darieck Scott notes how black writers feature the male rape figure in slavery as a mode "to represent/or *produce* pleasure from fanaticized identification with violated ancestors" (12; author's emphasis). In this way, pleasure functions paradoxically, gesturing to its literal meanings and to the history of violation and humiliation black subjects have endured as objects of pleasure for perverse enslavers. Scott explains, "Representations of the sexual exploitation of men as part of the historical trauma that in part produces blackness operate in the texts [that comprise his study] as almost therapeutic enactment, allowing re-conceptions of an identity paradoxically enriched, even empowered, by the suffering that constitutes it and that it psychically repeats" (12). I will analyze how O'Hara centers queer subjects in the telling of narratives of slavery, constructs pleasure as a refuge from the pornotrophic violence of enslavement and its legacies, and critiques notions of home for black and queer subjects, a space (when understood in terms of its Western, patriarchal, and heteronormative foundations) that has been particularly hostile to both.

By treading and troubling the line between pain and pleasure in slavery, Robert O'Hara makes space for a queer subject, largely unimagined in the black past, thereby offering a new conception of black identity as well. Matt Richardson asserts, "There is a queer limit to how we [black diasporic subjects] understand our history and ourselves" (3) and that the black queer is dead to black memory (10). Whether because of strictures of public decorum or the resistance to claiming nonnormative genders in black communities,[3] queer subjects have been historically marginalized in meditations on the black past. This marginalization is peculiar because the experience of slavery and the journey of the Middle Passage was inherently a queer experience. It was queer in the larger sense of the word because transporting millions of individuals across the Atlantic Ocean in a treacherous journey that would transform them from human beings into chattel was an inherently surreal and queer

---

3. See Matt Richardson's *The Queer Limit of Black Memory: Black Lesbian Literature and Irresolution*, 8.

experience.⁴ Omise'eke Natasha Tinsley expresses, "The black Atlantic has always been the queer Atlantic" (191). She goes further to highlight the same-sex bonds created in the ships' holds that endured long after the experience (191–92).⁵ In light of this powerful reconceptualization of the experience of the Middle Passage, Tinsley makes clear that we do a disservice to this history when we erase queer subjects.

Robert O'Hara stands among a number of contemporary black artists working to represent queer experience in slavery. Black creatives have increasingly produced work that restores queer subjects in histories of slavery. Karma Mayet Johnson in 2013 produced a theater piece entitled *Indigo, A Blues Opera* that tells the story of two enslaved women, Eliza and Bell, who fall in love and make their escape from slavery together. Also, Jewelle Gomez's 1991 Gothic novel, *The Gilda Stories*, tells the story of Gilda, a lesbian vampire, who escapes from life in slavery.⁶ By featuring black male queer subjects in the black past via the stage in his dramas *Insurrection: Holding History* and *Antebellum*, O'Hara provides an important complement to works like that of Gomez and Johnson. Because of his unique exploration of queer enslaved subjectivity in drama and his radical representation of pleasure and black sentience in the staging of slavery, his work most aligns with the book's project of tracing a practice in contemporary drama of presenting slavery anew through the framework of fugitivity.

"LOVE FOR SALE": FUGITIVE INTIMACIES IN *INSURRECTION: HOLDING HISTORY*

A radical reenvisioning of Nat Turner's 1831 revolt in Southampton County, Virginia (in a town then known as Jerusalem), *Insurrection: Holding History* deploys intimacy as an act of resistance. The drama stages revolutionary intimacies through the troubling of home, in the centering of queer subjects in the telling of slavery, and in the introduction of queer pleasure against a backdrop of sexualized violence against enslaved subjects. These forceful interven-

---

4. Spillers's seminal essay "Mama's Baby, Papa's Maybe: An American Grammar Book" develops a discussion on the way the trans-Atlantic slave trade disrupted conventional understandings of gender, thereby queering the enslaved subject.

5. Omise'eke Natasha Tinsley notes, "I began to learn *this* Black Atlantic when I was studying relationships between women in Suriname and delved into the etymology of the word *mati*. This word is the Creole women use for their female lovers: figuratively *mi mati* is 'my girl,' but literally it means *mate* as in *shipmate*—she who survived the Middle Passage with me" (192).

6. See also Richardson's *The Queer Limit of Black Memory* for a copious study on Black Lesbian literature and its engagement with history.

tions reflect the subtext of revolution that aligns with the spirit of Nat Turner. Pleasure and intimacy, then, become sites of revolt and freedom. *Insurrection* tells the story of Ron, a doctoral student of history at Columbia University and his 189-year-old grandfather TJ (voiced by a character named Mutha Wit) who is celebrating his birthday. TJ's timelessness calls up Aunt Ester, August Wilson's 285-year-old ancestor that figures largely in his oeuvre. Like Wilson, O'Hara includes a surreal figure that moves the depiction of slavery away from realism to a more fantastic representation of slavery.[7] Fashioned as a new-aged *Wizard of Oz,* the play sends Ron and TJ back in time from the 1995 setting of the play to the late nineteenth-century site of Nat Turner's slave rebellion and his grandfather TJ's "home." Once integrated into the slave community, Ron actually speaks against the cause of rebelling, warning them of the consequences to which they are not yet privy. Also present in the drama is a queer enslaved subject named Hammet (described as a "walking beauty"), who is Turner's assistant. Hammet and Ron, who is also homosexual, become enamored with one another, but must separate just as they are close to pronouncing love. Inhabiting the present as Ron and TJ are navigating the past are Ron's Aunt Gertha and her daughter Octavia, to which the narrative often returns. The two women often offer comedic interludes in the 1995 setting that also serve to disorient audiences. O'Hara notes that the play should be performed as if it were a bullet through time. Taking this into account, we should imagine such a bullet zig-zagging, maneuvering, and circulating within, through, and around time. Indeed this play resists linearity and chronological cohesion.

At the center of the drama is Nat Turner's story and Ron's impatience with institutional histories of Turner's narrative. In this way, the drama explores unresolved aspects of the slave past, its elisions, and its silences.[8] As the play begins, Ron is engaged in researching the history of Nat Turner's rebellion. Revisiting *The Confessions of Nat Turner* told to Thomas R. Gray, Ron laments that he has nothing new to say about this history, although the story won't let him go (18). This nagging desire that Ron has to tell Nat Turner's story likely comes as a result of the numerous gaps in dominant versions of Turner's narrative. Some historians challenge the veracity of the account Thomas R. Gray provided, arguing that Turner was coerced into giving a confession that Gray then embellished.[9] Gray even makes an appearance in *Insurrection* where, in the role of reporter, he confronts Nat Turner and declares in contemporary

---

7. See Richard Iton's *In Search of the Black Fantastic: Politics and Popular Culture in the Post-Civil Rights Era.*

8. See Suzan-Lori Parks's essay "Possession" in *The America Play and Other Works.*

9. See Daniel Fabricant's "Thomas R. Gray and William Styron: Finally, A Critical Look at the 1831 Confessions of Nat Turner."

vernacular, "Look you can give me your story or I can make it up and even if you do confess to me I'm probably gonna put in a little filler here and there so listen Nigga yo' silence will do you no benefit you dig?" (11). Here O'Hara embeds into the narrative the idea that the text Ron is reading is likely fiction—similar William Styron's 1967 fiction *The Confessions of Nat Turner*.[10] Therefore, even as Ron perceives his limitations in telling Turner's story, declaring, "i [sic] have nothing new to say about him or slavery" (18), there exists an underlying sentiment that Turner's story has yet to truly be told and that we might never have access to this history. Under these circumstances, O'Hara intervenes by adding his own take on Turner's story.

Confronted with the problematic discursive construction of Nat Turner's narrative and the fact that the dominant accounts of Turner's life have been voiced through white authors, O'Hara's drama "queries" and "queers" this history, according to Faedra Carpenter. Carpenter argues that *Insurrection* uses the "fantastical to emancipate African American history and identity from the bondage of compulsive white heteronormativity" (187). Indeed the underlying ethos of this drama is emancipation; however, I want to focus on the particular methods O'Hara draws upon to achieve this emancipation, namely as it relates to intimacy and pleasure. In centering these two affective registers, O'Hara not only emancipates black history and identity from dominant discourses and heteronormative frameworks, but he also constructs alternate spaces for the articulation of black subjectivity, which are enabled by intimacy and pleasure.

One key means by which O'Hara presents fugitive intimacies is through his reordering of narrative and time. O'Hara draws upon narrative strategies of time travel and other temporal disruptions as he depicts life in Nat Turner's nineteenth-century era and the contemporary conditions that constitute slavery's afterlives. Rebecca Balon argues that O'Hara's disruptions of time as a means to imagine queer enslaved subjects in *Insurrection* "encounters and thus reveals the obstacles to such a project posed by the ideological limits of the two identities"; she argues that O'Hara's method implicitly suggests that this reality can only be represented in a fantastic context (150). I contend, however, that such temporal disruptions occur throughout black dramatic representations of slavery irrespective of sexuality as we note in Wilson's *Gem of the Ocean* (chapter 2) and Branden Jacobs-Jenkins's *An Octoroon* (chapter 3) to point to notable instances. This book examines a number of dramas that experiment with temporal modes of representing slavery, which indi-

---

10. Also, if we consider the word "confession" itself, it implies a kind of intimacy, albeit a troubling one in which a person discloses intimate secrets to another. The subtext here affirms O'Hara's concerted effort to explore intimacy and slavery.

cates something more at work. These temporal disruptions are largely reflective of Calvin Warren's instructive notion of "black time," which posits that "slavery is not reducible an object-event of metaphysics" and that we need to reconceive of normative notions of time if we are to fully comprehend and represent the temporal deconstruction implicit in slavery (56). *Insurrection* issues a challenge to chrononormativity—the biopolitical practice that orders the social world and fixes bodies in time and space. This reordering upends a number of conceptions about the past that deny the enslaved physical and emotive agency. In this sense, it is thus necessary that time be disrupted in the telling of the narrative of slavery, especially when it implicates contemporary subjects.

Rather than attempt to tell some approximate version of Turner's story, O'Hara constructs an erotohistoriography, which according to Elizabeth Freeman treats the present as a hybrid and "uses the body as a tool to effect, figure, or perform that encounter" (95). In the case of Ron and TJ, this encounter is embodied in their specific social and historical positions with Ron's contemporary queer identity meeting the 189-year-old TJ who represents the slave past. Their journey to the past is initiated by an embrace between the two where Ron states, "holding history. i'm holding history in my arms. Gramps SPEAK" (20). By bringing Ron and TJ's body together in an embrace, O'Hara orients his configuration of this story in the context of familial connection. Ron is not merely touching or reading about history; he is holding it in his arms—his body and his ancestor's intertwined.

The infusion of time travel with familial intimacy is enacted through the practice of erotohistoriography. Elizabeth Freeman elaborates,

> [Erotohistoriography is a] way of imagining the "inappropriate" response of eros in the face of sorrow as a trace of past forms of pleasure. As a mode of reparative criticism, erotohistoriography honors the way queer relations completely exceed the present, insisting that various queer social practices, especially those involving enjoyable bodily sensations, produce forms of time consciousness—even historical consciousness—that can intervene into the material damage done in the name of development, civilization, and so on. Within these terms, we might imagine ourselves haunted by bliss and not just by trauma; residues of positive affect (idylls, utopias, memories of touch) might be available for queer counter- (or para-) historiographies. (120)

Through invoking familial love and connection within the context of slavery, O'Hara offers a history of slavery that is told through the body, through the confession, through the embrace. This intervention reimagines notions of connection and love, emotive states that were often denied in rhetoric about black sentience during slavery. Thus, to center love in the telling of the story of slavery clears space for new imaginings that also make room for differently situated bodies and unaccounted for identities.

The upending of time also underlies O'Hara's troubling of notions of home. The drama takes its cues from the already troubled notions of home, sexuality, and desire experienced by enslaved subjects and their descendants. The fact of the queer subject's nonnormative identity and the upending of conceptions of gender and sexuality brought on by the slave trade provide a mutually constitutive framework upon which to reimagine black sexuality and gender identification. In both *Insurrection* and *Antebellum,* home serves as an active metaphor that throws into sharp relief the vexed relations black subjects, especially black queer subjects, have with the concept. In one sense, home represents a place of no return, which serves a parallel sentiment for formerly enslaved peoples and queer subjects. In her preface to the groundbreaking collection *Black Queer Studies,* Sharon P. Holland asserts that "'Home' is a four-letter word. Functioning simultaneously as "a place of refuge and escape" (Holland, "Forward" xii), the concept of home for the queer holds as much pain as it does promise. Holland's choice of words is evocative for the discussion of slavery where notions of refuge and escape were constantly at play in the negotiation of life for the enslaved. Severed from homeland and forced into servitude, home represented a site to which the enslaved could not fully return. Even in the search for a home beyond the plantation that was enacted most often through escape, the enslaved was destined to live as a refugee—never truly finding home in America.[11]

The home has historically been the site of domestic violence and fraught domestic relations. Power dynamics in the home function as a model for political and social institutions across time. Thus, when contextualized in these terms, home often advances problematic ideologies in the perpetuation of normative gender frameworks that do not make space for queer subjects. Traditional home spaces are then insufficient locations for queer partnering and community. Robert O'Hara's dramas call attention to the need for queer subjects to imagine new spatial locations beyond the bounds of domesticity, something I will take up in more detail in my discussion of *Antebellum.*

The action in *Insurrection* is propelled by Ron's formerly enslaved ancestor TJ's request to go *home.* He says to Ron, "take me home ronnie. Drive me. Carry me. Push me. Take. Me. Home. Home . . ." (19). TJ's desperate request to be taken home, to his plantation home, disrupts conventional understand-

---

11. See Nicole Waligora-Davis's *Sanctuary: African Americans and Empire.*

ings of the enslaved's relationship to home. Just as we see in chapter 2 where Aunt Ester of *Gem of the Ocean* reimagines the bodies of those lost in the Middle Passage as constitutive of a resplendent City of Bones, TJ revises negative associations with his plantation home and instead claims it as a site of restoration. TJ's ability to assert a sense of home on the plantation, what Jacobs hauntingly refers to as "the house of bondage"—an environment rife with violence, dispossession, and dehumanization—performs a fugitive intimacy that allows him to define home beyond its abject terrors.

Once located in TJ's "homeland," O'Hara rewrites other familiar narratives of enslaved experience, taking power over them and their rendering of the black body as singularly abject and lacking agency. He focuses particularly on the erotics of torture that are characteristic of slavery. The bed in slavery, at once a symbol of sex and violence, becomes a site where notions of pleasure and desire get redefined in the drama. Reminiscent of Dorothy's home landing on and thus killing the wicked witch of the East in Oz, the bed that transports Ron and TJ to the plantation lands upon and kills the enslaver. The cast of the play, like the residents of Oz, break out into song—"He's Dead." The over-the-top camp performance destabilizes the emotional contexts of slavery, which are largely viewed through lenses of trauma and pain. Faedra Carpenter explains, "O'Hara applies the gay aesthetic of camp to create incongruous scenes marked by their self-conscious theatricality and humor. Thus, in one play, the monolithic topic of American slavery is viewed as both a subject of comedy as well as a subject of tragedy" ("Que(e)rying History" 194). Similar to the use of humor in Branden Jacobs-Jenkins's *An Octoroon*, the use of humor in the depiction of slavery offers the potential to communicate pleasure alongside political critique. O'Hara's killing of the enslaver via the bed reminds us of the bed as an instrument of torture in slavery (see Jacobs's enduring image of Luke chained to his enslaver's bed) and initiates an interrogation of the perverse sexual intimacies of enslaved life alongside emancipatory practices of intimacy and pleasure.

Once on the plantation, Ron witnesses the sexual dimensions of slavery's particular kind of political domination. First, the song "He's Dead" details the enslaver's physical and sexual brutality. The cast sings,

> from head ta toe my body aches
> my bent black back's about to break
> my sunburnt neck's gat a permanent crook
> he took my child befo' I gat a good look
> he sold my mama to a man named John
> he raped my sista just fo' fun

> he beat my father both black and blue
> If he had the chance he'd fuck you too (34)

The cast produces a jarring image as they detail the horrors of the slave experience while performing it in what O'Hara explains should be a "FULL-THROTTLE, NO-HOLDS-BARRED, 11:00, BROADWAY, SHOWSTOPPING, BRING DOWN THE HOUSE, PRODUCTION NUMBER, Chains and all" (32–33). Even though the full-throttle production number has the potential to obscure the enslaver's raping a woman "just fo' fun" or beating a man black and blue and even the possibility that the enslaver might "fuck you too" (observe that the "you" is not gender specific), the mixture of humor and horror merge in powerful tension. It must also be noted that the enslaver's name in the play is "Massa Motel." "Motels" (as opposed to the less charged term "hotel") are often associated with sexual indiscretions, secret trysts between lovers, and so on. Connecting the enslaver to this kind of location further defines him in contexts of sexual promiscuity. It also juxtaposes the notion of home and domestic space with the transient nature of motels as temporary housing. We can read the plantation home outside of traditional constructions of home and more aligned with the sexually inflected, impermanence of the motel. Even the title of the play is sexually charged with "insurrection" functioning as a homonym for "erection." Yet, in keeping with the revolutionary spirit of Turner's revolt and O'Hara's approach to representing it, "insurrection" here should be read in the context of resistance. The pleasure of sexual desire becomes imbricated in revolution.

On Massa Motel's plantation, pornotroping abounds. The perverse relationship between violence and sex is made prominent in a key scene in the play where an enslaved woman Izzie Mae is about to be beaten for not picking enough cotton. Ova Seea Jones, the plantation overseer, directs Izzie Mae to disrobe. He then demands that Buck Naked, a white male working-class figure who is aligned with and treated in a similar manner as the enslaved, tie her to the whipping post. As Ron looks on in horror, he requests that he be beaten instead. When the overseer asks Ron's name, Ron offers the name "Faggot" immediately signaling his queer identity. The overseer surveys Ron's body including his genitals with the whip and then directs Buck Naked to tie Ron up alongside Izzie Mae in order to be beaten. This scene is loaded with pornographic imaging and contexts all mediated through violence. The images of the nude Izzie Mae being strung up publicly in preparation to be whipped alongside the nude Ron who is also being prepared for whipping by a figure named "Buck Naked" produce an intensely erotic scene. Their literal and figurative nude bodies all become bound in a pornotropic/pornographic relation where violence and sex are intimately connected.

The sexual dimensions of violence against slaves in this context gives new meaning to the idea of "commodity fetishism." Karl Marx describes a commodity as "a very queer thing, abounding in metaphysical subtleties and theological niceties" (qtd. Ripstein 733). For Marx commodities become fetishized when we attempt to ascribe value to labor and material objects. The fetishism inherent in the possession of a body—that then is objectified and "made a thing" for the captor—arises as a result of the seductive nature of political domination over another human being. The fetish attached to the black body in slavery was most often realized through violence and sexual exploitation. If we read Marx's general use of the term "queer" in the context of O'Hara's play, the commodity here is "queer" as well—not easily contained in a singular meaning or idea. The fact that the whipping scene contains a heterosexual woman and a homosexual male shows the expansive reach of this domination and its queer underpinnings that are often elided in the name of the unspeakable. Not to diminish Izzie Mae's experience, but it is important that in this whipping scene O'Hara *includes* Ron, thereby establishing sex as embattled territory for black women as well as men.[12]

Significantly, both versions of *The Confessions of Nat Turner,* Gray's purportedly nonfiction work and Styron's fictive imagining, paint Nat Turner as an intensely violent individual and sexual predator. Gray's account depicts Turner as a callous murderer of women and children. Styron folds in a layer of queer subtext depicting Turner as a child being sold to a homosexual minister who then sells him away after Turner rejects his advances. Turner later in the novel goes on to rape white women. Styron's version has been widely critiqued as bolstering the myth of the black male rapist in the postlynching era.[13] Inevitably, Turner's story cannot escape the tendencies toward pornotroping of black subjects in slavery.

Insurrection rewrites the sexually brutalized enslaved subject and envisions him claiming power through the erotic. He does this primarily through showing intimate connection between two male queer subjects in his depiction of slavery.[14] Hammet, the queer enslaved subject, is central to this rewriting. As he enters the frame, Ron is instantly captivated by him. They exchange a number of passionate encounters and offer an unanticipated love story in this new

---

12. Maurice Wallace also discusses Paul D's narrative arguing that "the sodomitic threat was just as real during slavery as the heterosexual rape of women" (88).

13. For a contemporary reaction to the problematic tropes that Styron forwards, see *William Styron's Nat Turner: Ten Black Writers Respond* edited by John Henrik Clarke.

14. See Audre Lorde's "Uses of the Erotic: The Erotic as Power."

FIGURE 7. Nathaniel Andrew as Hammet and Breon Arzell as Ron in *Insurrection*. Used with permission from Tyler Core via Stage Left Theatre, Chicago, IL.

narrative exploration of Nat Turner's revolt. On their first encounter, Hammet "blows Sweet Air into RON's open mouth" (30). When they meet again, Hammet explains to Ron that he shook when he first met him. To this Ron asks Hammet if he likes boys, and Hammet responds "i lak you" (86). They kiss in this moment and Ron faints. Complete with its romance and mystique, their courtship becomes a central narrative within the larger one. Hammet in his close relationship to Nat Turner and his attraction to Ron allows for O'Hara to write queerness onto historical narratives of black hypermasculinity. While Hammet works with Turner to create one kind of social resistance, he also resists being rendered as victimized. He controls the fetish, the pleasure, which constitutes another kind of revolutionary act (see figure 7).

The ending of the drama reinforces O'Hara's centralizing of black queer subjects in narratives of slavery. TJ takes Ron into his arms as the insurrection is taking place—returning to the same embrace that propelled them on this journey. Just before his death, TJ tells him "you. mine. mi. proof. you. mine . . . PROOF" (103). That Ron—TJ's queer grandson—represents TJ's future and proof of his existence symbolizes a passing on of his legacy. In this sense, O'Hara not only writes the queer into the past but into the future.[15]

---

15. I do not want to suggest that this is an easy conclusion. I see this as O'Hara situating Ron between the past and the future as a rejection of the here and now. He then is able to rewrite the past and envision a potential future. As José Muñoz points out in *Cruising Utopia*,

Inasmuch as O'Hara compellingly narrativizes queer subjects into the past and future, the text ends in irresolution where Ron and Hammet's love relationship cannot be realized. On the subject of irresolution and how queer individuals continue to contest normative frameworks, Matt Richardson asserts that black lesbian writers are "beneficiaries of and contributors to a reconceptualization of black resistance to include gender variance as well as sexual transgression" (8). Irresolution, then, refuses a normative portrayal of black experience. Richardson also notes the significance of black people claiming gender and creative interpretations of the self in defiance of the efforts to dehumanize them. Under this rubric, there is a constant resistance to being brought in line with normative frameworks and ideologies—particularly ones that have historically marginalized black subjects. This is useful in thinking about how *Insurrection* ends. Returning to the search for home that compels TJ, Ron communicates his own thoughts about home and freedom to Hammet, telling him "you asked / what it feels like / to be free . . . lost / i [*sic*] feel lost sometimes / without a connection / without a linkage / without a / past" (97). For Ron, as a queer subject in the contemporary moment, his experience of freedom is one of loss and disconnection. It is only in his newly formed bond with Hammet that Ron experiences a sense of connection. The fugitivity of intimacy becomes a space of belonging and empowerment for Ron. However, the commencement of Turner's revolt thwarts a realization of Ron and Hammet's coupling. This occurs just as Ron is about to pronounce love for Hammet. Impulsively, Ron tells TJ that he doesn't want to return to the present. However, TJ reminds Ron that remaining in the past is an impossibility. Additionally, Hammet is subsequently killed in the revolt. O'Hara denies a traditional ending to their love story, thereby denying the possibility of their love story to be absorbed into a normative narrative of romance that ends in a pronouncement of love and a possible "happily ever after." He also does so in recognition that the conditions of slavery often disrupted the forming of bonds that could withstand the brutality of the institution.

ANTEBELLUM'S QUEER HAUNTED HOUSES

In his 2010 play *Antebellum,* O'Hara continues his exploration of queer bonds in the context of historical epochs where brutality reigned and how these intimate relations offered a degree of freedom. In this drama, however, O'Hara widens the lens to consider the legacies of slavery and its psychical impact

"Queerness is essentially about the rejection of a here and now and an insistence on potentiality or concrete possibility for another world" (1).

on those living in the US while also examining Berlin, Germany, during the Holocaust and how the logics of this genocide echoed the ideologies that made slavery possible. Although the slave era is not the primary subject and setting of the drama, it plays a significant role and progressively becomes central by the time the drama reaches its dénouement. O'Hara constructs both settings of the play as "bleeding into one another in the late 1930s." The two settings are interiors (one a plantation home and the other a German officer's library) and are joined so that they "read" as one home. While the drama is certainly concerned with exposing and countering the pornotropic violence projected onto the black body during slavery and beyond, my analysis of this work centers on how O'Hara experiments with the conception of the home space in his presentation of fugitive intimacies. He goes straight to the heart of domesticity where the heteronormative foundations of the home space get troubled. He also employs a transnational geographical location that allows for a challenge to questions of nation and the way nations imagine the past.[16]

The plot of the play is incredibly complex, but the dual narratives meet at the body of transsexual cabaret singer Gabriel, who later becomes Edna Black Rock. The play begins with Sara Roca, the wife of Ariel Roca, both of whom are Jewish and reside on Ariel's family's plantation in Atlanta. Sarah is excitedly preparing to attend the premiere of *Gone with the Wind* when Edna Black Rock arrives unexpectedly at her home. The two women make a connection, and Edna convinces Sarah to hire her as a maid (see figure 8). The setting then transitions to Nazi Germany where Gabriel, a black American male performer, is being held in an internment camp and is the sexual "slave" of Oskar von Scheleicher, a Nazi officer. During his time with Oskar, Gabriel involuntarily receives hormone treatments that transition him into a woman—he ultimately becomes Edna Black Rock. In another narrative twist, we learn that Gabriel/Edna was romantically involved with Sara's closeted husband Ariel while he traveled in Germany as a young man. When Edna arrives at Ariel's family home, the play explores a number of complex narratives regarding sexuality, the haunting presence of slavery in the American psyche, and the dangers of romanticizing the antebellum past.

Throughout *Antebellum*, notions of haunting and unresolved pasts figure centrally. Much like Toni Morrison's *Beloved* and its use of the specter to invoke the past, this text relies on Edna Black Rock to bind the past to the present and to force a reckoning with what has been suppressed. In Morrison's novel, when Beloved emerges, the text announces her: "A fully dressed

---

16. See Benedict Anderson's *Imagined Communities: Reflections on the Origins and Spread of Nationalism*.

woman walked out of the water" (50). She then voids endless amounts of water akin to a flooding. She also drinks cup after cup of water in an effort to quench her thirst (51). The flooding constitutes a metaphor for memory and the thirst a desire to recover loss. The all-consuming floods created by breeches in attempts to bandage over the past—to block it out and forget—have now arrived at 124 Bluestone Road. Edna Black Rock in many ways calls up Beloved when she appears at Sarah Roca's doorstep almost out of thin air. She is also incredibly thirsty, asking for cup after cup of water when she arrives. As Sarah is preparing for the premiere of *Gone with the Wind*, we are reminded again of the past being continually engaged in the present. Sarah, however, is largely uncritical of *Gone with the Wind*'s version of the past, even going so far as to dress up as they did in the "good ole days" (417). Edna issues a challenge to this, pushing her to think critically about just how much she knew of those days. We also learn that Sarah frequently sees spirits "floating around out there in them fields" (437). She says, "Some times I stand at that window there at night and I think I see them **rising**. . . . I discover things . . . shackles . . . bolts . . . **footprints** . . . . There are scratches on the trees along the edge of the field . . . a hidden alphabet I think . . . figures . . . **signs** . . . etched into **roots**" (437–38, playwright's emphasis). Sarah's descriptions call up images of slavery—the shackles, coded language and signs in the trees and roots. Thus, even as she is enraptured with the romantic tale of slavery promoted by *Gone with the Wind*, she is continually confronted in her own home with the past that the novel and film so thoroughly erase.

The erasure of the realities of the slave past in this moment not only has implications for understandings of slavery but also for the ability to recognize elements of slavery in other tragedies such as the Holocaust. What O'Hara does is bridge the two to show how the past, if not fully addressed, can repeat itself in devastating ways. In creating the parallel settings of late 1930s Atlanta and Nazi Germany, O'Hara suspends notions of place to show the endurance and dangers of unchecked brutality. In destabilizing place, O'Hara explores notions of homelessness in relation to race and sexuality as he does with *Insurrection*. Like *Insurrection*, he complicates these ideas of home to reveal how racial and sexualized oppression can render one homeless in the world. O'Hara utilizes the German setting to interrogate more thoroughly homelessness via the queer black American performer Gabriel and the closeted Jewish American Ariel. Gabriel, like many black Americans in this era, relocated to another country in the hopes of escaping the racial animus he experienced in the US. Although Gabriel is from New York, he identifies with the plight of black Americans in the South because it is not too distant from his own experiences of discrimination.

FIGURE 8. Jessica Frances Dukes as Edna Black Rock and Jenna Sokolowski as Sarah Roca, *Antebellum*. Used with permission from Stan Barouh © '09 via Woolly Mammoth Theatre.

There is no direct mention of this in the play, but it is worth noting that the 1930s—1935 in particular—was a time of social unrest in Harlem. The Harlem Riot of 1935 erupted because of intense job discrimination against black Americans, symbolized in the police killing of a young man accused of stealing a 10-cent penknife (Greenberg 406). This is also the cultural backdrop from which the now-disaffected Gabriel escapes. He articulates his feelings of homelessness in America to his suitor Ariel. In his attempt to warn Ariel to leave Germany, he tells them that Germany is turning into places like Mississippi, Alabama, and Georgia. To this, Ariel accuses him of paranoia, yet Gabriel reminds him, "You are white first in America, are you not?" (466). Gabriel attempts to help Ariel understand how racial discrimination and violence have made his life untenable in the US. He laments that he is always perceived as "colored," an identity that thoroughly marginalizes him in the US. He issues a final warning to Ariel: "All I'm saying is that America was built with my people's blood and Germany hopes to rebuild with the blood of your people. They have that in common and I can smell it" (469). This exchange folds in a number of complex issues regarding place and home enacted through the queer body. Gabriel echoes the voice of another, more prominent, black queer figure—James Baldwin, who, in a seminal 1967 essay "Negroes are Anti-Semitic Because They're Anti-White," explains that Jewish individuals cannot comprehend the ongoing strife black Americans experience in the land of their oppression. He writes: "For it is not here, and not now, that the Jew is being slaughtered, and he is never despised here, as the Negro is, *because* he is an American. . . . But America *is* the house of bondage for the Negro, and no country can rescue him." Notably, Baldwin draws upon Harriet Jacobs's formulation in the describing America as "the house of bondage for the Negro." Baldwin problematizes notions of "home" for black Americans and calls attention to the lingering effects of slavery. He also identifies a central conflict that inhibits connection between Jewish Americans and black Americans. O'Hara complicates this issue with the fact that Ariel and Gabriel are indeed lovers. Their love, however, is impossible to maintain because Gabriel is estranged from the US and Ariel is being progressively estranged from Germany (he is being followed and has experienced an assault). Ariel has also not revealed his homosexual identity to his family, who is positioned to pass down an inheritance to him funded by their profits from slavery. Gabriel and Ariel have formed an unsustainable bond that is further complicated by their histories. In many ways, the legacies of the past bear on their lives and make the realities they desire impossible.

As O'Hara dives deeper into the intersecting histories of slavery, the Holocaust, and how these social contexts make the possibility of a sustained relationship between Gabriel and Ariel an improbability, he works from the framework of erotohistoriography as a reparative act that inscribes positive affects (love, desire, and pleasure) amidst these traumatic events. O'Hara relies on ambiguous time constructs—noting the period as only the "late 1930s" rather than offering particular years, with the exception of one case where he is intentional about naming a setting as 1935 Berlin. Also, he writes the scenes so that they bleed into one another as opposed to clearly demarcating where Nazi Germany ends and the post-Reconstruction American South begins. He does this through the liminal figure, Gabriel, who is transitioning into Edna Black Rock. Gabriel/Edna functions as a bridge between the settings where in one instance they will be speaking to someone on the Roca Plantation and next they will be addressing Oskar in the German prison library space. The plantation setting keeps slavery present and, in many ways, serves as an index for the global social climate of the late 1930s.

Gabriel/Edna Black Rock's body mediates the traversing of space between Germany and the US and time between slavery, the Reconstruction, post-Reconstruction, and the Holocaust. It is through Gabriel/Edna Black Rock that O'Hara explores the perverse and potentially empowering intersections between pain and pleasure. Interestingly, rather than frame the pornotropic violence enacted in this play in the context of slavery, O'Hara depicts the sexual dimensions of violence under the rubric of Fascism as carried out through Oskar. When Oskar and Gabriel are featured together, their interactions are often as violent as they are pleasurable. For example, after a night together, Oskar proposes the idea that Gabriel serve as his house servant rather than reside in the prisoner quarters, Gabriel suggests that the arrangement resembles a marital one. At this, Oskar slaps Gabriel to the ground. He later asks Gabriel which of the guards rapes him when he is not near (441). The suggestion that Gabriel is regularly raped and the fact that he is currently being held as Oskar's slave illustrate how sexual violence was imbricated in the more generalized violence embedded in the Nazi prisons.

Another unexpected dimension to the sexual violence of the prison that Gabriel experiences is that Oskar has arranged for Gabriel to be transitioned into a woman. The state, now in complete control of his body, administers estrogen injections that cause Gabriel to progressively become a woman. The injections are painful, yet Gabriel's experience of them is largely framed in the context of intimacy. When Oskar administers one of the injections, the pain is so intense that Gabriel has to bite down on a bit in order to muffle his screams. Shortly after this Oskar kisses Gabriel declaring "I pick you" (472–73). Notably, the transition to a woman is also another way for Oskar to reconcile his attraction to Gabriel. By forcing Gabriel to perform heteronormativity, Oskar can then pursue his romantic interest in him without fear of admonishment.

Gabriel and Oskar's mutual affection further complicates their troubling relationship. They both express love for each other, and Gabriel teaches Oskar English. Oskar, however, knows the damage he has done to his reputation as a result of his intimacy with Gabriel, which he refers to as his open secret. Thus, he kills himself as recognition of this reality. Upon his death he says to Gabriel, "ICH LIEBE DICH!!!" translated as "I love you." To this Gabriel responds "... And I love you ... Oskar" (442). This exchange of love between men places Gabriel in more than just the singular context of pain and victimization. Rather, he has established a bond, albeit a perverse one, with his captor, thereby complicating our understanding of that experience altogether. Just as the pornotropic violence in *Insurrection* gets entangled with pleasure, Gabriel's embrace of his new identity as Edna Black Rock represents O'Hara's rewriting of the brutalized subject in a way that allows for a multidimensional depiction.[17]

---

17. I want to be careful to not romanticize this moment because O'Hara offers a thoroughly complex rendering of Gabriel's transition into Edna Black Rock. In one instance, Oskar finds him naked and bloodied after having cut himself (476–77). In this enigmatic moment where Gabriel doesn't speak, we can read his self-harming as a reflection of his internal turmoil during his transition.

Gabriel is essentially reborn as Edna Black Rock when she arrives on the Roca family plantation. It is also significant that the name Roca translates to "rock" in a number of languages most notably Spanish, so in essence, Edna Black Rock has assumed a connection to Ariel that binds them together in a kind of marital connection. Once Ariel has overcome the shock of Gabriel's transformation into Edna, they rekindle their romance and summarily disregard Sarah. After they make love in their act of reunion, the two look out onto the plantation fields. There Ariel shares with Edna that he, like Sarah, has seen spirits in the fields, saying that in his home he often recalled the presence of fear and that there were "things that were not to be remembered in this house" (478–79). Again, O'Hara frames the domestic space as a site of terror where the histories it holds are so devastating that they are not to be remembered. The foundations upon which the Roca home was built make it uninhabitable for Edna as a black subject, nor is it suitable to *house* the nonnormative relationship between Edna and Ariel.

Elaborating on how the past haunts the estate, Ariel describes his unearthing of an unmarked cemetery and looking into the water and seeing millions of faces "ones that did not make it to these shores" (479). In his revisiting of the Middle Passage, we see again the representation of this experience in the abstract. The event is remembered and represented through the imagery of the water rather than a literal representation of death. Like Wilson's *Gem of the Ocean,* the focus of the remembrance is on mourning as opposed to a more explicit depiction of the brutality. Ariel explains to Edna "as I looked into the water of this creek . . . as if it were a **crack** in the middle of this grassy tomb . . . **faces** . . . the dead staring through me . . . I knew . . . they had not been **mourned** . . . those that did not last the journey . . . I saw them that day . . . millions . . . dead . . . yet to be mourned . . ." (479, playwright's emphasis). Ariel's description of this moment is enabled by Edna's presence, particularly because she presses Ariel to confront his family's complicity with slavery. In this moment of confession to Edna, he releases his long-held feelings about the history of his family's land and his inability to negotiate life there. He explains to Edna that once he comprehended the death brought on by slavery, he could no longer live there and remain whole. In this moment that is framed in the joining of two lovers, one bisexual and the other now transgender, we see how O'Hara is voicing the story of slavery through queer individuals, thereby complicating public memory of this history with a queer narrative of love that the audience must hold alongside the history.

This drama, like *Insurrection,* ends with an unfulfilled partnership. Edna disrupts it by declaring to Ariel that Gabriel is dead and that they cannot be together. She reveals this, however, only after Sarah has been informed of their relationship and has confronted Edna. At the end of the play, as Edna is preparing to depart, Sarah enters, then shoots and kills Edna. Thus, even as Edna desires to pursue a life for herself—potentially one of fulfillment and romantic love—her life is ended. Although this moment can be read as a failure in the traditional sense, its failure actually has transformative potential.[18] The possibility of a love relationship forming between Ariel and Edna in the 1930s setting (with its attendant destructive racial and gender politics) represents a utopian vision, an idealized version of the world that works against the realities of their present society. The drama stops just short of imagining a world where the black and transgender Edna could openly cohabitate in an interracial relationship with the Jewish Ariel.

Although, Edna's killing constitutes a failure of one kind, José Muñoz allows us to read this failure differently. Muñoz explains that because utopia is always destined to fail, the conclusion one tends to draw is that queer utopias are also destined to fail. He continues,

> Despite this seeming negativity, a generative politics can be potentially distilled from the aesthetics of queer failure. Within failure, we can locate a kernel of potentiality. I align queer failure with a certain mode of virtuosity the helps the spectator exit from the stale and static lifeworld dominated by the alienation, exploitation, and drudgery associated with capitalism or landlordism. (*Cruising Utopia* 173)

Muñoz's notion of queer failure can also be productively read alongside Matt Richardson's conception of irresolution within black queer narratives. Irresolution challenges normative frameworks and forwards black resistance that includes and even centers black subjectivity. So, the failed partnering can be read as O'Hara's own enactment of fugitivity, in which he refuses to reconcile queer intimacy he depicts within normative frameworks or accepted notions of idealized endings. Edna and Ariel, in their failed coupling, offer a generative politics that causes audiences to reimagine the queer subject in Western history. The drama also reframes the home, refusing to depict it as site of domestic bliss and rather reveals it as a space of torture for enslaved subjects and as instrumental to the perpetuation of confining heteronormative social

---

18. Critic Bob Abelman reads the ending as anticlimactic and somewhat disappointing, explaining: "The play concludes as if the playwright painted himself into a corner with no reasonable way out. CPT's [Cleveland Public Theatre] overly dramatic presentation of this reinforces the impression that *Antebellum* is based on a brilliant concept that is sustained for most of the evening but, in the end, is gone with the wind."

structures. O'Hara's dramas allow the spectator to exit this space and rethink the past as well as the present.

Antebellum and *Insurrection* depict queer subjects in slavery and its aftermath who seek refuge in intimacy even as they exist under oppressive conditions. They refashion the pornotropic violence brought on by the domination of their bodies and find a space to resist this violence through pleasure and intimacy. In this way, we can understand their acts as performing fugitive intimacies. O'Hara not only envisions possibility through pleasure and intimacy, but he also critiques conceptions of home as a way of calling attention to how notions of home are problematic for black queer subjects. Thus, he refuses normative renderings of home that would serve to reinscribe black queer subjects into problematic spaces, thereby limiting the possibility for freedom. While his work has been read for its innovative disruptions of histories of slavery, it is O'Hara's intervention at the site of pleasure and intimacy that proves to be most consequential for his depiction of black and queer subjects. Turning our attention to matters of intimacy and pleasure reveals an unanticipated site of resistance that is rendered radical against the realities of all the ways slavery corrupted intimate acts and pleasure. In his dramas, O'Hara confronts and exceeds the queer limit of black memory. Contemplation on his radical representations of queer subjects during the slave era and its aftermath points us to an underexamined subject in our collective memory of slavery and American history from which queer subjects have often been erased in normative historical discourses.

EPILOGUE

Contemplating and Complicating Black Freedom

THE END of part 3 of Suzan-Lori Parks's *Father Comes Home from the Wars* is at once haunting and prophetic. Just as the drama's central figure Ulysses (once called Hero) prepares to read the Emancipation Proclamation to the enslaved subjects who remain on the plantation, the Runaway Slaves along with Ulysses's wife Penny and his antagonist Homer flee the plantation in search of freedom. When Ulysses explains to Odyssey Dog (his dog who can also speak) that everyone left before he could read the paper that declares them free, Odyssey intimates, "The Runaways, they still got to run" (159). Odyssey Dog's words suggest that in spite of any formal pronouncement of freedom, the act of escaping for the runaways must take place. That they "still got to run" can be read in a number of ways. The *still* signals an unrealized freedom of which the Runaways remain in search. Correspondingly, it suggests that their freedom won't be "real" until they achieve it themselves. The *still* also communicates that the proclamation on Ulysses's paper does not change the fact that The Runaways are fugitives. I end this book with a meditation on *Father Comes Home from the Wars* to explore how it utilizes the 1863 setting—the dawn of emancipation—to ask critical questions on the meaning of freedom. In doing so, I consider how Parks's drama theorizes notions of black fugitivity that I have examined throughout this book. *Father Comes Home*'s inconclusive ending points toward an uncertain future. In this sense, the notion that the Runaways "still got to run" gestures to a continuance of fugitivity that we can read in the context of the contemporary.

Set during the Civil War in the years 1862 and 1863, *Father Comes Home from the Wars: Parts 1, 2, and 3*, depicts a community of enslaved subjects negotiating the upheaval caused by the war and even exploiting this upheaval by escaping. The question of escape centers most squarely on the enslaved figure Hero, who has been offered freedom if he fights alongside his enslaver for the cause of the Confederacy. This impossible compromise becomes the primary conflict in part 1 of the drama. It is fitting that Hero has to make such a complex choice because we later learn that he should not be understood as a "hero" in the truest sense of the word. He has enacted a number of betrayals, particularly against the enslaved Homer. Hero informs his enslaver of Homer's plans to run away and performs the deed of chopping off Homer's foot as instructed by his enslaver after Homer is caught. Hero's enslaver promised freedom for assisting with Homer's capture; however, he never delivered on that promise (49). In a series of events, Hero's freedom is tied to unconscionable choices. Thus, from the drama's outset, Parks troubles notions of freedom and its costs. We learn in part 2 that Hero indeed joins his enslaver to fight as a Confederate soldier. There he meets Smith, a Union Army Captain, who has been captured by Hero's enslaver. In this section of the drama, Smith informs Hero that he is actually passing as white and was formerly enslaved. Smith encourages Hero to join him in running away and fighting with the Union Army, but he ultimately refuses. Before they separate, however, they contemplate their financial and human worth in a post-Emancipation America. Hero asks: "'I belong to the Colonel,' I says now. That's how come they don't beat me. But when Freedom comes and they stop me and ask and I say, 'I'm my own. I'm on my own and I own my ownself,' you think they'll leave me be?" (96). This question represents the many questions surrounding the status of formerly enslaved subjects in the wake of freedom. Parks captures the complications involved in transitioning an entire population from enslaved to free.

When Hero returns in part 3 as Ulysses (his changed name now carrying multiple significations from the Union Amy General Ulysses S. Grant to the literary figure in James Joyce's novel, which also signifies upon Homer's epic poem *The Odyssey* and upon which Parks, too, signifies in this drama) we learn that he has indeed survived the war though his enslaver did not. He also discloses that he has betrayed his wife Penny by coupling with an enslaved woman named Alberta. The drama ends ambiguously, as stated earlier, with Homer and Penny choosing to escape with a set of runaways. They do so, however, before learning that they have already been declared "free."

Parks's concern with the performativity of language in relation to freedom comes through at a number of times in the play. Considering words as "spells in our mouths," Parks asserts that language is physical and it is through digesting words that we are able to perform them on stage (*The America Play* 17). Language makes theater possible, but, as it relates to *Father Comes Home*, it also makes freedom possible. "The Truth will set you free / Even if the Master don't," the Oldest Old Man proclaims (15). In this instance Parks locates within language authority and authorship that transcends socially constructed dynamics of power. One need not wait for a formal declaration of freedom. The possibility to free one's self before emancipation is formally declared (lies within the individual). As *Father Comes Home* progresses, there is a continual reframing of power in relation to language. The Old Man later illumines, "Even though you are owned by another man / Your words are your bond. / They're part of your record. / Words and deeds both" (48). Just as the Old Man upends power dynamics of ownership through language, he also reorients the relationship between the bondage to which the enslaved characters are subject and places that power in the hands of those enslaved subjects. The subtext of the Oldest Old Man's words communicates to the enslaved subjects that their words are their bond and not the status of their existences, that instead of being bondspersons, they can use language to determine the strictures that bind them. Speech acts then become a form of self-possession. More than that, these same words become the record, thereby creating counternarratives of their lives. "Words and deeds" become interconnected to undermine the written language on deeds and bills of sale that deny the enslaved their humanity and agency. It is then fitting that the Runaways do not hear the words of the Emancipation Proclamation read by Hero/Ulysses, given that he proclaims that he cut out his soul and gave it up to his enslaver (156) and because the drama has already structured the narrative so that enslavers and other governmental power structures cannot determine the "free" status of black subjects. And if we follow the logic of emancipation as unrealized, it is clear that those words did little to grant true freedom to the formerly enslaved.

The drama in its use of language to reorient power away from enslavers and to the enslaved as well as its continual return to characters who voice uncertainty about what their lives will be once free keeps the question of freedom at the forefront of the drama. Indeed, *Father Comes Home from the Wars* reflects Parks's larger critical project of contemplating and complicating the meaning of black freedom in her dramas. With works such as *The America Play* and *Topdog/Underdog* that invoke Abraham Lincoln, issuer of the Emancipation Proclamation, Parks places in conversation the historical moment of emancipation and the condition of black subjects in its aftermath. Lincoln even appears indirectly in *Father Comes Home*. A feature character of the drama is "Penny," whose name calls up the currency that bears Lincoln's face. In the *LA Times*, Charles McNulty asserts, "Parks takes up a classic subject of drama—freedom—exploring it not just as an existential conundrum à la Sophocles but as a traumatic historical condition." Parks, in centering black American subjects ruminating the question of freedom, certainly frames freedom as an existential conundrum and traumatic historical condition. Yet, we should also understand the question of freedom as a future-minded one: How to attain and maintain freedom? How to enact freedom? Parks articulates similar questions as driving her work: "What do you do if you're allowed to own yourself? How can you own yourself even before freedom comes? And after freedom comes, what is the best use of yourself?" (McNulty). Parks's questions reinforce the notion that freedom during the American Civil War did not hinge on the war's outcome. In fact, Parks suggests through her ominous ending that emancipation has not yet been realized for black subjects. In her depiction of the unrealized transition from enslaved to free in *Father Comes Home from the Wars*, Parks reconceptualizes freedom.

Parks's drama also draws connecting lines across time to show a kind of psychic continuity between the "traumatic historical condition" of freedom and its ambiguous iterations for black subjects even today. In fact, *Father Comes Home from the Wars* addresses issues that extend beyond the Civil War and into Parks's own experience of receiving her father after his return from Vietnam. Parks contextualizes her father's service in Vietnam as an illustration of the limits of freedom for black men during this time. She says, "I always understood that my dad joined the army because it was the only place a black man could get a fair shake. The fact that the government was fucked up wasn't his problem. The government has been fucked up since day one. And my dad never gloried in war or his military service." That her father joined the army out of necessity signals Parks's own acknowledgement that even long after the Civil War ended freedom wasn't a given for black Americans. Much like Hero felt compelled to fight alongside his enslaver for the Confederate Army in order to attain freedom, Parks's father enlists in the US imperial project via war even as black Americans like him suffer the consequences of this power.

Interestingly, Parks finds inspiration in her father's military service in spite of its underlying tensions. The title of the play signals a return from the "wars," plural, although the Civil War was the featured conflict in the play and the Vietnam War featured singularly in Parks's life. In reading "wars" multiply, we can envision Parks gesturing to war, writ large, internal and external, atemporal and ongoing. Moreover, the fact that preparations for war are referred to as "rehearsals" bears significance for Parks theatrically. In many respects, Parks transforms "rehearsals for war" into rehearsals of freedom for black subjects. At the time that Parks was preparing to present *Father Comes Home from the Wars* in October 2014, that summer and into the fall of the same year US media was populated with images of protest and citizens staring down a militarized police force on the streets of Ferguson, Missouri, in the aftermath of the killing of Michael Brown. Imagery of the confrontation calls up battle. Black citizens took to the streets to make visible the subterranean war on black communities waged by the criminal justice system. The fight not only reveals the war but the quest for freedom on the part of the black protestors. Parks even includes a moment where Hero places his hands over his head in the iconic "hands up, don't shoot" gesture that became synonymous with Michael Brown and accounts of his murder at the hands of police. Sterling K. Brown, who starred as Hero/Ulysses in the 2014 Public Theatre production, recalls the emotionally charged backdrop of the performances and his personal connection to the events because he grew up in St. Louis, Missouri. He says,

> And so the resonance that [the question of freedom and self-ownership after slavery] has for me, in particular, being from St. Louis and doing this play in NYC—the incident with Mike Brown had transpired in Ferguson. The failure to indict happened while we were performing the show. And it was just heart-wrenching on a personal level for me. I go back to this statement from the Watchman: "Who watches the Watchman?" (Villarreal)

Father Comes Home from the Wars speaks to the relevance of the past in the present as well as the unresolved aspects of the past continuing to haunt the present.

The tensions of freedom that Parks captures in her drama link compellingly to Claudia Rankine's mixed media exploration of this subject matter in her celebrated work, *Citizen: An American Lyric,* which also entered public discourse in 2014. Like Parks's drama, *Citizen* explores the meaning of and particularly the limits of freedom through an archetypal representation of black experience where the names Citizen and Hero become problematized to reflect the complexity of such notions for black subjects. Just as there is no "hero" in Parks's drama, the black subjects in Rankine's work are not recognized as citizens with the right to articulate a full expression of their humanity without consequences. Rankine's title also intersects with August Wilson's character Citizen of *Gem of the Ocean,* featured in chapter 2. From Wilson to Rankine we see an ongoing interrogation of what citizenship means for black subjects and the realization that it has yet to be achieved. Collectively, these works reinforce the idea that the black citizen is still a fugitive within her/his own country, still running in search of freedom.

I want to consider Rankine's work alongside Parks because it articulates the aftermath of the unresolved emancipation that Parks makes clear with her ending. In bringing together prose, poetry, and the visual arts, *Citizen* offers a moving exploration of racial trauma from the microagressions[1] black individuals experience in the workplace to racial profiling and the pain of ongoing socially sanctioned violence against black subjects from Trayvon Martin and beyond. The work explores the failed realization of citizenship rights, particularly the denial of civic membership that Salamishah Tillet so powerfully articulates.[2] It also returns us to Chief Justice Taney's words reproduced at the open of this book in context of the *Dred Scott* case—that the Negro has no rights that the white man is bound to respect. Rankine poignantly communicates this in her work, calling attention to what Sharon P. Holland describes as the "unaccomplished shift from enslaved to free" in the white imagination.

I linger on the final image presented in Rankine's work, J. M. W. Turner's 1840 painting, *The Slave Ship: Slavers Throwing Overboard the Dead and Dying—Typhoon Coming On*, to contemplate slavery's continued resonance in the contemporary and how that is articulated in *Citizen* (see figure 9). The portrait depicts an ominous and sublime scene of panic out of fear of an oncoming storm provoking the ship's crew to throw enslaved subjects overboard so that they might be able to collect insurance money. They could not do so if the enslaved died onboard of natural causes. Body parts of the enslaved, particularly their legs and feet shackled with chains, become more visible upon deeper consideration of the portrait. Upon a closer look, one can see fish and other sea creatures waiting to feast upon the bodies. The devastation and carnage displayed in the image was powerful enough (in concert with other abolitionist efforts) to spur the British government in 1850 to call for an end to slavery in all Atlantic nations.

When queried on why she chose to end with an image from the slave era even though *Citizen* focuses almost exclusively on the present, Rankine explains,

> I didn't want to create false hope.... I thought, "Gosh, this problem has been around since the market—since black bodies were part of the market. When they were objects. When they were considered property." And that equation

---

1. Michael Woodford et. al. define microagressions as "everyday derogatory slights directed toward marginalized populations" (417).
2. See Salamishah Tillet's *Sites of Slavery: Citizenship and Racial Democracy in the Post-Civil Rights Imagination*.

FIGURE 9. J. M. W. Turner's *The Slave Ship: Slavers Throwing Overboard the Dead and Dying—Typhoon Coming On*

between whiteness and the black body as property of whiteness is the equation we can't get out of.... I wanted to end [*Citizen*] with Turner because people always say, "Well, I didn't know. It wasn't my intention. I wish I had known more about this...." But Turner knew better in the 1800s. He knew better. And this is 2015. So, there it was. The end. (Lydon)

Referring to the conflation of black bodies with property in slavery as an "equation we can't get out of" recalls Smith's words to Hero in *Father Comes Home* where he speculates, "Maybe even with Freedom, that mark, huh, that mark of the marketplace, it will always be on us" (98). Both sentiments interrogate the limitations of so-called freedom for black subjects. In her invocation of slavery in her work and her commentary on the choice to do so, Rankine identifies the central problem of race in the modern era as the perpetuation of black bodies as property. She makes clear that in spite of the progress made on issues of race and racism in America, the foundational experience of slavery continues to bear on the present.

Citizen also yields insight into why black fugitivity remains animated in black life long after slavery. For the black subject, the attempt to escape the dynamic of one's body continuing to be equated with property can be akin to an out-of-body experience. It means to be at once free and not free, citizen and noncitizen. Rankine narrates this separation from one's own body as well as the nation with the following:

> When you lay your body in the body
> entered as if skin and bone were public places,
>
> when you lay your body in the body
> entered as if you're the ground you walk on,
>
> you know no memory should live
> in these memories
>
> becoming the body of you.
> (144)

Here Rankine demarcates a private self (your body) with a public self (the body), the former representing the black subject as s/he defines him or herself and the latter signaling the body that the society has constructed. This subject resists interpolation into these realities ("no memory should live / in these memories") in an acknowledgement that these ever-repeating patterns must be disrupted in order to undo the equation.

Rankine goes further to highlight the pain of navigating a world that both sees and does not see you, where one experiences the injury of "feeling you don't belong so much / to you—" (146). The crisis of self-ownership for black subjects and the continued estrangement from the nation describes the conditions that motivate black subjects' ongoing strategies of escape in search of more emancipatory possibilities for their lives. Through the interactions that structure everyday experience, black subjects must often reckon with the reality of their sociopolitical confinement and non-belonging. Moreover, the implicit and ongoing viewing of black bodies as property challenges the black subject's right to define him/herself and to assert control over cultural myths that continue to constrain his/her existence.

Throughout this book, I have traced contemporary black drama's engagements with slavery, contextualized the development of these works with black theatrical precedents, and situated this growing body of work within the neo-slave narrative tradition. I also explored what I see as contemporary black drama's coalescence around the critical project of troubling our understandings of slavery and forwarding new representations of black subjectivity, past and present. I term these performance strategies—"performances of fugitivity" because this framework captures both the artistic and political implications of ongoing conditions of unfreedom for black creatives and black subjects writ large negotiating racial politics in America across time. Thus, I locate performances of fugitivity in the artistic endeavors to escape essentialized and contained notions of blackness while creating greater representational possibilities for black subjects. I also locate it in the subversive commentary underscoring the dramas, which suggests that the work of black political and social emancipation remains unfinished.

Moving from August Wilson's problematizing of citizenship against a post-Emancipation backdrop to Suzan-Lori Parks's own treatment of the subject, I develop an analysis on the limits of freedom that necessitate fugitivity. I consider how Wilson produces a counterarchive of material histories and upends familiar imagery of enslavement by presenting a visually abstract instantiation of the tortured black bodies of the Middle Passage, which reorients the gaze away from familiar images of brutalized black bodies and toward a more humanizing, nonexploitative depiction. I continue the analysis of how dramatists re-present black enslaved subjects via bodily and racially deconstructive practices with Lydia Diamond's *Harriet Jacobs* and Branden Jacobs-Jenkins's *An Octoroon*. Both dramas provide the opportunity to zoom in on how fugitivity can constitute an artful escape of objectification for black cultural producers. I also ruminate on this in my analysis of Robert O'Hara's dramas, *Insurrection: Holding History* and *Antebellum*, where queer experience becomes centered in the narrativizing of slavery. I consider queer fugitivity as a mode of resistant black performance that not only corrects the erasure of queer subjects from histories of slavery but also harnesses the affect of pleasure to make these representations possible while also expanding our conceptions of black affective experience. O'Hara's dramas also prompt a rethinking of home, which serves as an overarching concept that returns us to contemplations of belonging for black subjects. The black subjects who populate this book are often instantiated as bodies without a nation, in flight, and in search of liberation. Collectively, these dramas ask us to think otherwise in our engagement with the slave past.

The dramas I examine within this book constitute a new and radical approach to representing slavery that we have yet to fully consider. My work offers an invitation to examine this rich body of work on slavery and the innovative ways it depicts the institution, how it defamiliarizes representations of black bodies, troubles the gaze, and forwards new understandings of this history and blackness at once. Although critical movement has occurred in developing a theory for reading contemporary black dramas featuring slavery, my work offers a sustained study of drama's productive expansion of the capacities of the neo-slave narrative genre. In the same way that the neo-slave narrative seeks to tell counternarratives of slavery and speak to the sociopolitical zeitgeist of its era, contemporary black dramas about slavery offer a counternarrative of this history while drawing upon the body as an additional text with which to engage slavery. Moreover, through embodied performance, these dramas can speak to the affective and visual dimensions of black experience in compelling ways.

This book offers a thorough consideration of drama's place in an integral genre of black literary production. In more directly linking the genre as it is rendered in the form of the novel with black theatrical performance, we gain new possibilities for understanding both the neo-slave narrative genre as well as the black theatrical canon. It also continues the critical work of interrogating our received histories of slavery to make space for new readings of these histories. In doing so, theater is continually engaged in the act of "making history" as Suzan-Lori Parks would have it.

In its "Room for Debate" series, *The New York Times* called upon scholars and cultural critics to explore the question: "Do dramas about slavery stifle the tales of black lives now?" The conversation was sparked by rising sentiment that there are too many films in Hollywood being produced about slavery. (With The History Channel's remake of *Roots,* WGN's series "Underground" that features enslaved subjects plotting their escape, and films such as Nate Parker's *Birth of a Nation,* which is based on the Nat Turner story, it is true that slavery is indeed having a moment.) Responses to this question ranged from an indictment of Hollywood for exploiting histories of black suffering while not engaging contemporary black suffering to lamenting the limited roles this trend creates for black actors, to reminding audiences of how tales about slavery fill gaps in the American educational system, which has largely failed to engage the subject in a nuanced way ("Room for Debate").

Black theater featuring slavery demonstrates the necessity of the critical project of offering alternative narratives and perspectives to received histories of slavery. Black dramas offer space where the archive is interrogated and new understandings of the peculiar institution are advanced. They also offer a space for contemporary black subjects to negotiate feelings of unbelonging and to contextualize the troubling present with the slave past. In this sense, slavery can serve as a heuristic for articulating contemporary conditions of black life and returning to this history can provide a launching point for new articulations of blackness that complicate our understandings of black subjects, past and present.

The dramas taken up in this book do not simply retell the history of slavery. They re-present it in a way that enlarges the narrative possibilities for representing this history. If we consider performance as twice-behaved behavior, and always subject to revision, these dramas offer an active space to engage slavery as it passes through the culture and is performed by different individuals who interpret the work from various vantage points. These dramas, then, give black subjects the authority to participate in the narrativizing of their own histories and themselves in the process. As such, these performances of fugitivity can be most accurately read as rehearsals of freedom with each iteration moving the black subject ever closer to liberation.

WORKS CITED

Abelman, Bob. "'Antebellum' Writer's Concept is Brilliant, But Potential Not Quite Realized." *The News-Herald,* 27 Feb. 2012, www.newsherald.com/article/HR/20120227/NEWS/302279971. Accessed 1 July 2016.

"African Burial Ground Memorial." *General Services Administration,* www.gsa.gov/about-us/regions/welcome-to-northeast-caribbean-region-2/about-region-2/the-african-burial-ground. Accessed 14 July 2015.

Allen, Michael O. "Ground Zero Yields Burial Ground Relics." *New York Daily News,* 15 Nov. 2001, www.nydailynews.com/archives/news/ground-zero-yields-burial-ground-relics-article-1.920604. Accessed 11 July 2016.

Anderson, Benedict. *Imagined Communities: Reflections on the Origin and Spread of Nationalism.* Revised ed., Verso, 2006.

Bada, Valérie. *Mnemopoetics: Memory and Slavery in African American Drama.* P. I. E. Peter Lang, 2008.

Baldwin, James. "Negroes are Anti-Semitic Because They're Anti-white." *The New York Times,* 9 Apr. 1967, www.nytimes.com/books/98/03/29/specials/baldwin-antisem.html. Accessed 11 June 2016.

Balon, Rebecca. "Kinless or Queer: The Unthinkable Queer Slave in Toni Morrison's *Beloved* and Robert O'Hara's *Insurrection: Holding History.*" *African American Review,* vol. 48, nos. 1–2, 2015, pp. 141–55.

Baraka, Amiri (LeRoi Jones). *Home: Social Essays.* William Morrow and Company, 1966.

———. "Slave Ship." *The Motion of History and Other Plays.* William Morrow and Company, 1978. pp. 129–45.

Barfield, Tanya. *Blue Door.* Dramatists Play Service, 2007.

Bell, Bernard. *The Afro-American Novel and its Tradition.* U of Massachussetts P, 1989.

Bellamy, Maria. *Bridges to Memory: Postmemory in Contemporary Ethnic American Women's Fiction.* U of Virginia P, 2015.

Bent, Eliza. "Branden Jacobs-Jenkins: Feel that Thought." *American Theatre.* 25 May 2014. https://www.americantheatre.org/2014/05/15/brandenjacobsjenkins_appropriate_octoroon-2/. Accessed 12 June 2016.

WORKS CITED

Berryman, Ruby C. "Distilling Genocide into Drama: Adaptation of Holocaust and Slave Narratives to the Stage." *The Quint: An Interdisciplinary Quarterly from the North*, vol. 6, no. 4, 2014, pp. 82–112.

Best, Stephen. "On Failing to Make the Past Present." *Modern Language Quarterly*, vol. 73, no. 3, 2012, pp. 453–74, doi.org/10.1215/00267929-1631478.

Best, Stephen, and Saidiya Hartman. "Fugitive Justice." *Representations*, vol. 92, no. 1, 2005, pp. 1–15. *JSTOR*, doi 10.1525/rep.2005.92.1.1. Accessed 10 Aug. 2017.

Boucicault, Dion. *The Octoroon: A Broadview Anthology of British Literature Edition*, Broadview Press, 2014.

Brand, Dionne. *A Map to the Door of No Return: Notes to Belonging*. Vintage Canada, 2002.

Brantley, Ben. "Review: 'An Octoroon,' a Branden Jacobs-Jenkins Comedy about Race." *The New York Times*, 26 Feb. 2015, www.nytimes.com/2015/02/27/theater/review-an-octoroon-a-branden-jacobs-jenkins-comedy-about-race.html. Accessed 10 May 2016.

"The Breakfast Table: An Email Conversation about the News of the Day: John Lahr and August Wilson." *Slate*, 10–13 Sept. 2001, www.slate.com/articles/life/the_breakfast_table/features/2001/john_lahr_and_august_wilson/_2.html. Accessed 9 Feb. 2015.

Brecht, Stefan. "LeRoi Jones's *Slave Ship*." *The Drama Review: TDR*, vol. 14, no. 2, 1970, pp. 212–19.

Brooks, Daphne. *Bodies in Dissent: Spectacular Performances of Race and Freedom, 1850–1910*. Duke UP, 2006.

Brown, Kimberly Juanita. *The Repeating Body: Slavery's Visual Resonance in the Contemporary*. Duke UP, 2015.

Brown, Sterling K. Interview by Yvonne Villarreal. *Los Angeles Times*, 27 Apr. 2016, https://www.latimes.com/entertainment/arts/la-et-cm-sterling-k-brown-20160427-story.html. Accessed 10 July 2017.

Brown, William Wells. *The Escape; Or, A Leap for Freedom*. U of Tennessee P, 2001.

Bruce, La Marr Jurelle. "Mad is a Place; Or, the Slave Ship Tows the Ship of Fools." *American Quarterly*, vol. 69, no. 2, pp. 303–08, Johns Hopkins UP, 2017, doi:10.1353/aq.2017.0024.

Buckner, Joycelyn. "Performance Review: *Harriet Jacobs* by Lydia Diamond. Directed by Jessica Thebus. Kansas City Repertory Theatre. Copaken Stage, Kansas City. 30 October 2010." *Theatre Journal*, vol. 63, no. 3, 2011, pp. 460–62, doi: 10.1353/tj.2011.0084

Burnham, Michelle. "Loopholes of Resistance: Harriet Jacobs' Slave Narrative and the Critique of Agency in Foucault." *Arizona Quarterly: A Journal of American Literature, Culture, and Theory*, vol. 49, no. 2, 1993, pp. 53–73.

Butler, Judith. *Precarious Life: The Powers of Mourning and Violence*. Verso, 2004.

———. "What's Wrong with 'All Lives Matter'?" Interview by George Yancy, *The Stone, The New York Times*, 12 Jan. 2015, opinionator.blogs.nytimes.com/2015/01/12/whats-wrong-with-all-lives-matter/. Accessed 11 Apr. 2016.

Bynum, Tara. "Phillis Wheatley on Friendship." *Legacy*, vol. 31, no. 1, 2014, pp. 42–51.

Carpenter, Faedra. *Coloring Whiteness: Acts of Critique in Black Performance*. U of Michigan P, 2014.

———. "Robert O'Hara's *Insurrection*: Que(e)rying History." *Text and Performance Quarterly*, vol. 23, no. 2, 2003, pp. 186–204. *EbscoHost*, doi:10.1080/1046293032000141365

Carpio, Glenda. *Laughing Fit to Kill: Black Humor in the Fictions of Slavery*. Oxford UP, 2008.

Catanese, Brandi. *The Problem of the Color[blind]: Racial Transgression and the Politics of Black Performance*. U of Michigan P, 2011.

Chávez, Karma. "From Sanctuary to a Queer Politics of Fugitivity." *QED: A Journal in LGBTQ Worldmaking*, vol. 4, no. 2, 2017, pp. 63–70

Clarke, John Henrik, editor. *William Styron's Nat Turner: Ten Black Writers Respond*. Praeger, 1987.

Clarke, Kamari Maxine. "Transnational Yoruba Revivalism and the Diasporic Politics of Heritage." *American Ethnologist*, vol. 34, no. 4, 2007, pp. 721–34. *JSTOR*, www.jstor.org/stable/4496846. Accessed 24 Sept. 2017.

Colbert, Soyica D. *The African American Theatrical Body: Reception, Performance, and the Stage*. Cambridge UP, 2011.

Colbert, Soyica Diggs, et al. *The Psychic Hold of Slavery: Legacies in American Expressive Culture*. Rutgers UP, 2016.

"Columbia the Gem of the Ocean" Library of Congress. https://www.loc.gov/item/ihas .200000004/. Accessed 10 February 2019.

Commander, Michelle. *Afro-Atlantic Flight: Speculative Returns and the Black Fantastic*. Duke UP, 2017.

Cotter, William R. "The Somerset Case and the Abolition of Slavery in England." *History*, vol. 79, no. 255, 1994, pp. 31–56. *JSTOR*, www.jstor.org/stable/24421930.

Crawford, Margo Natalie. "The Inside-Turned-Out Architecture of the Post-Neo-Slave Narrative." Colbert, Patterson, and Levy-Hussen, pp. 69–85.

———. *Black Post-Blackness: The Black Arts Movement and Twenty-First-Century Aesthetics*. U of Illinois P, 2017.

———. "'What Was Is': The Time and Space of Entanglement Erased by Post-blackness." *The Trouble with Post-blackness*, edited by Houston A. Baker and Merinda Simmons, Columbia UP, 2015, pp. 21–43.

"Creating New Traditions: Maintaining Cultural Identity through New Burial Rituals. Burial #242." *The African Burial Ground*, U of California—Berkley, www.ocf.berkeley.edu/ ~arihuang/academic/abg/artifacts/culturalartifacts.html. Accessed 11 July 2016.

"The Culture of Gullah." *Museum of the City*, www.museumofthecity.org/project/the-culture-of -gullah/. Accessed 20 Sept. 2017.

Dezell, Maureen. "A 10-Play Odyssey Continues with *Gem of the Ocean*." *Conversations with August Wilson*, edited by Jackson R. Bryer and Mary C. Hartig. U of Mississippi P, 2006, pp. 253–56.

Diamond, Lydia. "The Author's America." Centerstage Theatre, Baltimore, MD. Perf. Tracie Thoms. 2012. *Vimeo*, uploaded by Centerstage, vimeo.com/49452938. Accessed Jan. 2015.

———. *Harriet Jacobs: A Play*. Northwestern UP, 2011.

Dickson-Carr, Darryl. *African American Satire: The Sacredly Profane Novel*. U of Missouri P, 2001.

Diouf, Sylviane A. *Slavery's Exiles: The Story of the American Maroons*. New York UP, 2014.

Dodd, Alexandra. "Dressed to Thrill: The Victorian Postmodern and Counter-Archival Imaginings in the Work of Mary Sibande." *Critical Arts*, vol. 24, no. 3, 2010, pp. 467–74. *Taylor & Francis Online*. dx.doi.org.ezproxy.tcu.edu/10.1080/02560046.2010.511883. Accessed 17 Sept. 2017.

Douglass, Frederick. *Narrative of the Life of Frederick Douglass*. Dover Publications, 1995.

Elam, Jr., Harry. *The Past as Present in the Drama of August Wilson*. The U of Michigan P, 2004.

———. *Taking it to the Streets: The Social Protest Theatre of Luis Valdez and Amiri Baraka*. The U of Michigan P, 1997.

Eng, David, and David Kazanjian. *Loss: The Politics of Mourning*. U of California P, 2003.

Eng, David and Shinhee Han. "A Dialogue on Racial Melancholia." *Psychoanalytic Dialogues*, vol. 10, no. 4, 2000, pp. 667–700.

Ernest, John. "The Reconstruction of Whiteness: William Wells Brown's 'The Escape'; Or a Leap for Freedom." *PMLA*, vol. 113, no. 5, 1998, doi: 10.2307/463245.

Fabricant, Daniel. "Thomas R. Gray and William Styron: Finally, A Critical Look at the 1831 Confessions of Nat Turner." *The American Journal of Legal History*, vol. 37, no. 3, 1993, pp. 332–61. *JSTOR*, doi: 10.2307/845661.

Fleetwood, Nicole. *Troubling Vision: Performance, Visuality, and Blackness*. U of Chicago P, 2011.

Ford, James Edward. "Introduction." *Black Camera*, vol. 7, no. 1, 2015, pp. 110–14. *Project Muse*, muse.jhu.edu/article/606132. Accessed 4 June 2017.

Foster, Frances Smith, and Nellie McKay. *Incidents in the Life of a Slave Girl: Contexts Criticism*, A Norton Critical edition, W. W. Norton and Company, 2001, pp. 278–94.

Foster, Verna. "Meta-Melodrama: Brandon Jacobs-Jenkins Appropriates Dion Boucicault's *The Octoroon*." *Modern Drama*, vol. 50, no. 3, 2016, pp. 285–305, doi: 10.3138/md.0792R.

Freeman, Elizabeth. *Time Binds: Queer Temporalities, Queer Histories*. Duke UP, 2010.

Frund, Arlette. "Phillis Wheatley: A Public Intellectual." *Toward an Intellectual History of Black Women*. Kindle ed., edited by Mia Bay, Farrah Griffin, Martha Jones, and Dianne Savage. The U of North Carolina P, 2015, pp. 35–52.

Gates, Henry Louis. *The Trials of Phillis Wheatley: America's First Black Poet and Her Encounters with the Founding Fathers*. E-Book ed., Basic Civitas Books, 2003.

Greenberg, Cheryl. "The Politics of Disorder: Reexamining Harlem's Riots of 1935 and 1943." *Journal of Urban History*, vol. 18, no. 4, 1992, pp. 395–441.

Gumbs, Alexis P. *Spills: Scenes of Black Feminist Fugitivity*. E-Book ed., Duke UP, 2016, ebookcentral.proquest.com/lib/TCU/detail.action?docID=4690047.

Halberstam, Jack *In a Queer Time and Place: Transgender Bodies, Subcultural Lives*. New York UP, 2005.

Handy, W. C. *Father of the Blues: An Autobiography*. Edited by Arna Bontemps, Da Capo Press, 1969.

Hannah, John. "'A World Made in My Image': Romare Bearden's Collagist Technique in August Wilson's *Joe Turner's Come and Gone*." *Reading Contemporary African American Drama: Fragments of History, Fragments of Self*, edited by Trudier Harris. Peter Lang, 2007, pp. 121–52.

Hansberry, Lorraine. *The Collected Last Plays*. Edited by Robert Nemiroff, Vintage Books, 1994.

———. *To Be Young, Gifted, and Black*. Edited by Robert Nemiroff, Signet Classics Reissue Edition, 2011.

Harney, Stefano, and Fred Moten. *The Undercommons: Fugitive Planning & Black Study*. Minor Compositions, 2013, www.minorcompositions.info/wpcontent/uploads/2013/04/undercommons-web.pdf. Accessed 10 Aug. 2017.

Harvey, David. "Dred Scott, John San(d)ford, and the Case for Collusion." *Northern Kentucky Law Review.* Vol. 41.1 (2014): 37–66.

"Harriet Jacobs Symposium—Timothy McCarthy 2." *YouTube,* uploaded by CentralSquareTheater, 17 Jan. 2010, www.youtube.com/watch?v=EAtcomRuKow. Accessed 15 Jan. 2015.

Harris, Chery. "Whitness as Property" *Harvard Law Review,* vol. 106, no. 8, 1993, pp. 1707–91.

Hartman, Saidiya. *Lose Your Mother: A Journey Along the Atlantic Slave Route.* Farrar, Straus, and Giroux, 2007.

———. *Scenes of Subjection: Terror, Slavery, and Self-Making in Nineteenth-Century America.* Oxford UP, 1997.

Haverson, Susan. "'Harriet Jacobs' Offers a Glimpse of Slavery." *Bay State Banner,* 3 Mar. 2010, baystatebanner.com/news/2010/mar/03/harriet-jacobs-offers-a-glimpse-of-slavery/. Accessed 10 May 2017.

Hill, Errol, and James Hatch. *A History of African American Theatre.* Cambridge UP, 2003.

Hirsch, Foster. "*Slaveship* by Leroi Jones." *Educational Theatre Journal,* vol. 22, no. 1, 1970, pp. 102–03.

Holland, Sharon Patricia. "Forward: 'Home' is a Four-Letter Word." *Black Queer Studies: A Critical Anthology,* edited by E. Patrick Johnson and Mae G. Henderson, Duke UP, 2005, pp. ix–xiii.

———. *Raising the Dead: Readings of Death and (Black) Subjectivity.* Duke UP, 2000.

Iton, Richard. *In Search of the Black Fantastic: Politics and Popular Culture in the Post-Civil Rights Era.* Oxford UP, 2008.

Jacobs, Harriet. *Incidents in the Life of a Slave Girl: Contexts, Criticism.* A Norton Critical Edition, edited by Nellie McKay and Frances Smith Foster, W. W. Norton and Company, 2001. pp. 1–158

Jacobs-Jenkins, Branden. *An Octoroon.* New York: Dramatists Playservice, Inc., 2015.

———. *An Octoroon.* SoHo Rep Production. 6 June 2014. New York Public Library Theatre on Film and Tape Archives. Accessed 20 November 2017.

Johnson, E. Patrick. *Appropriating Blackness: Performance and the Politics of Authenticity.* Duke UP, 2003.

Jones, Jacqueline M. "We 'the People': Freedom, Civics, and the Neo-Slave Narrative Tradition in August Wilson's *Gem of the Ocean.*" *Modern Language Studies,* vol. 46, no. 1, 2016, pp. 10–23.

Keizer, Arlene. *Black Subjects: Identity Formation in the Contemporary Narrative of Slavery.* Cornell UP, 2004.

Klammer, Martin. *Whitman, Slavery, and the Emergence of* Leaves of Grass. Penn State UP, 2010.

Knight, Christina. "'Fasten Your Shackles': Remembering Slavery and Laughing about it in George C. Wolfe's *The Colored Museum.*" *African American Review,* vol. 45, no. 3, 2012, pp. 355–69.

Littleway, Lorna. *Phillis Wheatley: The Celestial Muse.* 1979, Box 18, Folder 3. *The Camille Billops and James Hatch Collection.* Manuscripts and Rare Book Library, Emory U, 18 May 2015.

Levy-Hussen, Aida. *How to Read African American Literature: Post-Civil Rights Fiction and the Task of Interpretation.* New York UP, 2016.

Lott, Eric. *Love and Theft: Blackface Minstrelsy and the American Working Class.* Oxford UP, 1993.

Lorde, Audre. *Sister Outsider: Essays and Speeches by Audre Lorde.* Crossing Press, 2007.

Lydon, Christopher. "Claudia Rankine's *Citizen*." Radio Open Source: Arts, Ideas, and Politics with Christopher Lydon. 30 August 2016. http://radioopensource.org/claudia-rankine/. Accessed 30 August 2016.

Lyons, Bonnie. "An Interview with August Wilson." *Conversations with August Wilson*, edited by Jackson R. Bryer and Mary C. Hartig. UP of Mississippi, pp. 204–22.

Macharia, Keguro. "fugitivity." *Gukira—With(out) Predicates*, 2 July 2013, gukira.wordpress.com/2013/07/02/fugitivity/. Accessed 10 Sept. 2017.

May, Cedrick. *Evangelism and Resistance in the Black Atlantic, 1760–1835*. The U of Georgia P, 2008.

McAllister, Marvin. *Whiting Up: Whiteface Minstrels and Stage Europeans in African American Performance*. U of North Carolina P, 2011.

McCauley, Robbie. *Sally's Rape*. Moon Marked *and* Touched by Sun: *Plays by African-American Women*, edited by Sydné Mahone. Theatre Communications Group, 1994, pp. 211–38.

McKittrick, Katherine. *Demonic Grounds: Black Women and the Cartographies of Struggle*. U of Minnesota P, 2006.

McNulty, Charles. "Suzan-Lori Parks' 'Father Comes Home From the Wars' is an entrancingly intimate drama" Los Angeles Times, 18 April 2016. Accessed 20 August 2017.

Mitchell, Angelyn. *The Freedom to Remember: Narrative, Slavery, and Gender in Contemporary Black Women's Fiction*. Rutgers UP, 2002.

Morgan, Jennifer. *Laboring Women: Reproduction and Gender in New World Slavery*. U of Pennsylvania Press, 2004.

Morrison, Toni. *Beloved*. Plume, 1998.

———. "The Site of Memory." *Inventing the Truth: The Art and Craft of Memoir*, edited by William Zinsser. Houghton Mifflin, 1995, pp. 83–102.

Moten, Fred. *In the Break: The Aesthetics of the Black Radical Tradition*. U of Minnesota P, 2003.

Muñoz, José. *Cruising Utopia: The Then and There of Queer Futurity*. New York UP, 2009.

Myers, Victoria. "An Interview with Lydia R. Diamond." *The Interval NY*, 16 Feb. 2016, theintervalny.com/interviews/2016/02/an-interview-with-lydia-r-diamond/. Accessed 10 May 2017.

Nathans, Heather. "Visualizing August Wilson's *Gem of the Ocean*." *New England Theatre Journal*, vol. 19A, no. 1, 2008, pp. 75–86. *ProQuest*, library.tcu.edu/PURL/EZproxy_link.asp?http://search.proquest.com/docview/2277390?accountid=7090. Accessed 3 Feb. 2015.

Nemiroff, Robert. *To Be Young, Gifted, and Black: Lorraine Hansberry in Her Own Words*. Original drawings and art by Miss Hansberry and an introduction by James Baldwin, Prentice-Hall, 1969.

O'Hara, Robert. *Antebellum*. *The Methuen Drama Book of Post-Black Plays*. Edited by Harry Elam, Jr. and Douglas Jones, Jr., Methuen Drama, 2012, pp. 413–95.

———. *Insurrection: Holding History*. Theatre Communications Group, 1999.

Oczypok, Kate. "Pittsburgh Neighborhoods: History of The Hill District." *Pittsburgh Beautiful*, 2 May 2017, pittsburghbeautiful.com/2017/05/02/pittsburgh-neighborhoods-history-of-the-hill-district/.

Osborne, James F. "Counter-monumentality and the Vulnerability of Memory." *Journal of Social Archaeology*, vol. 17, no. 2, 2017, doi.org/10.1177/1469605317705445.

Parks, Suzan-Lori. *Father Comes Home from the Wars: Parts 1, 2, & 3*. Theatre Communications Group, 2015.

———. Interview by Mark Lawson. *The Guardian*, 21 Sept. 2016, https://www.theguardian.com/stage/2016/sep/21/suzan-lori-parks-interview-royal-court-father-comes-home-from-the-wars-obama . Accessed 10 July 2017.

———. *The America Play and Other Works*. Theatre Communications Group, 1995.

Patterson, Orlando. *Slavery and Social Death: A Comparative Study*. Harvard UP, 1982.

Pittman, Elizabeth. "Voicing the 'Law of the Sea' Commemoration and Cultural Nationalism in August Wilson's *Gem of the Ocean*." *Culture, Theory, Critique*, vol. 54, no. 1, 2013, pp. 19–36.

Plum, Jay. "Pleasure, Politics, and the Performance of Community: Pomo Afro Homos's *Dark Fruit*." *Modern Drama*, vol. 39, no. 1, 1996, pp. 117–31.

Pomo Afro Homos. *Dark Fruit*. *Staging Gay Lives: An Anthology of Contemporary Gay Theater*. Edited by John M. Clum, Westview Press, 1996. pp. 319–43.

Rankine, Claudia. *Citizen: An American Lyric*. Graywolf Press, 2014.

Rayner, Alice. *Ghosts: Death's Double and the Phenomena of Theatre*. U of Minnesota P, 2006.

Reed, Anthony. *Freedom Time: The Poetics and Politics of Black Experimental Writing*. The Johns Hopkins UP, 2014.

Reid-Pharr, Robert. *Conjugal Union: The Body, the House, and the Black American*. Oxford UP, 1999.

Richardson, Matt. *The Queer Limit of Black Memory: Black Lesbian Literature and Irresolution*. The Ohio State UP, 2013.

Ripstein, Arthur. "Commodity Fetishism." *Canadian Journal of Philosophy*, vol. 17, no. 4, 1987, pp. 733–48. *JSTOR*, www.jstor.org/stable/40231565. Accessed 14 July 2016.

Roach, Joseph. *Cities of the Dead: Circum-Atlantic Performance*. Columbia UP, 1996.

Roberts, Neil. *Freedom as Marronage*. Kindle ed., U of Chicago P, 2015.

"Room for Debate: Do Dramas about Slavery Stifle Tales of Black Lives Now?" *The New York Times*, 6 June 2016, www.nytimes.com/roomfordebate/2016/06/06/do-dramas-about-slavery-stifle-tales-of-black-lives-now. Accessed 10 July 2016.

Rushdy, Ashraf. *Neo-Slave Narratives: Studies in the Social Logic of a Literary Form*. Oxford UP, 1999.

Scott, Darieck. *Extravagant Abjection: Blackness, Power, and Sexuality in the African American Literary Imagination*. New York UP, 2010.

Scott, Dread. "Dread Scott: Decision." *Vimeo*, uploaded by Revolution Books, 4 June 2013, vimeo.com/69652042. Accessed 5 May 2014.

Scott, James C. *The Art of Not Being Governed: An Anarchist History of Upland Southeast Asia*. Yale UP, 2010.

Sellar, Tom. "In *An Octoroon*, Branden Jacobs-Jenkins Knocks Us Flat on Our Preconceptions." *The Village Voice*, 7 May 2014, www.villagevoice.com/2014/05/07/in-an-octoroon-branden-jacobs-jenkins-knocks-us-flat-on-our-preconceptions/. Accessed 10 May 2016.

Sharpe, Christina. "Black Life, Annotated." *The New Inquiry*. 8 Aug. 2014. thenewinquiry.com/black-life-annotated/. Accessed 10 Aug. 2017.

———. *In the Wake: On Blackness and Being*. Duke UP, 2016.

———. *Monstrous Intimacies*. Duke UP, 2010. Snodgrass, Mary Ellen. *August Wilson: A Literary Companion*. McFarland and Company, 2004.

Sonstegard, Adam. "Performing Remediation: The Minstrel, The Camera, and *The Octoroon*." *Criticism*, vol. 48, no. 3, 2006, pp. 375–95.

Spaulding, Timothy. *Re-Forming the Past: History, The Fantastic, and the Postmodern Slave Narrative*. The Ohio State UP, 2005.

Spillers, Hortense. "Mama's Baby, Papa's Maybe: An American Grammar Book." *Diacritics*, vol. 17, no. 2, 1987, pp. 64–81.

States, Bert. *Great Reckonings in Little Rooms: On the Phenomenology of Theater*. U of California P, 1985.

"Thelma Golden by Glen Ligon" from BOMBLive! Artists and Curators Series. 4 Mar. 2004. bombmagazine.org/article/3588/thelma-golden. Accessed 1 Aug. 2016.

Tillet, Salamishah. *Sites of Slavery: Citizenship and Racial Democracy in the Post-Civil Rights Imagination*. Duke UP, 2012.

Tinsley, Omise'eke Natasha. "Black Atlantic, Queer Atlantic: Queer Imaginings of the Middle Passage." *GLQ: A Journal of Lesbian and Gay Studies*, vol. 14, no. 2–3, 2008, pp. 191–215.

Vincentelli, Elisabeth. "*An Octoroon* Shocks and Awes with Outrageous Riff on Slavery." *New York Post*, 4 May 2014, nypost.com/2014/05/04/an-octoroon-shocks-awes-with-outrageous-riff-on-slavery/. Accessed 10 May 2016. Web.

Walcott, Rinaldo. "Fanon's Heirs." *Amerikastudien/American Studies*, vol. 59, no. 3, 2014, pp. 436–38.

Waligora-Davis, Nicole. *Sanctuary: African Americans and Empire*. Oxford UP, 2011.

Wallace, Maurice O. *Constructing the Black Masculine: Identity and Ideality in African American Men's Literature and Culture, 1775–1995*. Duke UP, 2002.

Wardi, Anissa J. "From 1727 Bedford Street to 1839 Wylie Avenue: Home in August Wilson's Pittsburgh Cycle." *University of Toronto Quarterly*, vol. 82, no. 1, 2013, pp. 44–61.

Warren, Calvin. "Black Time: Slavery, Metaphysics, and the Logic of Wellness." Colbert, Patterson, and Levy-Hussen, pp. 55–68.

Washington, Mary Helen. *The Other Black List: The African American Literary and Cultural Left of the 1950s*. Columbia UP, 2015.

Weheliye, Alexander G. *Habeas Viscus: Racializing Assemblages, Biopolitics, and Black Feminist Theories of the Human*. Duke UP, 2014.

Wilson, August. *Gem of the Ocean*. Theatre Communications Group, 2006.

———. *Joe Turner's Come and Gone*. Plume, 1988.

Williams, Linda. "Melodrama Revised." *Refiguring American Film Genres: History and Theory*. Ed. Nick Browne. U of California P, 1998, pp. 42–88

Wolbers, Marian. "Nomos, Mysticism, and Power Objects in August Wilson's *Joe Turner's Come and Gone*, *Gem of the Ocean* and *The Piano Lesson*." augustwilsonblog.files.wordpress.com/2017/03/nomos_mysticism_and_power_objects_in_august_wilson_by_marian_wolbers.pdf. Accessed 11 July 2016.

Wolfe, George C. *The Colored Museum*. Grove Press, 1988.

Woodford, Michael, et. al. "'That's So Gay': Heterosexual Male Undergraduates and the Perpetuation of Sexual Orientation Microagressions on Campus." *Journal of Interpersonal Violence*, vol. 28, no. 2, 2013, 416–35. *SagePub,* doi: 10.1177/0886260512454719 Accessed 3 Aug. 2016.

Woolfork, Lisa. *Embodying American Slavery in Contemporary Culture.* U of Illinois P, 2008.

Young, Harvey. *Embodying Blackness: Stillness, Critical Memory, and the Black Body.* U of Michigan P, 2010.

Zaytoun, Constance Kathryn. "*Gem of the Ocean* by August Wilson. Directed by Kenny Leon. Walter Kerr Theatre, New York City. 5 February 2005." *Theatre Journal,* vol. 57, no. 4, 2005, pp. 715–17. *Proquest.* library.tcu.edu/PURL/EZproxy_link.asp?http://search.proquest.com/docview/2079211?accountid=7090.

INDEX

Abelman, Bob, 134n18
African Burial Ground (New York), 68–69
African Grove Theatre, 17
"Afro-alienation," 41n13, 82, 90, 94, 103
Afro-Atlantic Flight: Speculative Returns and the Black Fantastic (Commander), 16n16
agency, 25–26
America Play, The (Parks), 66, 106, 138–39
Andrew, Nathaniel, 126 fig. 7
Angels in America (Kushner), 50
Antebellum (O'Hara), 122, 127–35, 130 fig. 8, 132n17, 134n18, 144; fugitive intimacies in, 115
Appropriate (Jacobs-Jenkins), 99
Arzell, Breon, 126 fig. 7

Bada, Valérie, 1n1, 17
Baldwin, James, 130–31
Balon, Rebecca, 120
Baraka, Amiri, 6, 17, 22, 27–33, 39n11, 63n7
Barfield, Tanya, 14–16, 15 fig. 2
Bearden, Romare, 64–65
Belizaire, "Rock," 3, 4 fig. 1
Bellamy, Maria, 6n8
Beloved (Morrison), 25, 115–16, 128–29
Bent, Eliza, 99, 99n15
Berryman, Ruby, 83n8
Best, Stephen, 12, 17
Black and Gay: A Psycho-sex Study (Dodson), 51
Black Arts Movement, 7, 26–27

blackface, 79–80, 82, 101
black feminist fugitivity, 36–49
Black Gay Men United, 50
black geographies, 59n2
"'Black' is a Country" (Baraka), 27–28, 31
Black left literary modernism, 22
black post-blackness, 7
black queer fugitivity, 49–53
Black Queer Studies (Holland), 122
Black Studies, 12
"black time," 33, 121
blindness, 21–22
Blue Door (Barfield), 14–16, 15 fig. 2
Bodies in Dissent: Spectacular Performances of Race and Freedom, 1850–1910 (Brooks), 4–5
body: fugitivity and, 12
Bolling v. Sharpe, 24
Boucicault, Dion, 99–103, 106, 108–9, 111
Box, The (Owens), 17
Branch, William, 17
Branner, Djola B., 50
Brantley, Ben, 106n19
Br'er Rabbit, 106, 106n19
Bridges to Memory: Postmemory in Contemporary Ethnic American Women's Fiction (Bellamy), 6n8
Brooks, Daphne, 4–5, 12, 23, 41n13, 77–78, 82, 90, 103
Brown, Kimberly Juanita, 6n8
Brown, Michael, 140

Brown, William Wells, 17, 77n1, 88. See also *Escape, The* (Brown)
Brown v. Board of Education of Topeka, Kansas, 24
Bruce Cheryl Lynn, 97 fig. 4
Butler, Judith, 74n9, 82
Bynum, Tara, 43n14

Carpenter, Faedra, 78n3, 82, 85, 99, 104, 120, 123
Carpio, Glenda, 100n16, 106
Catanese, Brandi, 86–87
Charleston church murders (2015), 70
Chase-Riboud, Barbara, 46
Chávez, Karma, 49–50
Citizen: An American Lyric (Rankine), 140–43
citizenship, 22, 63–64, 140–41
civic estrangement, 62
Clarke, Kamari Maxine, 16
Colbert, Soyica, 6n8
Colored Museum, The (Wolfe), 6, 33–37
Coloring Whiteness: Acts of Critique in Black Performance (Carpenter), 82
Columbia: The Gem of the Ocean (Baraka), 63n7
"Columbia: The Gem of the Ocean" (song), 63, 63n7
Commander, Michelle, 16n16, 35n8
commodity fetishism, 125
confession, 120, 120n10
Confessions of Nat Turner, The (Styron), 5–6, 119, 125
Craft, Ellen, 81
Crawford, Margo, 7, 26
Cruising Utopia (Muñoz), 126n15, 134

Dark Fruit (Pomo Afro Homos), 50–53
Davis, Angela, 35
Demonic Grounds: Black Women and the Cartographies of Struggle (McKittrick), 93n13
Diamond, Lydia, 78–79, 82. See also *Harriet Jacobs* (Diamond)
Diouf, Sylviane, 59
Dodd, Alexandra, 9n10
Dodson, Victor, 51
Door of No Return, 15
Douglass, Frederick, 9–10, 115

Drama of King Shotoway, or the Insurrection of the Caribs, The, 17
Dread Scott (performance artist), 2–4
Dread Scott: Decision (performance art), 2–4, 4 fig. 1
Dred Scott v. Sanford, 3
Drinking Gourd, The (Hansberry), 52–53; agency in, 25–26; blindness in, 21–22; commissioning of, 21; emancipation in, 26; performances of fugitivity in, 24–25; slaves in, 25; subjectivity in, 24–26
Du Bois, W. E. B., 103
Dukes, Jessica Frances, 130 fig. 8

Edmonds, Randolph, 17
emancipation: in *The Drinking Gourd*, 26
Emancipation Proclamation, 63, 65
Embodying American Slavery in Contemporary Culture (Woolfork), 6n8
Emerson, John, 3
Eng, David, 71
Equiano, Olaudah, 67
Ernest, John, 77n1
erotohistoriography, 121
Escape, The (Brown), 17, 77–78, 80–81, 88
Eustis, Oskar, 80n5
Evangelism and Resistance in the Black Atlantic (May), 43n14

failure, queer, 49
Father Comes Home from the Wars (Parks), 136–40, 142
Father of the Blues: An Autobiography (Handy), 56–57
feminism. See Black feminist fugitivity
Ferguson, Missouri, 140
fetishism, commodity, 125
Fierstein, Harvey, 50
"Follow the Drinking Gourd" (spiritual), 24
Ford, James Edward, 12, 78n2
forgetting, 16–18
Foster, Verna, 106n18
freedom: in *Antebellum*, 127–28; in black post-blackness, 7; in *Dark Fruit*, 50; in *The Escape*, 77, 81; in *Father Comes Home from the Wars*, 138–39; in fugitive acts, 55; in fugitive intimacies, 115–16; in fugitive time, 33, 107; in *Gem of the Ocean*, 56, 60–65, 75–76; in *Harriet Jacobs*, 89,

92, 94–95; in *Insurrection*, 127; in *Joe Turner's Come and Gone*, 58; in *An Octoroon*, 98–99; in performances of black fugitivity, 23; in *Phyllis Wheatley: The Celestial Muse*, 41–43; in revolutionary fugitivity, 27; in *Sally's Rape*, 46; in *Slave Ship*, 32

Freedom as Marronage (Roberts), 60

Freeman, Brian, 50

Freeman, Elizabeth, 121

Freud, Sigmund, 71

Frund, Arlette, 43n14

fugitive acts, 55, 62, 66, 70–71, 73, 76

fugitive intimacies: in *Antebellum*, 127–35, 130 fig. 8; in *Beloved*, 115–16; defined, 115; in *Insurrection*, 118–27, 126 fig. 7; time and, 120–21

fugitive time, 32–36, 107

fugitivity: in Black Studies, 12; body and, 12; defined, 78n2; in Ford, 12; home and, 12–13; political sense of, 11–12

Gates, Henry Louis, 38–39, 39n11

gays. *See* black queer fugitivity

Gem of the Ocean (Wilson), 7, 54, 120, 123; as commemorative text, 76; as countermonument, 62–70; and *Joe Turner's Come and Gone*, 56–58; and marronage, 59–62; Middle Passage in, 56–58, 61, 63–64, 66–68, 71, 74–75; mourning in, 70–75; post-Emancipation in, 55–56

geographies, black, 59n2

Gilda Stories, The (Gomez), 118

Gomez, Jewelle, 118

Gordon-Reed, Annette, 46

Graham-Brown, Lawrence, 3, 4 fig. 1

Gray, Thomas R., 119–20

Gross, Seymour, 39n11

Guare, John, 50

Gullah Sea Island, 16

Gumbs, Alexis Pauline, 38

Gupton, Eric, 50

Haiti, 60

Halberstam, Jack, 12, 49–50

Hamilton (Miranda), 80n5

Han, Shinhee, 71

Hancock, John, 42

Handy, W. C., 56–57

Hannah, John, 64–65

Hansberry, Lorraine, 21, 24, 37. *See also Drinking Gourd, The* (Hansberry)

Harlem Renaissance, 17

Harlem Riot, 130

Harney, Stefano, 12

Harriet Jacobs (Diamond), 79, 82–98, 86 fig. 3, 97 fig. 4, 144

Harris, Cheryl, 81–82

Hartman, Saidiya, 2, 9, 12, 23, 48n19, 71–72, 74, 101, 116–17

haunting, 128–29, 133

Hemmings, Sally, 38, 46–47

Hill District, Pittsburgh, 59–62

Holland, Sharon Patricia, 58, 122

Holocaust, 128–29, 131–32

home, 122–23, 129, 134–35; fugitivity and, 12–13

Homer, 137

homosexuality. *See* Black queer fugitivity

Hopkins, Pauline, 17

imperialism, 37, 69

Incidents in the Life of a Slave Girl (Jacobs), 84, 87–88, 90–91, 93–95, 114–15

Indigo, A Blues Opera (Johnson), 118

"In Search of Our Mothers' Gardens" (Wheatley), 39

In Splendid Error (Branch), 17

Insurrection: Holding History (O'Hara), 115, 118–27, 126 fig. 7, 135, 144

In the Break (Moten), 10n11

irresolution, 49

Jackson, Eliza, 54

Jacobs, Harriet, 84, 87–88, 90, 93–95, 114–15. *See also Harriet Jacobs* (Diamond)

Jacobs-Jenkins, Branden, 78–79, 82, 99n15, 112n24. *See also Octoroon, An* (Jacobs-Jenkins)

Jamison, Angelene, 39n11

Janice, Obehi, 89

Joe Turner's Come and Gone (Wilson), 56–58, 64

Johnson, James Weldon, 24

Johnson, Karma Mayet, 118

Jones, Jacqueline, 7

Jubilee (Walker), 5

Keizer, Arlene, 6, 6n7
King Hedley II (Wilson), 60
Klammer, Martin, 52n22
Kushner, Tony, 50

La Cage aux Folles (Fierstein), 50
Lahr, John, 69
Leap for Freedom, A (Brown), 17
lesbians, 127. *See also* black queer fugitivity
Levy-Hussen, Aida, 6n8, 33
liberatory narrative, 6n7
Lincoln, Abraham, 65, 106
Littleway, Lorna, 38–43
"long emancipation," 2
Lose Your Mother: A Journey Along the Atlantic Shore (Hartman), 71–72
lynching, 14, 55, 60, 111–12, 111n23
Lyons, Bonnie, 54

Macharia, Keguro, 12
"Mama's Baby, Papa's Maybe: An American Grammar Book" (Spillers), 41n12, 118n4
marronage, 59–62
Marx, Karl, 125
May, Cedrick, 42n14
McAllister, Marvin, 78, 80, 82
McCauley, Robbie, 6, 38, 43–49
McKittrick, Katherine, 59n2, 68, 75, 93n13
McNulty, Charles, 139
memory, 16–18
"Meta-Melodrama: Brandon Jacobs-Jenkins Appropriates Dion Boucicault's *The Octoroon*" (Foster), 106n18
Middle Passage: in *The Colored Museum*, 34; in *Gem of the Ocean*, 56–58, 61, 63–64, 66–68, 72–75; in *Phyllis Wheatley: The Celestial Muse*, 39; as queer experience, 117–18; in *Slave Ship*, 28–29, 31; Wilson on, 71
Millhand's Lunch Bucket (Bearden), 64
minstrelsy, 78–80, 82, 101
Miranda, Lin-Manuel, 80n5
Mitchell, Angelyn, 6, 6n7, 90
Mnemopoetics: Memory and Slavery in African American Drama (Bada), 1n1
Monstrous Intimacies (Sharpe), 6n8

Morrison, Toni, 10, 25, 115–16, 128–29
Moten, Fred, 10n11, 12, 23, 82n7
mourning, radical, 70–75
Muñoz, José, 49, 126n15, 134

Nathans, Heather, 67, 88
Neal, Larry, 27
"Negroes are Anti-Semitic Because They're Anti-White" (Baldwin), 130–31
Neighbors (Jacobs-Jenkins), 99, 112n24
neo-slave narrative, 5, 23, 143, 145; *Harriet Jacobs* as, 89–91; *The Slave* as, 28; staging, 5–11
New York City African Burial Ground, 68

Obama, Barack, 13, 13n13, 84–87, 98
Octoroon, An (Jacobs-Jenkins), 79, 82, 98–113, 105 fig. 5, 110 fig. 6, 116, 120
Octoroon, The (Boucicault), 99–102, 108–9
Odyssey, The (Homer), 137
O'Hara, Robert, 115, 117–18. *See also Antebellum* (O'Hara); *Insurrection: Holding History* (O'Hara)
"On Failing to Make the Past Present" (Best), 17
Osbourne, James F., 62
Owens, Clifford, 3, 4 fig. 1
Owens, Daniel W., 17

Parks, Suzan-Lori, 7, 10–11, 66, 103, 106, 136, 138–39. *See also Father Comes Home from the Wars* (Parks)
patriarchy, 37
Patterson, Robert, 6n8
Peculiar Sam, or the Underground Railroad (Hopkins), 17
performances of fugitivity, 11–13, 143–44; and black feminist fugitivity, 36–49; and black queer fugitivity, 49–53; defined, 5, 23; and fugitive time, 32–36; revolutionary, 27–32
performances of whiteness, 78–83, 85–86, 86 fig. 3, 89, 98–113, 105 fig. 5, 110 fig. 6
"Performing Remediation: The Minstrel, The Camera, and *The Octoroon*" (Sonstegard), 100n17
Peters, John, 43

Phyllis Wheatley: The Celestial Muse (Littleway), 38–43
Piano Lesson, The (Wilson), 64
Pittman, Elizabeth, 64
Pittsburgh, PA, 59–62
Plessy v. Ferguson, 24
Pomo Afro Homos (Postmodern African American Homosexuals), 50–53
Psychic Hold of Slavery, The (Colbert, Patterson, and Levy-Hussen), 6n8

queer experience, Middle Passage as, 117–18
queer failure, 49, 134
queer fugitivity. *See* Black queer fugitivity
queer subject, 117–18

racial melancholia, 70–75
radical mourning, 70–75
Raisin in the Sun, A (Hansberry), 37
Rankine, Claudia, 70, 140–43
Rayner, Alice, 66, 96
Reed, Anthony, 33
Reid, J. C., 17
Repeating Body, The (Brown), 6n8
revolutionary fugitivity, 27–32
"Revolutionary Theatre, The" (Baraka), 27
Richardson, Matt, 49, 118n6, 127
Roach, Joseph, 8–9, 75n11
Roberts, Neil, 60–61
Rushdy, Ashraf, 6, 6n6, 7–8

Salaam, Kalamu ya, 27
Sally's Rape (McCauley), 6, 38, 43–49
Sandberg-Zakian, Megan, 83, 93n14
scenes of objection, 10, 10n11
Schary, Dore, 21
Scott, Darieck, 115–17
Scott, James C., 59
"separate but equal" doctrine, 24
September 11 attacks, 68–69
Seven Guitars (Wilson), 60
sexual pleasure, 116–17
sexual violence, 124–26, 131–32
Sharp, Granville, 42
Sharpe, Christina, 2n2, 6n8, 12, 30, 115

Sheppard, Leslie Ann, 86 fig. 3
Sibande, Mary, 9n10
"Site of Memory, The," 10
Sites of Slavery: Citizenship and Racial Democracy in the Post-Civil Rights Imagination (Tillet), 6n8
Six Degrees of Separation (Guare), 50
Slave, The (Baraka), 28–31, 33
slave market, 40–41, 47–48, 48n19
slavery: afterlife of, 2; in *The Drinking Gourd,* 25; in *Harriet Jacobs,* 83–98, 86 fig. 3, 97 fig. 4; in *Insurrection,* 121–22; in Littleway, 40–41; long shadow of, 1; and performances of whiteness, 79–83; in *Sally's Rape,* 46–48; turn toward, in black drama, 13. *See also* Middle Passage
Slave Ship (Baraka), 6, 17, 28–29, 31–33
Slave Ship, The: Slavers Throwing Overboard the Dead and Dying—Typhoon Coming On (Turner), 141, 142 fig. 9
Sonstegard, Adam, 100n17
Spaulding, Timothy, 6, 6n7
Spill: Scenes of Black Feminist Fugitivity (Gumbs), 38
Spillers, Hortense, 11, 37, 41n12, 116, 118n4
staging: of neo-slave narrative, 5–11
States, Bert, 65–66, 96
"Steal Away" (spiritual), 25
Stewart v. Somerset, 42
Stowe, Harriet Beecher, 11, 35, 107n20
Styron, William, 5–6
subjectivity, 24–26, 36–38, 78

Taney, Roger B., 3
Tanner, Obour, 43n14
theater, 65
Till, Emmett, 24
Tillet, Salamishah, 6n8, 62, 107n20, 141
time: "black," 33, 121; fugitive, 32–36, 107; fugitive intimacies and, 120–21; "traumatic," 33
Tinsley, Omise'eke Natasha, 118, 118n5
"To the Right Honorable William Earl of Dartmouth" (Wheatley), 39–40
Topdog/Underdog (Parks), 106, 138–39
"traumatic time," 33

Trials of Phillis Wheatley, The: America's First Black Poet and Her Encounters with the Founding Fathers (Gates), 39n11
Trump, Donald, 13n13
Trumpets of the Lord (Johnson), 24
Turner, J. M. W., 141, 142 fig. 9
Turner, Nat, 5–6, 31, 118

Uncle Tom's Cabin (Stowe), 11, 35–36, 107n20
Undercommons, The: Fugitive Planning and Black Study (Moten, Harney, Halberstam), 12

VenJohnson, Genevieve, 86 fig. 3
Vincentelli, Elisabeth, 111n23
"Voices from the Days of Slavery," 109n22

"wake work," 2n2
Walcott, Rinaldo, 2
Walker, Alice, 39
Walker, Margaret, 5
Wallace, Maurice, 125n12
Warren, Calvin, 17, 121
Washington, Mary Helen, 22
Wheatley, Phyllis, 38–40, 39n11, 41n13
White, Marvin K., 50

whiteness: and Afro-alienation, 82; in Butler, 82; as category, 77n1; in *Harriet Jacobs*, 83–98, 86 fig. 3, 97 fig. 4; minstrelsy and, 78–79; in *An Octoroon*, 98–113, 105 fig. 5, 110 fig. 6; performances of, 78–83, 85–86, 86 fig. 3, 89, 98–113, 105 fig. 5, 110 fig. 6
"Whiteness as Property" (Harris), 81–82
Whiting Up: Whiteface Minstrels and Stage Europeans in African American Performance (McAllister), 78
Whitman, Walt, 51n21, 52, 52n22
Williams, Bert, 35
Williams, Linda, 110–11
Wilson, August, 7, 54–56, 64–65, 69. See also *Gem of the Ocean* (Wilson)
Wilson, Wilmer, IV, 3, 4 fig. 1
Wolbers, Marian, 65
Wolfe, George, 6, 33–37
women. *See* Black feminist fugitivity
Woods, Ryan, 110 fig. 6
Woolfork, Lisa, 6n8
Wright, Richard, 55

Yellin, Jean Fagan, 83, 93n14
Yoruba language, 16
Young, Harvey, 47n18, 86

Zaytoun, Constance Kathryn, 69–70

BLACK PERFORMANCE AND CULTURAL CRITICISM
VALERIE LEE AND E. PATRICK JOHNSON, SERIES EDITORS

The Black Performance and Cultural Criticism series includes monographs that draw on interdisciplinary methods to analyze, critique, and theorize black cultural production. Books in the series take as their object of intellectual inquiry the performances produced on the stage and on the page, stretching the boundaries of both black performance and literary criticism.

Staging Black Fugitivity
    STACIE SELMON MCCORMICK

Contemporary Black Women Filmmakers and the Art of Resistance
    CHRISTINA N. BAKER

Reimagining the Middle Passage: Black Resistance in Literature, Television, and Song
    TARA T. GREEN

Conjuring Freedom: Music and Masculinity in the Civil War's "Gospel Army"
    JOHARI JABIR

Mama's Gun: Black Maternal Figures and the Politics of Transgression
    MARLO D. DAVID

Theatrical Jazz: Performance, Às .ẹ, and the Power of the Present Moment
    OMI OSUN JONI L. JONES

When the Devil Knocks: The Congo Tradition and the Politics of Blackness in Twentieth-Century Panama
    RENÉE ALEXANDER CRAFT

The Queer Limit of Black Memory: Black Lesbian Literature and Irresolution
    MATT RICHARDSON

Fathers, Preachers, Rebels, Men: Black Masculinity in U. S. History and Literature, 1820–1945
    EDITED BY TIMOTHY R. BUCKNER AND PETER CASTER

Secrecy, Magic, and the One-Act Plays of Harlem Renaissance Women Writers
    TAYLOR HAGOOD

Beyond Lift Every Voice and Sing: The Culture of Uplift, Identity, and Politics in Black Musical Theater
    PAULA MARIE SENIORS

Prisons, Race, and Masculinity in Twentieth-Century U. S. Literature and Film
    PETER CASTER

Mutha' Is Half a Word: Intersections of Folklore, Vernacular, Myth, and Queerness in Black Female Culture
    L. H. STALLINGS

www.ingramcontent.com/pod-product-compliance
Lightning Source LLC
Chambersburg PA
CBHW030139240426
43672CB00005B/191